Screening Images of American Masculinity in the Age of Postfeminism

Screening Images of American Masculinity in the Age of Postfeminism

Edited by Elizabeth Abele
and John A. Gronbeck-Tedesco

LEXINGTON BOOKS
Lanham • Boulder • New York • London

Published by Lexington Books
A wholly owned subsidiary of The Rowman & Littlefield Publishing Group, Inc.
4501 Forbes Boulevard, Suite 200, Lanham, Maryland 20706
www.rowman.com

Unit A, Whitacre Mews, 26-34 Stannary Street, London SE11 4AB

British Library Cataloguing in Publication Information Available

Library of Congress Cataloging-in-Publication Data Available

ISBN 978-1-4985-2582-4 (hardcover)
ISBN 978-1-4985-2583-1 (e-book)

∞™ The paper used in this publication meets the minimum requirements of
American National Standard for Information Sciences—Permanence of Paper
for Printed Library Materials, ANSI/NISO Z39.48-1992.

Printed in the United States of America

To Renie,
the perfect traveling companion

Contents

Recovering Masculinities

Masculinities for Men and Women

Negotiated Masculinities

Loving Anti-Heroes

List of Images

CHAPTER 1

CHAPTER 2

CHAPTER 3

CHAPTER 4

CHAPTER 5

CHAPTER 6

CHAPTER 7

CHAPTER 8

CHAPTER 9

Introduction

Liberating American Masculinity

Elizabeth Abele

The chapters in this volume engage prominent film and television texts that directly interrogate images of US masculinity that have appeared since the second-wave feminist debates of the 1960s and 1970s. Rather than using "postfeminist" as a blanket definition of contemporary gender constructions, the chapters of *Screening Images of American Masculinity in the Age of Postfeminism* most often use the term in its temporal sense, designating the period from the late 1980s on—as a period when feminist concepts had clearly impacted American society and culture, even as many remained suspicious of the term itself.

Whether acknowledged or not, our current society clearly owes a debt to feminism for the contemporary conversations about ideals of American masculinity. As Michael Kimmel asserts, "Far from being only about the loss of power, feminism will also enable men to live the lives we say we want to live" (*Misframing* 222). From this vantage point, feminism becomes less about limiting male professional opportunities or familial control than about allowing men to also make choices, for more meaningful work or to be a part of the family that they love.

Defining the relationship between US masculinity and American feminist movements of the twentieth century is a complex undertaking. Since second-wave feminism is generally presented as "women's liberation," there is the implication that men were the captors—or at the very least, in no need of liberation themselves. However, feminism's process of revealing and questioning the artificial limitations placed on women by society—allowing women to enter arenas previously considered suited to "men only"—cannot help but reveal the social construction of men as well, constructions that may create as many limitations as privileges. Feminism has therefore created both changes in American masculinity as well as the tools to discuss and critique those changes.

The cultural texts examined in this volume do not present a unified response to feminism nor to its counter-movements, but instead interrogate various models of masculinity presented through film and television, asking what gender constructions these texts promote or question. Though it is clear that second-wave feminism has influenced American society in a way that cannot be undone—marking this as a different age than period prior to second-wave feminism—the status of these changes remains an active debate. Yvonne Tasker and Diane Negra note that the term "postfeminism" refers to a wide range of assumptions that imply the "pastness" of feminism. Yet they likewise observe that postfeminist culture works "to incorporate, assume or naturalize aspects of feminism" (3), so that feminism in its multiple iterations is simultaneously past and vibrantly present. Some critics use the term as defining a set of gender roles in the twenty-first century, distinct from pre-second-wave feminist constructions: Elana Levine notes the term's common usage to describe the "hegemonic gender politics of contemporary western culture" (140). One quality of this new hegemony that Hannah Hamad has explored is the requirement of postfeminist masculinity for involved fatherhood, "privileging masculine subjectivities, and the concomitant elision of motherhood" ("Hollywood" 102). Yet this construction assumes that contemporary fatherhood always comes at the expense of mothers, without benefit to this generation of children.

What makes the postfeminist period interesting is to observe not only the new "norm" of postfeminist gender constructions, but as importantly how feminism, third-wave feminisms, queer studies, and masculinity studies continue to actively critique media and society. Katherine Farrimond uses the term (post)feminism "as an indicator of such cultures of 'bothness' which situate themselves as a part of and apart from feminism. The (post)feminist cultural text takes a selective approach not only to feminism as a political position and cultural history but also to related cultural narratives" (44). Joel Gwynne and Nadine Muller similarly see the potential of the postfeminist period "offering liberating possibilities to women as a discourse indicative of a post-traditional era characterized by dramatic changes in social relationships and conceptions of agency" (2). I would suggest that rather than seeing postfeminism as necessarily a step backward from gender equality, that it might operate more as a plateau—with liberating possibilities available to *men and women*, while interrelated gender movements continue to challenge social relationships, including definitions of male and female roles. Film and television texts that explore American masculinity as a work in progress can serve as indicators of what social progress has occurred, where we have stalled, and what new issues have arisen from changes in the gendered landscape.

Scholars have noted the value in examining popular culture as one measure of social change, as a barometer of shifting values and aspirations, if not yet reality. Media cultural theorists Michael Ryan and Douglas Kellner have described the relationship between social history and media as "a process of discursive transcoding, . . . emphasiz[ing] the connections between the representations operative in film and the representations which give structure and shape to social life. . . . Film is the site of a contest of representations over what social reality will be perceived as being and indeed will be" (12–13). American Studies scholar Alan Nadel makes a similar argument for the value of cultural studies, connecting film to the marketplace: "Films are particularly useful in analyzing that subtext in that they are commercial products that represent a large collaborative consensus about ways to commodify a culture's values, to which commercial success lends affirmation" (4). Television likewise operates in this intersection of social values, narrative, spectacle, and the marketplace, while allowing for a more extended and intimate relationship with characters as well as their development than is possible with a single film.

In her review of postfeminist media scholarship, Levine suggests that "it does feminist critiques a disservice to classify particular instances as wholly disruptive of dominant discourses or as all-out efforts of containment against such disruptions" (141). The chapters in this collection resist this "either/or" approach, revealing the traps and the possibilities within specific popular texts whose dynamics have found an audience. In the media texts selected, particular cultural values are actively debated, values that are key to evolving definitions of American masculinity. Instead of portraying contemporary men as bemoaning their loss of power, the chapters of *Screening Images of American Masculinity in the Age of Postfeminism* explore these shifts in gender portrayals as enacted across the past decades in various genres.

CRACKS IN THE FOUNDATION: US MASCULINITY BEFORE FEMINISM

With various factions pointing to a late twentieth-century "crisis in American masculinity," there is the implication that at one point men were *not* in crisis, that their roles had once been stable and well-defined—perhaps holding in mind the perfect icons of pre-Vietnam manhood, ignoring the cracks in US ideology that have long been a part of American culture. For example, Nina Baym refers to the "melodramas of beset manhood" dating back to Cooper and Melville, particularly in literature valorized by American (male) literary critics. This continual crisis may actually have less to do with feminism than with the inordinate value this culture has placed on an unsustainable ideal of American masculinity.

Mid-twentieth century psychologists and sociologists, including Erich Fromm, Carl Rogers, and Abraham Maslow, wrote extensively of the psychological costs to American men of the "power" they possessed. Fromm saw this American male existing as a commodity, with no value placed on his human qualities "except if he can sell them, except if he can be successful, except if he is approved by others" (23). The empty profit that these men got in return was captured in fiction by Sloan Wilson's *The Man in the Flannel Suit* (1955) and in nonfiction by William H. Whyte's *The Organization Man* (1956).

On television and in the comic papers, fathers, like Ozzie Nelson, Ricky Ricardo (Desi Arnaz), and Danny Thomas, rarely seemed in control when they returned from work. As Leslie Fiedler commented, "Dagwood Bumstead . . . goes to work every day and welcomes the tyranny of Blondie as quite what his own inadequacy demands and merits" (340).[1] Since these incompetent family men rarely found the promised fulfillment from the workplace, they sought the illusion of triumph offered by the Westerns and war movies that dominated the big screen. But as Robert B. Ray notes "the genuine threats posed by World War II to traditional American ideologies surface only in the cracks of films consciously intended to minimize them" (31). While many films allowed the official "Hero" to enjoy the fruits of his victory, others frankly showed the outlaw Hero's yearning for the pleasures of community and domesticity from which he had been banished, as in *Shane* (1953), *The Searchers* (1956), and *The Man Who Shot Liberty Valance* (1962).

Predating Betty Friedan's observations in *The Feminine Mystique* (1963), Marshall McLuhan in *The Mechanical Bride* (1951) painted the media's images of ideal American masculinity as equally sterile as that of the American housewife: "so the cowboy is as non-erotic as the hard-driving executive. He is emotionally hardened and unresponsive to any but a tiny area of experiences. He can act, but he cannot feel. . . . Both are rigidly adolescent and non-receptive to experience" (157). Following World War II, the Western became the most prevalent genre on film and television, reflecting the value of the cowboy with American men of the period, both working class and the executive. Like Friedan, McLuhan points to an ideal—perhaps a masculine mystique—promoted by capitalistic ideology and popular culture, that likewise proves limiting and unfulfilling. He specifically notes that these masculine roles are sexually and emotionally repressive, counterparts to the ideal of the suburban housewife—that McLuhan referred to as the "love-goddess assembly line" (37).

As an example of a prefeminist awareness of the constraints of ideal masculinity, the award-winning Western *High Noon* (1952) directly calls into question society's rigid and dehumanizing expectations of postwar manhood. In the film, outlaw Henry Miller is reported to be returning to Hadleyville on the noon train to exact vengeance on the town and the Marshall that convicted him. Though Will Kane (Gary Cooper) had retired that morning—marrying the Quaker Amy Fowler (Grace Kelly)—he pledges to face Miller at noon, rather than to leave as planned with his new wife. As Kane makes the rounds throughout the community to recruit deputies, one by one his constituents refuse to stand by him—despite acknowledging their sincere debt to him. In the end, the only one who stands by him is his wife, Amy, who despite her religious ideals shoots a man in the back to save her husband. The film ends with Will and Amy riding away in the midday sun, as Kane disgustedly drops his badge in the dust.

In McLuhan's terms, Kane rejects the "rigidly adolescent and non-receptive to experience" position of the cowboy, choosing a more emotionally mature life. Kane's masculinity is never in "crisis" or in need of recuperation. It is the society that is in crisis, expecting one man to carry the burden of all. In the end, it is a woman who takes action and has Kane's back—"masculine" qualities that we would expect from the male leaders. In the end, Kane rejects the burden of "ideal" masculinity to build something new with his wife.

The significance of Kane's reluctant hero is marked by the anger *High Noon* aroused in traditionalists John Wayne and Howard Hawks[2] at its release. Hawks objected: "I didn't think a good sheriff was going to go running around town like a chicken with his head off asking for help, and finally his Quaker wife had to save him." Yet *High Noon*'s function as a touchstone of American masculinity was likewise confirmed by its mis-identification by *Die Hard*'s (1988) villain Hans (Alan Rickman): "This time John Wayne does not ride off in the sunset with Grace Kelly"; John McClane (Bruce Willis) corrects him: "That's Gary Cooper, asshole." Cooper's Kane represented an alternative path to that of Wayne (and like Kane, McClane chooses his wife over empty duty). Overall, the myth that American masculinity was stable and fulfilling prior to feminism ignores the major effort that it took to create this façade, as reflected in both popular culture and critical texts.

Second-wave feminism recognized the dehumanizing expectations of twentieth-century men. As early as 1974, Friedan noted that "men weren't really the enemy—they were fellow victims suffering from an outmoded masculine mystique that made them feel unnecessarily inadequate when there were no bears to kill" (*Christian* 1). In a 1970 *Washington Post* interview clearly titled "'Women's Liberation' Aims to Free Men, Too,"[3] Gloria Steinem declared "We want to liberate men from those inhuman roles as well," making involved fathers an original goal of feminism. As with women, the combination of patriarchy and American capitalism limited men prior to feminism to specific roles—including those of jock, hero, distracted genius, executive, and lone wolf—that were reinforced by film and television images. Significantly, unlike the female roles, which were explicitly connected to community life, the successful male roles often existed alone or in homosocial environments. Therefore it is not surprising that for contemporary male screen protagonists, emotional connections emerge as a challenge as great (or greater than) traditional masculine goals of duty, triumph, or professional success.

MASCULINITY SINCE SECOND-WAVE FEMINISM

The chapters of this volume look at constructions of masculinity that began to appear toward the end of George H. W. Bush's presidency continuing into the twenty-first century. In discussing second-wave feminism's impact on American men and masculinity, it has been more common for men's groups as well as cultural critics to view feminism in negative terms.[4] Whether this late-twentieth-century crisis was real is actually less important than its consistent portrayal. David Savran writes: "The self-appointed guardians of male spirituality are unanimous in imagining masculinity as a fragile and vulnerable commodity—oppressed with 'internalized oppression'" (296). It is significant that unlike the crisis in confidence of the 1960s and 1970s, internal factors (social, physical, psychological) rather than external events (like Vietnam or Watergate) were presented as the cause.

These analyses capture the shallow understanding and portrayal of feminism as a foe of masculinity to be overcome. Concurrently, masculinity studies emerged as a more inclusive perspective, involving scholars who often identify as pro-feminist rather than postfeminist.[5] Masculinity theorist Stephen M. Whitehead has made a call to men of this century, similar to that of Erich Fromm: "we must fashion new bonds of trust and intimacy, a necessary adaptation if we are to alleviate the physical and psychological consequences of existential disorientation" (171). Previously, Tania Modleski inserted a similar hope in her critique of 1990s postfeminist films: "I like to think that despite the disturbing contradictions . . . a time will come when we may join together to overthrow the ideology that . . . is ultimately responsible for the persecutions suffered by people on account of their race, class, and gender" (134).[6]

The authors of these following chapters have chosen textual examples that follow protagonists who actively struggle with the conflicting messages about masculinity, attempting to find a path that serves their respective lives—even if they fail. Though these figures may share some qualities with a self-congratulatory construction of postfeminist masculinity, these protagonists are more often works in progress, acknowledging the limits of their negotiations and self-actualization. The conversations *within* these texts about American masculinity are more often open-ended, allowing both male characters and male viewers a wider range of choices. These chapters also cover a wide range of genres: from action and fantasy to dramas and romantic comedy, providing a broad platform for not only the (de)construction of the American male protagonists' masculinity but also for the consideration of those masculinities through a critical lens.

The first section "Recovering Masculinities" follows the journeys of male protagonists who have been wounded, physically as well as psychologically, by traditional masculinity. Over the course of the narrative, the protagonists each attempt to find a more satisfying existence, with varying success. In "Fashioning Flexibility: Racial Neoliberalism and the Vicissitudes of Masculinity," Michael Litwack confronts head-on the ambivalence of locating progressive elements within "postfeminist" masculinities, as embodied by the figure of Sonny Crockett in Miami Vice (1984–1990). Though a Vietnam vet and a vice cop, Crockett does not fit into the traditional model of these identities, appearing more like a fashion model. Litwack's chapter reads the prominence of Crockett's flexible, softer, reconstructed (white) masculinity within the entangled genealogies of whiteness, gender regulation, and neoliberalism in the United States. In "'Any Closer and You'd Be Mom': The Limits of Postfeminist Paternity in the Films of Robin Williams," Katie Barnett interrogates Williams's unique persona, particularly the great lengths that his 1990s characters were willing to go to for the rewards of fatherhood, literal, and surrogate. His films affirmed fatherhood as the "salvation" for men perceived to be in crisis, while his characters availed themselves of paths not available to most men. Like Sonny Crockett, a more fluid masculinity is tied to a deliberate performance, fitting in with film scholar David Greven's assessment of the early 1990s "as a period in which masculinity became self-aware" (13).

The following pair of chapters addresses films that appeared post-9/11, an event which added another layer of critique to traditional US masculinity, with the physical attacks on American soil and the challenges to America's global policies. With "The Bourne Refusal: Changing the Rules of the Game?" Mary T. Hartson argues that Jason Bourne's amnesia and questioning of his own identity over the course of *Bourne Trilogy* (2002; 2004; 2007) highlight his alienation from the military-industrial complex, a patriarchal order that has failed to protect its sons. Bourne actively resists his heroic construction—in particular the role of "soldier"—at the same time that he cannot help but perform it, a reflection of the very real challenges of veterans to re-integrate themselves into their domestic lives. John A. Gronbeck-Tedesco moves the focus to a more ordinary man with "Rethinking the Nation and the Body Politic: *The Wrestler* and the Demise of American Exceptionalism," situating the film *The Wrestler* (2008) at the intersection of nationhood, gender, and the body. Like the *Bourne* trilogy, this film specularizes (and feminizes) the traumatized male body as a symbol of the nation. In this critically acclaimed independent film, the spectacle and commodification of the working-class body through wrestling presents conflicting images of manhood, without the comforting traditions of the US triumphalist cinema, reflecting the malaise of postindustrial, post-9/11 America.

While the first section examined texts that focused on male woundedness and crisis, the chapters of "Masculinities for Men and Women" concentrate on texts in which the masculinity of the figures has been designed to appeal to both male and female audiences. In *Mechanical Bride*, McLuhan described the gender-segregated strains of American culture—"the horse opera" and "the soap opera," advocating the fusion of the traditions and their values of "action and feeling, office and home" (157); this section examines the implications of these fusions. In 'Subverting the Master's Hero: *Firefly*'s Malcolm Reynolds as a Feminist-Inflected Space Cowboy," Laura L. Beadling examines the value of this blending of masculinity with feminine values. Matching *Firefly*'s (2002-3) genre fusion as a space Western, the ship's captain Malcolm Reynolds presents an appealing gender fluidity, by simultaneously displaying virile mastery while embracing feminist values and respecting female colleagues. Not coincidentally, Beadling also situates Malcolm's masculinity within a mixed gender crew, who each present an individual blend of masculine and feminine qualities. In "When Eleven Year-Olds *Kick-Ass*: The Gender Politics of Hit Girl," Keith Friedlander directly addresses the ambivalent value of the gender transgression when traditionally masculine qualities are embraced more fully by characters who are not male. The true hero of Matthew Vaughn's 2010 movie adaptation of the comic series *Kick-Ass* is actually not the titular male Kick-Ass, but the female Hit-Girl, who further complicates the superhero model as an eleven-year-old, serving as a foil to the male superheroes and villains in this text. The film adaptation radically shifts the reading of Hit-Girl as exploited victim to a figure of ultimate girl power. By keeping both readings of Hit-Girl in play, the chapter examines (masculine) violence as a sign of both power and pathology, available to males and females alike.

The third section "Negotiated Masculinities" extends the examination of gender transgressions to highly successful professional men who work with (and love) women who are equally independent and accomplished. In these series, the protagonists are shown in constant negotiations as they improvise constructions of family and masculinity appropriate to their particular situation. In "'I'm Listening': Analyzing the Masculine Example of Frasier Crane," Dustin Gann demonstrates that the gauntlet of relationships Crane formed and professional challenges he endured mirror the struggles of American men adjusting to second-wave feminism. As the series *Frasier* (1993–2004) explored the intersection of a creative workplace and non-traditional family structure, Frasier's masculinity was seen in the context of a range of masculinities, as he interacted with women who explored their greater range of professional and personal choices. With "Hanging with the Boys: Homosocial Bonding and Heterosexual Bromance Coupling in *Nip/Tuck* and *Boston Legal*," Pamela Hill Nettleton likewise turns to the gender-integrated professional workplace, to explore the homosocial bonds between the lead protagonists. While the homosocial bonding classically found in the American Western deliberately excluded femininity—as the male characters avoided emotional intimacy with women—the bromances at the center of *Nip/Tuck* (2003–10) and *Boston Legal* (2004–08) instead provide a relief from the intensity and instability of their professional and personal relationships with strong women. Nettleton sees these series as offering hope for a greater acceptance of expansive masculinities and same-sex couplings, while also potentially falling into the backlash trap of shoring up patriarchy and demonizing women.

The last chapter of this section expands the concept of the professional workplace to include a band of superheroes, as Derek S. McGrath dissects Whedon's reconfiguring of the superhero blockbuster in "Some Assembly Required: Joss Whedon's Indecisive Gendering in Marvel Films' *The Avengers*." With *The Avengers* (2012), director Joss Whedon moved from television to film, bringing to the superhero genre his talent at making action attractive to male and female audiences—as Beadling notes in her chapter on *Firefly*. McGrath traces how this blockbuster evokes and revises the tropes of traditional genres—challenging constructions of masculinity, sexuality, race, and family, while modeling cross-gender collaborative practices.

The final section "Loving Anti-Heroes" looks at how shifting definitions of masculinity can be observed as well in anti-heroic protagonists, as borderline-sociopaths struggle to maintain personal connections. Instead of justifying their protagonists' emotional and moral sacrifices to their self-defined duty, these texts ultimately reveal a complicated relationship to their protagonist and his choices. The concerns facing contemporary manhood are reflected through the prism of the 1950s–60s in Maureen McKnight's chapter "The Falling Man: The Agency of Nostalgia in *Mad Men*." In her reading, Mad Men (2007–15) invites viewers to visit a pre-feminist past, while at the same time disrupting this idealized masculinity. This chapter specifically examines Don Draper's own nostalgia that simultaneously longs for closed frontiers as well as perfect family moments. In "'Out Like a Man': Straddling the Postfeminist Fence in *Dexter* and *Breaking Bad*," Brenda Boudreau explores the pressures that even anti-heroes fail to conform to postfeminist hegemonic masculinity. Despite flouting the law as a serial killer and a high yield meth producer, respectively, the protagonists of both series find it more difficult to disregard their obligations as husbands and fathers. As these men struggle to balance the contradictions traditional and feminist masculinity, Boudreau notes how these negotiations relate to women, particularly as the wives of the anti-heroes become scapegoats, both within the universe of these long-running series and with the shows' audiences.

My own chapter "Last Men Standing: Will Smith as the Obsolete Patriarchal Male" closes the section, examining *I Am Legend* (2007) both within the context of millennial zombie apocalypse films and of Smith's most recent films, where he represents the last adult male of his kind. While Smith established his career with protagonists that energized American masculinity, his millennial protagonists are aloof figures of authority who demonstrate the limits of traditional, rigid masculinity. In contrast, male characters with more fluid masculinity in other zombie films or in supporting roles within these Smith vehicles are more likely to survive and to build emotional connections. Smith's evolving persona raises questions about our culture's growing acceptance of African American masculinity as *American masculinity*.

Ultimately, *Screening Images of American Masculinity in the Age of Post-feminism* plots both the ongoing negotiations and wider opportunities presented by US television series and film over the past decades. As bell hooks notes, "Mass media are a powerful vehicle for teaching the art of the possible. Enlightened men must claim it as the space of their public voice and create a progressive popular culture that will teach men how to connect with others, how to communicate, how to love" (103). Taken together, these chapters interrogate "the possible" screened in popular movies and television series, confronting the multiple and competing visions of masculinity in circulation on film and television in the postfeminist age. *Screening Images of American Masculinity in the Age of Postfeminism* maps how these cultural texts may open new imaginations of masculinity not *after* or *beyond* feminism but, rather, in its very wake.

NOTES

1. Michael Kimmel similarly describes post-World War II breadwinners who took refuge in their basement workshops and scouting as "assert[ing] their manly pride in workmanship as they united to fight against becoming faceless workers" (*Manhood* 101).

2. Fred Zinneman publicly brushed aside the attacks by Wayne and Hawks, who reportedly made *Rio Bravo* (1959) to show a more appropriate response from a town in a similar situation.

3. This article was excerpted from a commencement address at Vassar College. Significantly, Steinem has said that it "was prepared with great misgivings about its reception, and about the purpose of speaking at Vassar."

4. In her two books *Backlash: The Undeclared War against American Women* (1991) and *Stiffed: The Betrayal of the American Man* (1999), Susan Faludi captured the most common narratives about men in the postfeminist age. Tania Modleski's *Feminism without Women: Culture and Criticism in a "Postfeminist" Age* (1991) and Fred Pfeil's *White Guys: Studies in Postmodern Domination and Difference* (1995) focus on male figures that dominate, co-opt or crumble in the face of strong female characters.

5. Activists like Rob Okun, author of *Voice Male: The Untold Story of the Pro-Feminist Men's Movement* (2014), use the term "pro-feminist" rather than "feminist men" to mark their support of feminist goals, while avoiding the possibility of co-opting the feminist movement.

6. Suzanne Hatty wrote of the 1990s masculine-crisis films, "Here we are perhaps witnessing a crisis *within* the construct of masculinity" (181). Instead of seeing these figures as hopelessly floundering, Hatty observes the resolution of this crisis through a more fluid masculinity.

WORKS CITED

Farrimond, Katherine. "The Slut That Wasn't: Virginity, (Post)Feminism and Representation in Easy A." Ed. Joel Gwynne and Nadine Muller. *Postfeminism and Contemporary Hollywood Cinema*. New York: Palgrave, 2013. 44-59. Print.

Fiedler, Leslie. "Mythicizing the Unspeakable." *Journal of American Folklore* 103 (1990): 390-99. Print.

Friedan, Betty. *The Christian Science Monitor* 1 April 1974: 1. Web. 10 Jan. 2013.

Fromm, Erich. *Escape from Freedom*. New York: Holt, 1941. Print.

Greven, David. *Manhood in Hollywood from Bush to Bush*. Austin: U of Texas P, 2009. Print.

Hamad, Hannah. *Postfeminism and Paternity in Contemporary US Film: Framing Fatherhood*. New York: Routledge, 2014. Print.

———. "Hollywood Fatherhood: Paternal Postfeminism in Contemporary Popular Cinema." *Postfeminism and Contemporary Hollywood Cinema*. Ed. Joel Gwynne and Nadine Muller. New York: Palgrave Macmillan, 2013. 99-115. Print.

Gwynne, Joel and Nadine Muller, ed. *Postfeminism and Contemporary Hollywood Cinema*. New York: Palgrave, 2013. Print.

Hatty, Suzanne E. *Masculinities, Violence and Culture*. New York: Sage, 2000. Print.

hooks, bell. *The Will to Change: Men, Masculinity, and Love*. New York: Atria, 2004.

Kimmel, Michael. *Manhood in America: A Cultural History*. New York: Free, 1996. Print.

———. *Misframing Men: The Politics of Contemporary Masculinity.* New Brunswick: Rutgers UP, 2010. Print.

Levine, Elana. "Feminist Media Studies in a Postfeminist Age." *Cinema Journal* 48.4 (2009): 137–43. Web. 8 Aug. 2014.

McLuhan, Marshall. *The Mechanical Bride: Folklore of Industrial Man.* Boston: Beacon, 1951. Print.

Modleski, Tania. *Feminism without Women: Culture and Criticism in a "Postfeminist" Age.* New York: Taylor, 1991. Print.

Nadel, Alan. *Flatlining on the Field of Dreams: Cultural Narratives in the Films of President Reagan's America.* New Brunswick: Rutgers UP, 1997. Print.

Ray, Robert B. *A Certain Tendency of the Hollywood Cinema, 1930–1980.* Princeton: Princeton UP, 1985. Print.

Ryan, Michael and Douglas Kellner. *Camera Politica: The Politics and Ideology of Contemporary Hollywood Film.* Bloomington: Indiana UP, 1988. Print.

Savran, David. *Taking It Like a Man: White Masculinity, Masochism, and Contemporary American Culture.* Princeton: Princeton UP, 1998. Print.

Tasker, Yvonne and Diane Negra. *Introduction. Interrogating Postfeminism: Gender and the Politics of Popular Culture.* Durham, NC: Duke UP, 2007. 1–25. Print.

Whitehead, Stephen M. *Men and Masculinities.* Cambridge: Polity, 2002. Print.

RECOVERING MASCULINITIES

Fashioning Flexibility: Racial Neoliberalism and the Vicissitudes of Masculinity

Michael Litwack

INVESTIGATING THE "CRISIS OF MASCULINITY"

This chapter considers the "crisis of masculinity" as a racial trope that manages and reconsolidates the imperatives of whiteness and heteropatriachy through the guise of their renunciation. In the 1980s, the perils and promises of a putatively waning white male authority emerged as a prominent fixation on US television. Whereas the filmic images of Sylvester Stallone's *Rambo* and Arnold Schwarzenegger's *Terminator* each resembled, in Barbara Creed's memorable phrase, an "anthropomorphised phallus" (65), TV action dramas and procedurals increasingly turned to images of white masculinity that were considerably more flaccid. Writing in 1985 for *TV Guide*, for example, critic Alex Karras noted affirmatively the inauguration of sensitive and vulnerable male leads on contemporary serials, citing the proliferation of "three-dimensional" male characters that were unafraid to express their emotions on crime dramas like *Hill Street Blues* (NBC, 1981–1987) and *Magnum P.I.* (CBS, 1980–1988) (qtd. in Spangler 107–8). In this estimation, the usual suspects said to have initiated a challenge to (an implicitly white) patriarchal masculinity—namely, feminism in its liberal incarnation—were re-scripted as productive opportunities to fashion more fluid male identities, thereby offering some men, in the volitional and market-oriented idiom of "choice," a broader range of options for their gendered self-constitution.

Perhaps more than any other program of its era, show-runner Michael Mann's prime-time series *Miami Vice* (NBC, 1984–1989) staged the alleged crisis of white male identity as an occasion to author "new" forms of masculinity. Starring Don Johnson as detective and Vietnam veteran Sonny Crockett, *Vice* was noted for its quick-cut techniques and stylistics of visual excess that placed the expansion of new male consumer markets at the center of its narrative. Broadcast in stereo—the novel signature of NBC at the time—and remembered more for its close-ups of Crockett's shiny pastel blazers and expensive sports cars than its plotlines, *Vice* branded an emergent mode of white hipster masculinity that linked consumption practices to the making of white male identities able to *adapt* to the aftershock of US imperial ventures in Southeast Asia as well as political changes wrought by both insurgent and hegemonic forms of feminism and multiculturalism.

The hit crime drama, as its namesake implies, was set in the South Beach section of Miami and centered on the Metro-Dade Police Department Vice Squad that, as one critic wryly commented, doubled as an "affirmative action heaven" (Rosaldo 212) comprised of Crockett, his black partner Ricardo Tubbs (Philip Michael Thomas), the Latina detective Gina Navarro Calabrese (Saundra Santiago), and Chicano Lieutenant Martin Castillo (Edward James Olmos), among other officers. Following in the generic footsteps of secret agents Alexander Scott (Bill Cosby) and Kelly Robinson (Robert Culp) from the adventure series *I Spy* (NBC, 1965–1988), *Vice* was part of a broader "integrationist aesthetic" that surfaced in the 1980s, pairing together white and African American male cops (Wiegman 117).[1] Yet while upon *Vice*'s debut Michael Mann reported that Thomas's Tubbs would be "nobody's Tonto"—a confused reference to the Lone Ranger's submissive and stereotyped Indigenous sidekick—by the second season it became apparent that Johnson was to be the series' real star, a point observed by fans, critics, and even Mann himself (see Abalos; Breznican). In its pretense to multiculturalist incorporation, then, Johnson's Crockett was the unquestioned centerpiece of the program, with episodes generally focusing on his (often unsuccessful) undercover operations in the domains of narcotics and sex work. Indeed, Crockett's capacity for an adaptable masculinity was overdetermined by his very profession as an undercover detective.

Critical receptions of *Miami Vice*'s portrayal of masculinity have often fallen into two camps. For many, the program's commitment to law and order as well as its somewhat playful rehashing of the cowboy genre contained "an inherent conservativeness reminiscent of Reagan, as well as a distinctly neoconservative notion [of] . . . the heroic male image" (Trutnau 45; see also Feuer 102–4). Others, however, located a transgressive potential in the program's notorious display of the eroticized male body, arguing that the series intriguingly disrupted heterosexual voyeuristic conventions (King 283-84). What is striking about these assessments, though, is the "choice" with which the critic seems to be presented: either the series remains embedded in a conservative ideology of heteronormative, phallic masculinity or *Vice*'s affinity with male exhibitionism and non-mastery presents a progressive alternative to more "traditional," "static," and "firmer" masculinities grounded in the coercions and mandates of a patriarchal order. But, as I argue, this implicit "choice" between the rigidly patriarchal, on the one hand, and the flexibly innovative, on the other, confounds an analysis of the racial impulses that expand and demarcate these fields of masculine possibility.

In this chapter, I suggest that considering *Vice* in terms of a specifically neoliberal racial and gendered logic may provide a more comprehensive account of how Crockett's re-fashioning of the male *subject* through a seeming embrace of historically feminized tropes maintains the *predicate* of white male supremacy.[2] Broadly, I understand neoliberalism as a social formation in which the principles of the economic market are now sanctioned as the singular imagination for political freedom. The neoliberal "man of enterprise and production" is framed as a flexible and self-activating subject who must constantly reinvent himself in order to participate in an economized grid of social life (Foucault 147). Neoliberalism is in fact itself profoundly flexible, a "political rationality," Wendy Brown writes, "that exceeds positions on particular issues and that undergirds important features of the Clinton decade as well as the Reagan-Bush years" (37). In the terms of personal agency and individual responsibility, neoliberal rationalities idealize adaptable (rather than rigid) subjectivities suited for what

Figure 1.1. Don Johnson as Sonny Crockett sports a florescent suit as he broods over his cocktail. *(Miami Vice)*

David Harvey and others have identified as the flexible organization of late capitalism: the acceleration of turnover time in production and exchange, the demand for labor's innovation and malleability, and capital's increased investment in the socialization of affect, style, taste, and creative production. In recent years, scholars have called for a renewed attention to neoliberalism as a constitutively racial project, one that elaborates and extends racialized strategies of policing, expropriation, and state-sanctioned violence (see Goldberg; Melamed; Reddy). This chapter seeks to contribute to this analysis of the peculiar alchemy of race, gender, sexuality, and nation that composes the texture of neoliberal formations in the United States, focusing on the vexed representational contours of white masculinity established in *Miami Vice*. Examining neoliberal multiculturalism as a gendered visual and political logic, I trace how *Vice* registers the conjunctural racial and sexual contradictions that dovetail with the ascendancy of a neoliberal ethos of self-enterprise and self-malleability. If, as Sarah Banet-Weiser suggests, "gender identity is constructed in the present 'postfeminist' cultural economy as . . . a flexible, celebratory identity category that is presented in all its various manifestations as a kind of product one can buy or try one" (202), I maintain that the racialization of flexibility itself has contoured such "postfeminist" itineraries. My polemical aim is to show that the unproblematic celebration of newly adaptable white heterosexual masculinities, such as Sonny Crockett's, is mediated by gendered and sexual protocols of racial formation that structure contemporary configurations of neoliberalism in the realm of US public culture.

To explore the series' broader narrative treatment of white masculinity, I focus on the episode "Duty and Honor" (3.15), which stages a crisis of white masculinity within a transforming political-economic milieu marked by numerous transformations in 1980s US culture. While "Duty and Honor" is atypical because Crockett's partner, Tubbs, is largely absent, this absence is arguably only an exaggerated version of Tubbs's waning centrality to the show, his representational amputation so to speak. First aired during the third season on February 6, 1987, "Duty and Honor" tracks Crockett as he tracks a mysterious killer who has murdered several women in South Beach. The episode opens with a flashback to a 1972 crime scene in Saigon where a young Lieutenant Castillo (Edward James Olmos) enters a hotel room to find a dead Vietnamese woman and the words "VC WHORE" scrawled on the wall in the woman's blood. The episode then cuts to present-day Miami, and we learn that this killer has reappeared in Florida, committing a similarly brutal variety of murders. In the episode's plot, protagonist Crockett, with the vice squad, must apprehend this killer. As Crockett interviews Vietnam veterans in the Miami area, viewers learn that the killer—referred to only as "The Savage" (Michael Wright)—was castrated by a sex worker, whom he had tried to assault while stationed in Southeast Asia. Since his mutilation, the Savage has sought revenge against the woman who castrated him by murdering any prostitute he can find (leaving his calling card of "VC WHORE" at the murder scenes).

Upon one reading, "Duty and Honor" appears to confirm some of the inaugural tenets of feminist media criticism: in the face of castration, the program offers a surplus of masculinity so as to contain—in fact, to massacre—that which poses the threat of feminization. For instance, TV studies scholar Lynne Joyrich uses "Duty and Honor" as a point of departure to assert that "a common strategy of television is . . . to construct a violent hypermasculinity—an excess of 'maleness' that acts as a shield [against the feminine]" (165). Although I am convinced by Joyrich's argument, permit me to pose a different set of questions, one provoked by the architectonics of race and gender that scaffold the US American idiom of neoliberalism: How might a certain condensation of "violent hypermasculinity" come to make narrative sense only through racialized representational practices and narrative codes that have gained mutated force in the contemporary? And how, moreover, might *Vice*'s championing of the image of an enlightened, fashionable, and highly vulnerable white male agent of the state function to recuperate a national symbolics of masculinity and "resolve"?

In *Miami Vice*, a diegetic preoccupation with masculine inadequacy announces—as it responds to—historically particular anxieties over the place and meaning of white heterosexual masculinity in a culture where, as Ron Becker puts it, a "once-unquestioned hierarchy regulating sexuality (and structuring gender) was increasingly questioned" (35). Confronted with the failure of a certain white heteropatriarchal ideal, *Vice* enacts an object lesson in proper(tied) male citizenship in a world represented as profoundly at odds with patriarchal masculinity and its structuring fantasy of male egoic wholeness. Yet *Vice*'s affirmative turn to male violability and dynamism itself sustains the prerogative of white masculine personhood. Indeed, Crockett's newly privileged form of flexible masculinity surfaces as discursively legible only through the activation of antiblack iconographies of pathological gender and sexuality and the articulation of these iconographies to neoliberal ideals of masculine cosmopolitanism and self-enterprising innovation in the domain of gender. Reading the elasticity of white heteropatriarchy discloses that the lure of a flexible, reconstructed (white) masculinity cannot be disentangled from the deeply entwined contradictions of racial violence and gender regulation that sustain the contemporary US social formation.

THE BODY POLITICS OF FLEXIBILITY

In Miami, it would seem that the threat of castration lurks around every corner—especially for Sonny Crockett. Unlike most male lead TV characters, Don Johnson's Crockett was known more for how he *looked* than for what he *did*. As the object of a sexualized gaze that adored his lean figure, Crockett would model the latest Armani suits each week as he cruised down South Beach. Not only did Crockett lack mastery over the authorial gaze, but he also lacked mastery at work and in the bedroom. Although highly eroticized, divorcé Crockett was repeatedly punished for encounters with women or unable to achieve a (hetero)sexual relation. Sonny's ex-wife Caroline Crockett-Ballard (Belinda Montgomery) and his son Billy (Ryan St. Leon; later Clayton Barclay Jones) move to Atlanta when Caroline is offered a new job, with Sonny conceding that his detective lifestyle often places them in danger. Even when Sonny does finally find "true love" during *Vice*'s second season with Dr. Theresa Lyons (Helena Bonham Carter), she is portrayed as a maniacal, controlling heroin addict who disrupts Sonny's law (both the paternal law and the juridical law he is paid to enforce). And, for a television detective, Crockett was surprisingly bad at catching his villain, often failing to locate his suspect or suffering emotional trauma in the process of the investigation. Moreover, while Crockett's past military service in Vietnam functioned as a crucial backstory, but his service was a subject that he preferred to avoid.

If castration is rendered an inevitability for the 1980s US American man, *Vice* takes up a strikingly pedagogic function, prescribing how to proceed after one has recognized the facticity of this castration. "Duty and Honor" dramatizes a moment of coming into (non-)recognition of the ostensibly castrating effects of Vietnam, consumerism, feminism, and occupational and (hetero)sexual failure in the neoliberal "New Economy" through its peculiar doubling of Crockett and the Savage.[3] Through the figuring of Crockett, *Vice* rewrites various failures of heteronormative white masculinity—failures embedded in and propelled by neoliberal transformations—as the condition of televisual adventure and exploration: exciting opportunities to self-construct a cosmopolitan identity. Like Crockett, the man may acknowledge castration and progress forward through a dynamic movement between the masculine and the feminine that may ironically bolster his power. Or, like the Savage, the man may deteriorate into a state of psychosis in which he can neither acknowledge nor confirm his castration in a "respectable" way.

In the structure of the episode "Duty and Honor," the Savage's violence has a surprisingly quotidian quality: in murdering the woman who castrated him and her stand-ins, he reaches the logical ends of patriarchy. While the Savage's violence certainly functions as retribution for the (bodily and psychic) trauma of feminization, it also marks an inability to acknowledge truth of this castration—genitally, symbolically, and culturally. This failure to deal with, even to recognize, castration becomes formalized in the episode's key murder scene, in which the Savage kills a sex worker in his motel room. After her murder, the Savage raises his arm into the frame, spreading his victim's blood on the wall, signifying his mastery over the woman. Just as in the case of the pornographic "money shot"—which paradoxically serves as our visual evidence of the male orgasm (making male heterosexuality intelligible) even as it requires the man to "pull out" (making heterosexuality, according to a certain cultural logic, unrealizable)—the Savage's violent rampage produces him as at once possessing and in dispossession of his penis. The Savage is inaugurated as a split-subject or, more accurately, as in psychosis. Unable to recognize his castration, he seeks to penetrate the woman as if he had not already been castrated. However, unlike Jacques Lacan's description of the psychotic who refuses to accept the (m)Other's castration and, as such, fails to succumb to the symbolic law, the Savage repudiates his own lack and thus his very position within the symbolic and political economy of (sexual) difference. Crucially, he does not merely repress this wound of/to masculinity but forecloses it, installing instead an altered vision of the real, one simultaneously before and outside the complex of castration. For Lacan, as for Crockett upon investigating the murder, the problem is *"not that of the loss of reality*, but [rather] of the mainspring of what takes its place" (178). The Savage's refusal to accept the fact of castration therefore instantiates not only a disavowal of his corporeal lack but also a racialized manifestation of a primitive psychosexual backwardness, an incapacity to function within a shifting politico-economic field represented as always-already castrating. On the one hand, this revaluation of the castration thematic indicates a strategy by which the white male subject reconciles and resources a putative waning of authority through an imaginary identification with injury and marginaliza-tion. On the other, it alerts us, symptomatically, to the repressed ritualization of lynching and sexual terror that underwrites the racial institution of castra-tion in US modernity, and that continues to organize the white male embrace of suffering and fragmentation in its "postfeminist" iteration.

IMAG(IN)ING RACIAL *VICE*

Miami Vice narrates Crockett's phallic failure in a celebratory manner. Crockett resources his masculinity in an entrepreneurial spirit, allowing him to reconcile the narrative instance of feminization by moving flexibly across social spaces and identities. For example, Crockett's remarkable ability to primp in the mirror, fail to achieve orgasm, unsuccessfully pursue his target, then moments later go undercover as a South Beach john, all confirm his failure or non-mastery. Nevertheless, this non-mastery produces Crockett's ascendancy as the heroic subject of televisual representation, allowing him to achieve victory by the program's conclusion. Yet it is only Crockett's market prowess—his access to the latest trends and styles—that authorizes him to emerge virtually unscathed from this series of diegetic castrations. Although Crockett's exhibition of traditionally defined "feminine" characteristics would not necessarily function as a source of empowerment for women nor for the queer man, Crockett's white hetero-male body provides a location from which his gender fluidity and anti-masculinism performs, ironically, a reconsolidation of white patriarchal power. Indeed, it is finally Crockett who lives and the Savage—along with countless unnamed and faceless women—who must die.

While *Vice* therefore retraces the topography of desirable masculinity outside the imperatives of occupational success and sexual mastery, the episode "Duty and Honor" affirms this alternative model of consumerist white masculinity only through the hypervisible figuration of black male violence, particularly violence against the non-black woman. Here, the proliferation of white hetero-masculinities that flirt with "the feminine" demands the image of a stubbornly anachronistic and illiberal stock figure positioned at the radical threshold of our governing logics of capital accumulation: a subject antagonistic to the dominant post-Fordist rationality of the malleable. As Kaja Silverman remarks, "the differentiation of the white man from the black man on the basis of the black man's hyperbolic penis . . . places the white man on the side of 'less' rather than 'more' and, so threatens to erase the distinction between him and the white woman" (131). In *Vice*'s scene of divided belief, if the Savage's phantasmatic penis serves to legitimate Crockett's pursuit (and self-pursuit) through the specters of miscegenation and the penetrability of the female body, it also radically disrupts his own fantasy of corporeal integrity. By calling into question the bodily dissimilitude between the white man and the white woman—and with it, the psychic and social valence of the white man's organ—the (imaginary) overexposure of the black male penis makes legible the constitutive racial violence that undergirds the white heteronormative romance, its requisite promulgation of ritual and gratuitous brutality against the black body.

Yet it is not only the Savage himself who cannot recognize the "truth" of his castration. *Vice* sutures the viewer to a psychic space of split belief where we both know and cannot know the Savage's lack. Halfway through the episode, it is revealed that the Savage was "emasculated" by a "Viet Cong whore." The Savage nonetheless sustains his position as a hypermasculine and hypersexual war machine, which, on a certain register, repudiates the viewer's knowledge of loss qua castration. In contrast to the pastels and dark greys that characterize shots of Crockett's attire and setting—constructing him as at once gritty and glamorous—we often find the Savage barely visible, as a ghostly threat that can only marginally be located (epistemologically but also visually) through a nervous combination of tracking and following shots. *Vice*'s sustained preoccupation with the Savage's deviant, surplus masculinity despite the fact of his mutilation proves a disturbing confrontation between the structure of (racial) fetishism and what Frantz Fanon shows to be the collapse of the signifiers "black" and "penis."[4] In other words, the tele-visual fact of blackness interdicts Crockett's (and the viewer's) ability to register the Savage's literal castration and the national economy of masculinity that hinges upon it.[5]

In a fascinating doubling early in the episode, shots of the Savage cruising the streets of Miami in search of a prostitute are interspersed with shots of Crockett, as it were, cruising his suspect. But Crockett once again cannot perform adequately: while the Savage's quest culminates in murder, he fails to determine the identity of the criminal. It is Crockett, in fact, who is presented as multiply castrated. As Joyrich maintains, "In the logic of the episode, this castration is infectious—after the introductory flashback to the initial crime in Vietnam, the episode begins as Sonny Crockett is interrupted at the height of a sexual encounter by the news of the latest homicide" (168). But unlike the Savage, who psychotically attempts to hypermasculinize himself in the face of castration, Crockett leaves the scene of botched seduction peacefully yet without climax.

This simultaneous affirmation and denial of emasculation marked by Crockett's movement between male heterosexual prowess and emotional understanding, feminized consumption and masculinized pursuit, produces Crockett in terms of a gendered ambivalence that saves him from psychosis: a location that would make the recognition of castration a structural impossibility.[6] These parallel castrations suggest that "Duty and Honor" is not concerned with reconstructing social life prior to castration ("the reality that is lost") but rather with the various modalities through which masculine subjects (cannot) deal with their knowledge of psycho-social castration ("the reality that takes its place"). In question is *not* the failure of heteronormative masculinity but *the failure to acknowledge this failure, the incapacity to self-manage the inevitability of this breakdown.*

In stark contrast to Crockett, the Savage is produced as exceptionally backward in his failure to acknowledge this changing terrain of masculinity. "Lagging behind in the [teleological] march toward sexual and gender cosmopolitanism" (Manalansan 99), and always dressed in an unseemly long black trench coat while lurking in the shadows of Miami's dimly lit streets, the Savage is an untimely figure whose jerky movements and washed-out aesthetic mark him as out of place but also out of time. The Savage is psychically trapped in the killing fields of Southeast Asia but also, we are to assume, in a static masculine-as-mastery model of gender normativity: a regression to criminalized (black) hypermasculinity that becomes inextricable from his racial and sexual difference. The Savage's ghost-like status—his ability to be everywhere and nowhere all at once—also proffers the assassin as the return of Crockett's hypermasculine repressed. In fact, the coupling of Crockett and the Savage produced through the use of ideational montage throughout "Duty and Honor" establishes the pair as surprisingly similar.

This anxious possibility that the cop and his object of pursuit may be more alike than different becomes most apparent in one of the episode's crucial doublings in which Crockett goes undercover to locate the Savage. In the scene's opening shot, the camera pans a group of drunk white men sitting on the streets of Miami, tilting upward to expose Crockett posing as a potential john. The scene then cuts to the Savage on the same street in search of a woman to murder. Interestingly, the same music plays throughout the sequence, and there is neither a dramatic crescendo nor a sudden climactic accent upon the entrance of the Savage. Likewise, both men look equally pensive as they cruise the streets of South Beach. Mirroring the Savage's movement, the detective appears at home in the *mise-en-scène* populated by criminalized populations such as sex workers, drug users, and homeless people. In these few moments before the Savage emerges in Crockett's field of vision, the differences between protagonist and criminal become illegible, making us forget, however briefly, that these men are not here for the same reason.

When he does become aware of the Savage, the camera becomes intensely identified with Crockett's gaze, scanning the killer and culminating with a wide shot of the Savage's body that hints that Crockett may be cruising for sex as much as for justice. Yet this twin articulation of the Savage as an object of both erotic longing and recalcitrant otherness requires that the woman enter into this scene to secure Crockett's precarious heterosexuality and to emphasize that the Savage is not a proper object choice (neither of desire nor identification). Posing as a prostitute, fellow Detective Gina Navarro Calabrese crosses the street to provoke the Savage, flirting with him in broken Vietnamese. Throughout, Crockett looks onward, orchestrating Calabrese's action, fully in control of the gaze. As the camera pulls back to increase the shot's depth of field, a tall building becomes visible in the frame. Having the same shade of blue as Calabrese's blouse, the building appears as an extension of her body—as if she possessed the phallus.

Encountered with the woman's prosthesis as well as her verbal injunction that threatens to return him to a pre-oedipalized world in which the mother's voice dominates (or worse, threatens to propel him into a postfeminist gendered reality in which the woman can ostensibly "make herself heard"), the Savage becomes increasingly angry, violently grabbing and shaking Calabrese; it is almost as if he cannot control himself.[7] In this gesture, Crockett and the Savage's masculinities become strikingly opposed to one another, especially in relation to questions of self-sovereignty and self-discipline. If, up until this point, the Savage incarnates what Angela Y. Davis has theorized as the myth of the black rapist, his unrestrained reaction to Calabrese establishes this propensity for violence as an inability to resource one's masculinity respectfully and responsibly. The neoliberal politics of self-management meet the sexual logics of white supremacy, though no introduction seems necessary.

The Savage's criminalized inability to deal with the woman on her own terms foregrounds the Savage's incapacity for self-regulation, even to exist in language when faced, quite literally, with the feminine. The Savage's radical negation, and his later availability for violent death, suggests that, in *Vice*, the very category of male heteronormativity becomes realigned around a set of entrepreneurial aims, including one's capacity for sovereign self-regulation and one's capacity to leverage one's gender in a self-enterprising manner. This contraction between entrepreneurial virility and masculine restraint is buttressed by fetishistic shots of Crockett's expensive sports car—a symbol of (male) economic prowess—that jet across the screen after the detective establishes his racial and sexual difference in relation to the killer. Through this coupling, then, an anxiety over Crockett's *feminine* and *consumer* excess is sublimated into an anxiety over *racial* and *masculine* excess that is issued through the Savage's body. It is therefore in the name of narrative closure and episodic regeneration that the racial abject must be killed off—expelled from *Vice*'s televisual body so as not to risk de-naturalizing Crockett's putatively reconstructed masculinity and disclosing his own imbrication within a regime of masculinist state violence.

RECONSTRUCTING MASCULINITY
IN THE MULTICULTURALIST FRAME

"Duty and Honor" occupies what Ann Laura Stoler has branded as the complex pivot between "rupture and recovery" in the operatives of racism (200). The episode resuscitates the founding narratives of the US racial order of things only later to retract these narratives by positioning the Savage as a victim of the Vietnam War: a war machine that, through the episode's closed-circuit tauto-logic, becomes indistinguishable from the Savage's. He is at once causality and casualty of this violence; his immobility in the field of gender requires that he be fully immobilized. The episode both cites and covers over the specular sexual violence of lynching vis-à-vis its representation of the castrating Vietnamese woman, functionally obscuring the lynching at the hands of the Miami police with which "Duty and Honor" concludes and through which Crockett's self-actualization takes shape. By the same token, the only form through which US militarism and gendered violence can be explicitly evoked is through the figuration of the Savage. When Crockett interviews veterans to learn the Savage's identity, he finds one man who served with the assassin in Vietnam. The veteran comments: "they called him the Savage. His code name, ya know? Heard he had over forty VC kills. Most of them behind enemy lines. They say he was so good, he killed over half the poor commies in their sleep. In their sleep, believe that?" This myopic projection of US imperial violence onto a racialized form of masculine aggression depends upon the black male as inflexible and unreconstructed subject. Moreover, this subtractive homology of "blackness," "hypermasculinity," and "violence" requires that the Savage's sexual predation be made identical with US state violence such that a racialized and regressive masculinity becomes marshaled as the primary impediment to the program's neoliberal dream of male comradeship across difference.

This series of citations and immediate displacements—of white racial terrorism onto the Vietnamese woman, of US imperial power onto the blackened racial grotesque, of sexual violence as a central tactic of war onto the phantasmatic black male rapist—each secure the double premises of antiblackness *and* its disavowal by positing a multicultural world that is continuously interrupted by unassimilability of the black figure. Crucially, "Duty and Honor" labors to disarticulate its legitimation of the Savage's murder from a "defense of *white* womanhood from Black men's irrepressible rape instincts" (Davis 185, emphasis mine) that the episode might otherwise seem to conjure: his first victim is Vietnamese, Detective Navarro is Latina (though passing as Vietnamese), and the appellation "VC WHORE" is written at each crime scene in his victims' blood. Yet in the episode, racial blackness becomes a limit-point for inclusion within *Vice*'s multiracial detective squad and within Miami as a racially and ethnically diverse global city. In this respect, the Savage's corporeal amputation at once mirrors and necessitates the striking absence of African American Detective Tubbs from the episode—his textual excision. For if the pairing of black and white male protagonists in the action-adventure genre functions to contain and "resolve" the problem of race through the assumed bonds of masculinity, Tubbs's presence in the antiblack imaginary of the episode would risk exposing the ruse of race-transcendence that animates Tubbs and Crockett's friendship.[8]

For this reason, the Savage can only be redeemed through a narrative of victimhood—an act of feminization but also of deracination—as the precondition of his entry into the national, even international, family of brothers. As South Vietnamese officer Nguyen Van Trang (Haing S. Ngor) states at the episode's conclusion, "Only when we found [the Savage] did I realize that this sick man was nothing but the victim and weapon of war." This racial triangulation precariously binds together the white, black, and Asian (American) men under the sign of US national victimhood, though it does so through the eclipse of the long and highly differentiated history of US racial violence, both domestic and foreign, proffering an image of a traumatized post-Vietnam War US (masculine) multicultural subject that transforms the nation's involvement abroad from active intervention to "passive suffering."[9] In the synecdochic structure of *Vice*, Crockett too emerges as a vulnerable subject of passive victimization, as the icon of a fragmented and wounded masculinity that re-establishes his (police) power and its ethical legitimacy. This final invocation of the killer as weaponized victim ultimately interpellates the Savage into a nationalist frame of universal masculine suffering, one that is regenerated and sustained through his requisite death.[10] Again, the appeal to the pathos of a generalized condition of castration obviates the racial structuration of sexual violence that organizes the US national symbolic of masculinity. After all, "Duty and Honor" assures us, all men are in fact now wounded.

CONCLUSION

Flexible masculinity in the episode "Duty and Honor" refashions the terrain of white masculinity by encouraging the viewer to take pleasure in white supremacist fantasies while condemning the masculinist nation-state logics to which these fantasies are fundamentally braided. *Vice*, in short, wants it both ways. The program allows the white male subject to pursue these phantasms and, at the same time, disavow any participation in their governing logics through the discursive initiation of a figure who is visualized as stubbornly anachronistic and inflexible. How else could *Vice* torture and mutilate the Savage—surely, a structuring fantasy that underwrites the material and psychic archaeology of whiteness—and then proceed as if it is Crockett who must actually manage the crisis of castration?

In this chapter, I have sought to demonstrate that established iconographies—gendered and sexualized iconographies of race—have formed the conditions of possibility for the much-heralded thrall to flexible and mobile models of (white) masculinity. I have argued that the failure of a certain kind of white masculine ideal is in fact constitutive of—as opposed to disruptive to—the co-productions of white supremacy and heteropatriarchy. While Crockett is shown to embody a dynamically enterprising and malleable masculinity that copes with various figurations of injury and violation, it is the structuring persistence of sexualized racial violence that inaugurates this field of white possibility and that sustains its performative coherence. In this way, *Miami Vice* encounters, as it constitutes, the impossibility of thinking the so-called postfeminist lure of (masculine) flexibility without thinking its indebtedness to a particular vision of racial modernity and the contemporary realignment of this vision under the sign of neoliberal freedom.

NOTES

1. *Vice* was arguably the most successful of several TV dramas appearing around 1987 that featured the interracial buddy formula including *Magnum P.I.* (CBS, 1980–1988), *The A Team* (NBC, 1983–1987), and *Sonny Spoon* (NBC, 1988).

2. My account of "resourcing" masculinity bears the imprint of the work of Beverly Skeggs.

3. The very logic of castration, as foregrounded here, emerges in the historical instance through specific political, cultural, and economic configurations that are inextricable from the racial and sexual agencies of the nation-state. What is dubbed "castration" thus traffics—productively, I hope—between a popular idiom and a more properly psychoanalytic one.

4. Fanon writes in one well-known passage that "the black man has been occulted. He has been turned into a penis. He *is* a penis" (147).

5. As Hiram Perez has effectively pointed out in his discussion of the racial-sexual violence that underwrites the history of lynching, "the castrated penis must itself become fantastic in order to sanction genocidal violence" (185).

6. As James Lyons has written in his study of *Miami Vice*, "Crockett's status as a veteran was employed to give his handsome playboy persona an edge of soldier steel, thus reconciling differently desirable aspects of masculinity" (9).

7. For this account of the gendered voice and its inscription in audiovisual media, see Doane esp. 346.

8. On the interracial buddy formula, see Guerrero and Wiegman. On antiblack racism in the wake of multiracialism and multiculturalism, see Sexton.

9. In her monograph *The Oriental Obscene*, Sylvia Shin Huey Chong argues such a positing of the United States as passive sufferer was one among several narratives that comprised the broader national phantasmatic of the Vietnam era and its racial afterlife.

10. Significantly, if unsurprisingly, this precarious incorporation into a national enterprise of masculinity requires an effacement of the long and ongoing history

of black anti-imperialism and internationalist critique of US empire. On the theory, politics, and organization of African American solidarity with decolonization and anticolonial movements during the Vietnam War, see, for example, Taylor.

WORKS CITED

Abalos, Brenda. "Straightness, Whiteness, and Masculinity: Reflections on 'Miami Vice.'" *Race and Ideology*. Ed. Arthur Spears. Detroit: Wayne State UP, 1999. 167–80. Print.

Banet-Weiser, Sarah. "What's Your Flava? Race and Postfeminism in Media Culture." *Interrogating Postfeminism: Gender and the Politics of Popular Culture*. Ed. Yvonne Tasker and Diane Negra. Durham: Duke UP, 2007. 201–26. Print.

Becker, Ron. *Gay TV and Straight America*. New Brunswick, NJ: Rutgers UP, 2006. Print.

Breznican, Anthony. "'Miami Vice' Makes Series of Changes." *USA Today* 26 July 2006. USAToday.com. Web. 22 Jan. 2015.

Brown, Wendy. *Edgework: Critical Essays on Knowledge and Politics*. Princeton: Princeton UP, 2005. Print.

Chong, Sylvia Shin Huey. *The Oriental Obscene: Violence and Racial Fantasies in the Vietnam Era*. Durham: Duke UP, 2012. Print.

Creed, Barbara. "From Here to Modernity—Feminism and Postmodernism." *Screen* 28.2 (1987): 47–67. Print.

Davis, Angela Y. *Women, Race, and Class*. New York: Vintage Books, 1983.

Doane, Mary Ann. "The Voice in Cinema: The Articulation of Body and Space." *Narrative, Apparatus, Ideology: A Film Theory Reader*. Ed. Philip Rosen. New York: Columbia UP, 1986. Print.

Fanon, Franz. *Black Skin, White Masks*. Trans. Richard Philcox. New York: Grove, 2008. Print.

Feuer, Jane. *Seeing Through the Eighties: Television and Reaganism*. Durham: Duke UP, 1995. Print.

Foucault, Michel. *The Birth of Biopolitics: Lectures at the Collège de France, 1978–1979*. Trans. Graham Burchell. Basingstoke: Palgrave, 2008. Print.

Goldberg, David. *The Threat of Race: Reflections on Racial Neoliberalism*. Oxford: Wiley-Blackwell, 2008. Print.

Guerrero, Ed. "The Black Image in Protective Custody: Hollywood's Biracial Buddy Films of the Eighties." *Black American Cinema*. Ed. Manthia Diawara. New York: Routledge, 1993. Print.

Harvey, David. *The Condition of Postmodernity*. Oxford: Blackwell, 1990. Print.

Joyrich, Lynne. "Critical and Textual Hypermasculinity." *Logics of Television: Essays in Cultural Criticism*. Ed. Patricia Mellencamp. Bloomington and Indianapolis: Indiana UP, 1990. 156–72. Print.

King, Scott Benjamin. "Sonny's Virtues: The Gender Negotiations of Miami Vice." *Screen* 31.3 (1990): 281–95. Print.

Lacan, Jacques. "On a Question Prior to Any Possible Treatment in Psychosis." *Ecrits: A Selection*. Trans. Alan Sheridan. New York: W. W. Norton, 1977. Print.

Manalansan IV, Martin F. "Colonizing Space and Time: Race and Romance in Brokeback Mountain." *GLQ* 13.1 (2007): 97–100. Web. 11 Apr. 2014.

Lyons, James. *Miami Vice*. Malden, MA: Wiley-Blackwell. 2010. Print.

Melamed, Jodi. *Represent and Destroy: Rationalizing Violence in the New Racial Capitalism*. Minneapolis: U of Minnesota P, 2011. Print.

Reddy, Chandan. *Freedom with Violence: Race, Sexuality, and the US State*. Durham: Duke UP, 2011. Print.

Rosaldo, Renato. *Culture and Truth*. Boston: Beacon, 1989. Print.

Perez, Hiram. "You Can Have My Brown Body and Eat It, Too!" *Social Text* 23.3–4 (2005): 171–91. Print.

Sexton, Jared. *Amalgamation Schemes: Antiblackness and the Critique of Multiracialism*. Minneapolis: U of Minnesota P, 2008. Print.

Skeggs, Beverley. "Uneasy Alignments, Resourcing Respectable Subjectivity." *GLQ* 10.2 (2004): 291–98. Web. 15 June 2014.

Silverman, Kaja. *The Threshold of the Visible World*. New York: Routledge, 1996. Print.

Spangler, Lynn. "Buddies and Pals: A History of Male Friendships on Prime-Time Television." *Men, Masculinity, and the Media*. Ed. Steve Craig, Thousand Oaks: Sage, 1992. 93–110. Print.

Stoler, Ann Laura. *Race and the Education of Desire*. Durham: Duke UP, 1995. Print.

Taylor, Clyde, Ed. *Vietnam and Black America: An Anthology of Protest and Resistance*. Garden City, NY: Anchor, 1973. Print.

Trutnau, Jean-Paul. *A One Man Show? The Construction and Deconstruction of a Patriarchal Image in the Reagan Era*. Victoria: Trafford, 2005. Print.

Wiegman, Robyn. *American Anatomies: Theorizing Race and Gender*. Durham: Duke UP, 1995. Print.

"Any closer and you'd be Mom": The Limits of Postfeminist Paternity in the Films of Robin Williams

Katie Barnett

Throughout the 1990s, Robin Williams was a ubiquitous presence on the Hollywood screen. The actor colonized the family comedy market in a period when family films were big business in Hollywood, starring in a number of the decade's biggest hits (*Mrs. Doubtfire*, *Jumanji*, *Aladdin*, *Hook*, to name but a few). In many of these films, Williams takes on the role of father—whether literal or surrogate—providing a model of masculinity which is filtered through a distinctly paternal prism. It is this rendition of masculinity through fatherhood, and the extent of its ability to subvert the postfeminist masculine "crisis" that this chapter will explore.

In many of his films, there inevitably comes a point at which Williams is compelled to run through a rapid repertoire of personae. As a staple of his comedy films in particular, this compulsion to cycle through split-second renditions of various different identities, presents an opportunity for Williams to demonstrate his unique performative prowess, often in a brief interlude from the main plot. Indeed, this ability is his hallmark: "I do voices," his character Daniel Hillard tells his social worker in *Mrs. Doubtfire* (1993), when asked if he has any special skills. In highlighting Williams's impressive vocal dexterity, the inclusion of this rapid-fire identity cycle suggests a wider cultural preoccupation in the United States at the time: the crisis of masculinity.

During the 1990s, the concept that American men—particularly straight, white, middle class men—were in a state of crisis regarding their masculine identity gained particular traction in Hollywood. While debate continues over the validity of such a crisis, particularly with regard to claims of lost power in a postfeminist landscape, on screen it formed a persistent undertone to the portrayal of American men, as Hollywood struggled with the fragmentation and shifting definitions of straight, white masculinity. Williams's trademark casting on and off of voices and identities mirrors this atmosphere of crisis in which men were perceived to be floundering, unsure of how to "be" a man. As Williams bounces between Zen monk and Rastafarian, Sean Connery and Ronald Reagan, Marlon Brando and John Wayne, he reveals the anxieties at the heart of the contemporary crisis of masculinity. These anxieties come to hang on one overarching question: which version of manhood would be enough to secure masculine survival beyond the millennium?

A discussion of postfeminist Hollywood fatherhood necessarily acknowledges Stella Bruzzi's seminal work on fatherhood and masculinity in Hollywood cinema, *Bringing Up Daddy* (2005). Bruzzi identifies the enduring importance of the father figure in Hollywood and, noting the relative dearth of material addressing the father on screen, demonstrates how fatherhood has long been a fundamental facet of Hollywood masculinity. Bruzzi characterizes the 1990s and early 2000s as a period of "fragmentation" and pluralization, as cinema's fathers emerge into a postfeminist landscape where masculinity has been destabilized by perceptions of crisis (153). Despite the growing diversity of male representation, however, fatherhood remains a persistent theme, a recurrent touchstone for men seeking purpose or redemption. Building on this, Hannah Hamad's recent work on postfeminism and paternity marks a crucial intervention in the study of fatherhood on film, in particular her identification of "postfeminist culture's paternal imperative" (*Postfeminism* 91). Here, Hamad astutely recognizes the desire to re-cast men as fathers on screen, and in doing so rehabilitate their precarious masculinity. While Hamad focuses primarily on twenty-first-century Hollywood, however, this chapter seeks to address the twentieth-century roots of the "paternal imperative" Hamad identifies, and draw an explicit link between fatherhood as a form of masculine survival and the cultural preoccupations and anxieties of pre-millennial US society.

Moreover, despite an emerging body of scholarship focusing on fatherhood as an expression of masculinity in Hollywood, both pre- and post-millennium, scant attention has been paid to Williams's recurring incarnation as father and the way in which his star persona is woven around the ambiguities of paternity that assert themselves in cinema at the end of the twentieth century. The reliance on fatherhood that Hamad identifies in the latter-day star personas of Brad Pitt, Bruce Willis, and Clint Eastwood was already well established a decade previously, in the ebullient figure of Williams. As one of 1990s Hollywood's most visible and bankable male stars, a consideration of Williams's films through the prism of fatherhood remains overdue, not least because of the diverse nature of his paternal performances. Before fatherhood became a "prominent selling point" and a reliably profitable theme in twenty-first-century Hollywood (Hamad, "Hollywood" 101), it significantly informed Williams' on-screen masculinity. His roles routinely embody the dominant tropes of postfeminist fatherhood as identified by Bruzzi, Hamad, Yvonne Tasker (2008) and Michael Kimmel (2012), among others: sensitive new man, adolescent man-child, the father who realizes the redemptive value of family. As such, the establishment and endurance of Williams's on-screen fatherhood offers another window through which to view postfeminist masculinity in Hollywood.

This chapter seeks to intervene in the discussion of postfeminist fatherhood by highlighting its potency—and its limitations—as addressed through Williams's paternal star performances. It focuses on the decade leading up to the millennium, namely the period between Williams's appearance as John Keating in *Dead Poets Society* (1989) and his performance as Dr. Know in *A.I.: Artificial Intelligence* (2001). Returning to his exclusive alma mater, the idealistic Keating quickly transcends his role as English teacher to become an inspirational figure of guidance to a group of boys on the brink of manhood. In him, the boys find an alternative to the unemotional, unsympathetic fathers to whom they have become accustomed. Keating, in fact, becomes a father figure in his own right, a role established when he bestows upon his students the secret rituals of the Dead Poets Society, a group that they duly restart. His paternal legacy is finally cemented in the film's late, rousing scene in which the boys take to their desks to salute him with Walt Whitman's own words: "O Captain, my Captain!" Although Keating faces dismissal after one boy's suicide, fundamentally his act as surrogate father outlasts his physical presence.

The entire essence of Keating's character is bound up in this move toward the paternal. Fulfilling his function as a father-substitute, he reveals a benevolent alternative to the cold, authoritarian fathers around him. Twelve years later, Williams lends his voice to the omniscient Dr. Know in *A.I.*, an encyclopaedic hologram who retains access to all the knowledge in the universe. Dr. Know has none of Keating's human warmth and ability to inspire, yet he retains an essence of the same paternal elements that Keating displays. In his ability to provide answers to the young "mecha" David (Haley Joel Osment), Dr. Know occupies the same paternal spectrum that dominates Williams's films throughout the 1990s. David is desperate to locate the Blue Fairy, who he believes can transform him into a human child, thus enabling David's desire for maternal love. Dr. Know's offer of guidance is something of a façade, however. A search engine with a human persona, he can only process David's words, not his emotions. As such, Dr. Know is a disillusioning image of substitute fatherhood, reflecting an element of paternal disenchantment prevalent in the construction of late 1990s masculinity, the paternal "desertion" and "betrayal" identified by Susan Faludi at the heart of the contemporary crisis (596).

Dead Poets Society and *A.I.* demonstrate the enduring reliance of Williams's star persona on fatherhood. They also illustrate both the benefits of postfeminist paternal masculinity, and hint—particularly in *A.I.*—at its failures. With this in mind, this chapter is concerned with the representations that occur between these two paternal poles, focusing in particular on Williams's role in *Mrs. Doubtfire.* Fatherhood was a persistent theme in 1990s Hollywood, as films from *Die Hard* (1988) to *The Lion King* (1994), *Kindergarten Cop* (1990) to *Falling Down* (1993), drew on the figure of the father as a point of anxiety, redemption, and veneration. During this period, Williams's films continually revisit the paternal figure in a variety of guises—biological and surrogate, capable and erratic, responsible and unorthodox—all through the prism of Williams's affable star identity. As such, his films during this period provide a means through which to interrogate the use of fatherhood as what I have deemed a saving mechanism. In discussing the crisis of masculinity, Kord and Krimmer note that "culturally, it is often played out in the domestic realm," and this inclination is mirrored in the films discussed next (37). The extent to which fatherhood is able to provide men with a tangible future during a period of uncertainty and crisis drives this chapter, as the familiar sight of Williams cycling through a variety of split-second identities only momentarily obscures the fact that overwhelmingly, the version of masculinity that Williams's characters choose is rooted in a domestic vision of fatherhood.

BEYOND NEVERLAND:
FATHERHOOD AND THE QUEST FOR SURVIVAL

At first glance, to equate Williams with fatherhood perhaps runs counter to the popular star image of the actor wisecracking his way through numerous zany, larger-than-life roles. In *Mork and Mindy* (ABC, 1978–1982), his first major television acting role, Williams plays the alien Mork, a clueless but ultimately lovable being trapped in the body of a grown man. This role set into motion a distinctive trend in Williams's subsequent film career: that of the man-child character, whereby the body of Williams is often inhabited with the brains, attitude or maturity of a child. Films such as *Toys* (1992), *Jumanji* (1995), and *Jack* (1996) all demonstrate the man-child persona in action and furthermore, as Nicole Matthews observes, Williams "has made a career out of being a father who acts in a childlike manner: playing games and creating domestic disasters" (112). Less indulgently, Matthews's assessment finds some common ground with Kord and Krimmer, who suggest that the childishness at the heart of many of Williams's roles, in particular Daniel in *Mrs. Doubtfire*, "disqualifies him from fatherhood" (41). Such a dismissive reading of Williams's on-screen paternity, however, belies the tensions that underlie his performances. As Bruzzi observes, there is often a complex relationship between "unconventionality and competence" at play (178). Williams's repeated incarnation as the exuberant, often eccentric, man-child does not preclude the conviction of his paternal performance, or indeed his suitability as a father.

Certainly, beneath this repeated portrayal of immaturity and frivolity, perhaps nowhere better acknowledged than in Williams's depiction of the original boy who never grew up, Peter Pan, there lies a strong inclination toward the paternal role as a source of redemption and survival. This redemption is arguably only reinforced by the popular notion of Williams as a somewhat immature figure, as he is compelled to grow up in order to survive. In *Hook*, Peter Pan eventually *does* grow up, refuting the most fundamental aspect of J. M. Barrie's original character.

Peter begins the film as an inattentive, workaholic father, a common trope employed in Hollywood during this period. In the words of Captain Hook (Dustin Hoffman), he is "a cold, selfish man who drinks too much, is obsessed with success, and who runs and hides from his wife and children." To teach him a lesson, Hook spirits Peter's two young children away to Neverland, where Peter must venture once again in order to rescue them from the clutches of his long-time nemesis. Following Hook's defeat, Peter returns from Neverland transformed and determined to be a better dad. "I can't stay and play," he tells the rest of the Lost Boys, as his priorities finally become clear. "I did what I had to do, and now I have to go back." Though the original Peter Pan made an eternal life in Neverland, here Williams's Pan is one who recognizes his future in fatherhood. With a fresh understanding of his paternal responsibilities, Peter escapes the endless childhood of Neverland and the grown-up narcissism of his workaholic lifestyle to pursue a productive future in the real world, where his long-term legacy rests in his children. If this, too, may be deemed a form of parental narcissism, it is one rendered entirely acceptable in Peter's bid for masculine survival.

In choosing fatherhood, Williams's characters reflect a wider trend in Hollywood during the same period: that of "redirecting masculine characterizations from spectacular achievement to domestic triumph" (Jeffords 166). A renewed emphasis on fatherhood as a source of masculine accomplishment has its roots in the veneration of the "new man" and the spate of single father films during the 1980s. Equally, however, it can be connected to the persistent spectre of the future that dominated pre-millennial discourse in the United States, and the desire to access this future, transcending the crisis of masculinity. President Clinton seized on the metaphor of "building a bridge" to the future, repeatedly utilizing this imagery as he counted down to the dawn of the twenty-first century. Such a focus on the future runs counter to the competing notion of masculine crisis, a state that posited the apparent "end" of masculinity as it was popularly conceived. Accessing the promise of Clinton's bright, resolutely American future, therefore, was tinged with uncertainty. Fatherhood—particularly the image of "new," emotionally involved fatherhood favored in late twentieth-century popular culture (Griswold 6–7)—provided an answer worthy of the millennial future on offer. In returning their focus to the family and investing not in themselves (rejecting the hyper-consumer lifestyle of the yuppie) but in the next generation, American men could begin to envisage their future once more.

Lee Edelman's theory of reproductive futurism illuminates this desire to live on through the child. Writing post-millennium, Edelman discusses the act of sacrificing one's own immediate desires for the knowledge that reproduction offers its own, more long-term survival: that is, the opportunity for an element of immortality achieved by channeling one's self through subsequent generations. In focusing on fatherhood and the legacy inherent in the father-child relationship—what Peter Blos has referred to as the "generational continuum," through which sons are compelled to consolidate the father's legacy—men could rediscover the possibility of a future (6). David Greven's assessment of Hollywood masculinity in the period between the Bush presidencies suggests a "struggle between narcissistic and masochistic modes of manhood" and, paradoxically, the drive toward fatherhood highlights the former mode: paternity as a solution to mortality (4). Much of the rhetoric surrounding fatherhood in the 1990s focused on the problems caused by absent fathers, shoring up fatherhood for the sake of the children. Edelman's theory reveals that this apparent paternal sacrifice is in fact rooted in the narcissistic desire to exist beyond the self: "to live longer than everyone else, and to know it," as Elias Canetti frames it (65). As Hollywood began to deal with the crisis of masculinity during the 1990s, fatherhood became a reliable source of second chances and belated deliverance. What Hamad characterizes as the "recuperative" effects of paternity, I would go further and delineate as necessary to survival (*Postfeminism* 90). In a society both fascinated and apprehensive about crossing beyond the year 2000, fatherhood became an anchor on which to hang troubled masculinity and enact the desire of continuance.

The fact that so many of Williams's roles during the decade rest on his primary characterization as a father—whether literal, as in *Hook, Mrs. Doubtfire,* and *What Dreams May Come* (1998), or surrogate, as in *Aladdin* (1992), *Patch Adams* (1998) and *Good Will Hunting* (1997)—reveals the pervasive reach of this model of masculine survival. In essence, Williams becomes the poster boy for paternal redemption, as the often childish, immature persona he cultivated during this period is channeled toward responsibility, with meaning attained through paternal performance. The exuberant, selfish individual must not be allowed to triumph over a wish to see oneself immortalized in the next generation.

This message is rendered clearly in *Aladdin*, in which the Genie is a constant source of wit and energy, a role that again relies on Williams's vocal ability. Released from his lamp, the Genie agrees to administer the young man's wishes if Aladdin will uphold his end of the bargain: to permanently set the Genie free with his third wish. Here, the Genie's first instinct is toward his own wellbeing. Yet as he begins to take on a paternal role toward Aladdin, dispensing romantic advice and general guidance, his priorities undergo a significant shift. He offers to forgo his permanent release from the lamp so that Aladdin may marry Jasmine, the Sultan's daughter, thus prioritizing Aladdin's desires—as the surrogate son—over his own. In the end, both Aladdin and the Genie get their wish, but not before the Genie comes to his selfless conclusion. Though *Aladdin* is more fantastical, meaning, and the prospect of an immortal legacy, is still ultimately rooted in a realization of fatherly instincts.

FROM ZERO TO HERO:
THE POWER OF FATHERHOOD IN *FATHER'S DAY*

The ability of fatherhood to save the beleaguered man in crisis is made particularly apparent in *Father's Day* (1997), in which Williams portrays Dale Putley, an eccentric and over-emotional man whose accomplishments amount to a failed career as a writer. Dale's first on-screen appearance shows him attempting to kill himself. Setting fire to his notebooks, he bids a dramatic goodbye to his "life's work" before inserting the barrel of a gun into his mouth. "For years I've thought about killing myself," he observes morosely. "It's the only thing that's kept me going." Dale is a failed man who sees no future for himself, with nothing to look forward to beyond the act of suicide. Yet Dale is saved by the promise of fatherhood. A phone call from his ex-girlfriend Collette (Nastassja Kinski) interrupts his suicide attempt, informing him that he may be the father of her runaway teenage son, Scott (Charlie Hofheimer). Dale is one of three contenders for the mantle of biological father, along with Collette's husband Bob (Bruce Greenwood) and her lawyer ex-boyfriend Jack (Billy Crystal). Together, Dale and Jack mount an impromptu road trip, motivated by their potential paternity to try to find Scott. They are followed by a particularly inept Bob, the face of weak, passive fatherhood against Dale and Jack's active quest.

This activity becomes crucial to successful fatherhood in *Father's Day*. Bob's deficient masculinity is rendered in his inability to change a flat tire, stranding him at a remote gas station and and removing from the narrative, in favor of two would-be fathers who will stop at nothing to find Scott. Dale and Jack are transformed into pursuers and protectors, determined to save the boy who may or may not be their son and, in doing so, save themselves. Though neither has entertained the idea of fatherhood before, they become embroiled in a competition to "prove" which one of them has claim to paternity. Jack is triumphant in his discovery that he and Scott have "the same toes," but Dale is equally convinced by the "whirly" hair that he and Scott share. When Jack crows, "no match, you lose, I'm the father," a clear link is drawn between winning and fatherhood: to lose is to face a return to a previous, meaningless existence that, for Dale in particular, is unthinkable.

Of the three men, Dale is perhaps the bluntest about the power of fatherhood to save him: "I need this kid," he tells Jack, when Jack suggests they should give up on finding the missing boy. Dale's reasoning is simple enough: while Jack has had a successful career and lives happily with his wife Carrie (Julia Louis-Dreyfus), Dale has never accomplished anything. Scott symbolizes the potential for success, and thus for survival: a different kind of "life's work" that promises a future far beyond that of a failed novel. Dale provides a clear example of survival-through-fatherhood in a period of crisis, binding Williams's star persona to the concept of fatherhood as a saving mechanism.

MRS. DOUBTFIRE: PATERNITY, PRIVILEGE, AND POWER

Perhaps the most revealing of Williams's fatherhood films is *Mrs. Doubtfire*, in which his character Daniel stands on the brink of divorce from his wife Miranda (Sally Field). Desperate to spend more time with his three children following the separation, Daniel resorts to cross-dressing as an older Scottish housekeeper, the eponymous Mrs. Doubtfire. A huge box office success in 1993, the film addresses a number of contemporary domestic issues that reflect wider cultural preoccupations in American culture at the time: divorce, the power of the family court, working mothers, and fathers' responsibilities to their children. The latter was a particularly potent issue during the 1990s. A myriad of social problems were attributed to the effects of neglectful fatherhood, including truancy, underage pregnancy, drug use and educational underachievement (Baskerville 695). Clinton made a number of references to the ill-effects of fathers who did not take responsibility for their children, in his 1994 State of the Union address observing, "we cannot renew our country

Figure 2.1. **Hands-on dad: His children are pleasantly surprised as Daniel (Robin Williams) collects them from school.** *(Mrs. Doubtfire)*

when children are having children and the fathers walk away as if the kids don't amount to anything."

Daniel, however, is the epitome of involved fatherhood, the antithesis of those fathers that Clinton castigates for abandoning their responsibility to the next generation. In the film's early scenes, we discover that Daniel is reading *Charlotte's Web* to his younger daughter Nattie (Mara Wilson), performing all the voices. He meets his children outside school, and organizes a memorable twelfth birthday party for his son Chris (Matthew Lawrence). The opening scene of the film shows Daniel at work, providing the voice of a cartoon bird, yet he walks out on his contract when his character lights up a cigarette, protesting that the cartoon is promoting smoking to a young audience.

Perhaps unusually amidst the more common Hollywood fare of executive fathers who are defined by their jobs, Daniel identifies himself almost entirely by his relationship with his children. In court, facing the reality of not being able to see them every day, he protests: "I have to be with my children. It's not a question, really, I mean I have to be with them, sir, please." Here Daniel's fatherhood is an almost spiritual endeavor, as evidenced on a subsequent court date in which he tells the judge, "I'm addicted to my children, sir. . . . Don't take my kids away from me." Daniel has moved beyond the proscriptive equation of father-breadwinner, and is an avid proponent of hands-on, emotionally engaged fathering.

Mrs. Doubtfire, then, can be seen as relatively progressive alongside other popular family films that emerged in Hollywood during the same period, such as *Kindergarten Cop*, *The Santa Clause* (1994), and *Liar Liar* (1997), which feature neglectful fathers who realize belatedly that they are missing out on the value of the father-child relationship. Notably, all these films center on a divorced man, outside the family home. As a result, their authority is diminished, and their masculine identity loses coherence amidst this familial fragmentation. While the aftereffects of divorce are only one aspect of the contemporary crisis of masculinity, its exposure in Hollywood during this period highlights the value of a solid paternal presence in the quest for masculine survival.

Rather than building to the conclusion that fatherhood is the surest means of male survival, *Mrs. Doubtfire* begins with this conceit as read. Paternity is the very essence of Daniel's character. In the recording studio, his first thought is not for his paycheck, but for his responsibility to his own, and other, children. "If you want a check, stick to the script," Daniel's boss warns him. "If you want to play Gandhi, do it on somebody else's time." His boss may be scathing about the choice he makes, but Daniel doesn't doubt where his loyalties lie. The subsequent scene, in which Daniel rushes to his children's school to meet them at the gates, is almost romantic in nature. On a sunlit San Francisco afternoon in a neat, middle class district of the city, the crowd parts in front of Daniel, revealing three smiling children who are as delighted to see their father as he is to see them. *Mrs. Doubtfire*, as a result, does not hinge on the realization of a bad father belatedly recognizing the joys of fatherhood. In placing the value of fatherhood front and center, the film nevertheless reveals the boundaries—both spoken and unspoken—of this survival.

The first of these limits is the effect of socioeconomic factors on Daniel's ability to focus on his own fatherhood. Daniel and Miranda have a comfortable, middle class lifestyle, residing in a large family home in a smart, affluent suburb. Unusually, it is Miranda who takes on the role of breadwinner, as partner in her own successful interior design company. Daniel, despite his erratic working habits and his propensity for getting fired, is also capable of earning a good salary: his employment may be sporadic, but the work he does is skilled and quite lucrative. The value of this economic position cannot be underestimated when considering Daniel's ability to transcend the masculine crisis through fatherhood.

First, Daniel's privileged economic status enables him to spend a great deal of time with his children. At the Hillards' first custody hearing, faced with a restrictive visitation schedule, he implores the judge to reconsider: "One day a week. That's not enough.. . . . I know it seems like a lot but for me it's not enough, really. I haven't been away from them for more than one day since the day they were born." The fact that Daniel has barely spent a day away from his children is evidence of his paternal commitment; it is also testament to his unusual privilege. Daniel does not need to work long hours out of the family home. Instead, as the film's early scenes make clear, he has the luxury of time with his children, a luxury born of affluence.

Neither is being fired the disaster that it would be for most fathers. Daniel is free to walk out on his job without a backward glance, even fulfilling the cathartic desire to tell his boss to "piss off" on his way out the door. It is Daniel's economic privilege that allows him to put his moral concerns for his children first, rather than their material needs, which are already amply met.

Second, when faced with limited visitation hours—amounting to odd evenings and weekends—Daniel is able to sacrifice a great deal of time and money in his masquerade as Mrs. Doubtfire. In his first evening as Mrs. Doubtfire, Daniel realizes his cooking skills are severely lacking, as he mangles the recipe and sets fire to Mrs. Doubtfire's false breasts. Seeking a quick fix that will not result in his dismissal, Daniel opts for a home delivery service that provides gourmet meals. Peeling off $100 bills for the delivery driver, Daniel is able to salvage the evening with Miranda none the wiser, an option that is again reliant upon his privileged economic standing. Equally, the time required for Daniel's enterprise as Mrs. Doubtfire is considerable. The performance not only demands time for Daniel to don his elaborate disguise, but time for Daniel to be available as Mrs. Doubtfire, both in her scheduled after-school hours, and for trips to the pool and meals out to which she is invited by Miranda.

Even his shipping job at a television company is a condition of the family court judge rather than a way of making ends meet. Daniel is not at risk of being destitute, even when he is unemployed; rather, the court wishes to see him gainfully employed as a condition of his custody case. Insulated from the realities of falling job security and long working hours that may hinder other fathers in pursuing a meaningful relationship with their children, Daniel is free to exercise an emotionally attached, hands-on version of fatherhood that allows him to harness paternity as a way through the crisis of masculinity. Daniel's recognition that his own future and therefore his own survival lies in fatherhood is not in itself remarkable; perhaps instead it is the recognition that he can indulge this paternal desire, unrestrained as he is by the demands of being the breadwinner.

Daniel's privileged economic status is impossible to decouple from his particular unique skills as a voice artist and accomplished actor. Even his shipping job is short-lived once he is able to demonstrate his prowess in front of a camera. Once again, this allows him to transcend the situation of many other fathers in his position. Daniel is rendered "special," and in retaining this status he is permitted more access to his children than might otherwise be offered to a divorced father. Eventually discovered in his masquerade as Mrs. Doubtfire, Daniel's access to his children is further restricted by the judge. Yet as a television presence, his children are still able to "see" him every day. In the process, Daniel retains access to the family home even when, ostensibly, he is banned from the premises. Furthermore, Daniel's heartfelt advice to children of divorce on his show (again in the guise as Mrs. Doubtfire) reaches the ears of Miranda, who is finally compelled to reverse the court's decision and invite Daniel back into his children's lives. His own survival as a father threatened by divorce, Daniel is able to overcome the possibility of disenfranchisement in a way that is inextricably linked to his uniqueness. As a saving mechanism, fatherhood is still most available to men of privilege.

Likewise, Daniel's plan to spend more time with his children disguised as their housekeeper is not one that would be available to many disenfranchised fathers. Daniel can have his make-up artist brother Frank (Harvey Fierstein) "make [him] a woman." Utilizing Frank's skills with heavy-duty plaster, Daniel brings his female alter ego to life using his own skills as an actor. In addition, he performs an array of unsuitable candidates over the phone to Miranda, convincing her in the process that Mrs. Doubtfire is the only viable choice to look after their children. Daniel's predicament may be recognizable to a large number of divorced or separated fathers; his way out of his powerless position, however, relies upon the skill available to him as a privileged minority. His solution is so extraordinary that it casts doubt on his reflection as an "everyman" kind of dad.

It is worth noting, however, that Daniel's unique performative abilities, as well as his evident love and affection for his children, do not deflect the attention of the family court. The audience is sure of Daniel's commitment to his fatherhood from the very beginning, yet the court remains unconvinced by his emotional pleas. Here, *Mrs. Doubtfire* engages with a common criticism of the family court in the United States, that of its unnecessary dispossession of good fathers in divorce proceedings.

At the Hillards' initial hearing, the judge, while acknowledging his reluctance to deprive the Hillard children of "an obviously loving father," is clear in his demarcation of the most suitable parent. He guarantees a devastated Daniel a follow-up hearing, stating: "I'm giving you three months, Mr. Hillard. Three months in which to get a job, keep it, and create a suitable home. If this proves to be a possibility for you, I will consider a joint custody arrangement when we reconvene." The judge immediately reduces Daniel's fatherhood to the quantifiable criteria of employment and residency, relegating his emotional attachment to his children in the process. The court remains beholden to a traditional performance of fatherhood—namely, that of the provider—that diminishes Daniel's relationship with his children while demanding the fulfilment of measurable criteria.

Again, the focus shifts back to Daniel's economic position: financially stable, he can rent an apartment and begin turning it into a "suitable home." What the court's intervention and subsequent conditions reveal is the difficulty of rendering fatherhood as salvific for any man, regardless of extenuating factors. As *Mrs. Doubtfire* reveals, the future on offer through fatherhood is slowly diminished with every condition placed upon it before it is recognized as valuable: in this case, the necessity of providing a home and financial support before regular contact is permitted. This requirement is further complicated by the fact that in the 1990s, the economy was an unstable place for many American men: as Faludi suggests, "[t]he role of the family breadwinner was plainly being undermined by economic forces that spat many men back into a treacherous job market during corporate 'consolidations and downsizings'" (595). In maintaining an economic demand on fathers, the family court is revealed as a significant barrier to many men's attempts to find meaning in fatherhood.

A discussion centering on Daniel's performance of fatherhood, inevitably, comes to rest on his adoption of the Mrs. Doubtfire persona. There is a distinctly paradoxical attitude towards fatherhood in the United States during this period: on the one hand, the father is deemed responsible for many problems afflicting the American family, yet on the other hand he is held up as the saviour of this very same unit. In Daniel's reconstruction as Mrs. Doubtfire, the same mixture of anxiety and desire is revealed. Daniel must be permitted to return to the family home and retain an influence over his children. Yet this return is tempered by the fact that Daniel's only hope of re-entry into the family is in disguise as his female alter-ego.

However, the unavoidable maternal appropriation that underlies Daniel's adoption of the Mrs. Doubtfire disguise reveals some of the most fundamental limitations at the heart of postfeminist paternity as a form of masculine survival. Tania Modleski's work on maternal marginalization as a feature of Hollywood's fatherhood films is testament to the longevity of the theme; drawing on this, Hamad argues that "the appropriation and/or marginalization of motherhood" has become increasingly normalized (*Postfeminism* 17). *Mrs. Doubtfire* succeeds in achieving both. Miranda is largely sidelined; however, in recognizing fatherhood as a source of masculine survival, Daniel turns toward a fatherhood heavily influenced by the maternal. As his brother remarks on putting the finishing touches to Mrs. Doubtfire's face mask, "any closer, and you'd be Mom."

It is not simply in appearance that Daniel comes to resemble a no-nonsense matriarch. Prior to their separation, Daniel and Miranda's parenting roles are defined neatly along the lines of indulgence and discipline. However reluctant she is to be the authoritarian parent, Miranda is nevertheless under no illusion about her role in the family: "I bring home a birthday cake and a few gifts," she snaps after the fiasco of Chris's birthday party. "You bring home the goddamn San Diego Zoo and I have to clean up after it!" Daniel, meanwhile, is the "fun" parent, more interested in surprises than schoolwork. Yet as Mrs. Doubtfire, Daniel becomes the epitome of responsibility. He enforces the house rules, banning television until homework has been completed, chastising Chris for bad language, and ensuring the children do their share of the household chores. Mrs. Doubtfire is equally concerned with the housework, and her cooking and cleaning begins to surpass Miranda's own high expectations. In essence, Mrs. Doubtfire moves not into the space left by Daniel, but the space left by a working Miranda, a case of the (incognito) father out-mothering the mother.

Thus the power of fatherhood to lift men out of the masculine crisis is revealed to come at the expense of the mother in *Mrs. Doubtfire*. Miranda is relegated to the sidelines as Daniel continues to expand his influence as Mrs. Doubtfire. Even when he is exposed and punished by the family court, his visitation reduced to supervised sessions, it is from Miranda that Daniel derives his final grab for power. As Mrs. Doubtfire, he maintains a presence in the Hillards' home, beamed into their living room daily via his new television show. It is on the set of this television show that Miranda finally visits Daniel, armed with an apology and a firm acceptance of blame. "I don't want to hurt our children," she tells him, before proceeding to tear up the custody agreement and assure Daniel that he can visit the kids whenever he likes. Daniel is finally able to execute his fatherhood in a way that benefits both himself and his children, but for this to happen Miranda must relinquish an aspect of her own parental autonomy and authority within the home.

CONCLUSION

What *Mrs. Doubtfire* reveals is both the redemptive possibilities of fatherhood and the underlying limitations that render it inaccessible to many men. In dealing specifically with the aftermath of Daniel's divorce, in itself an increasingly common occurrence by the 1990s, many of these limitations are exacerbated by Daniel's exclusion from the family. Though the film is concerned with the restrictions placed upon Daniel's fatherhood by the family court, it reveals its own restrictions on masculine survival through fatherhood. In doing so, the paternal veneration apparent in Williams's 1990s canon of films provides a solution to the crisis of masculinity that, in the end, remains lacking.

Mrs. Doubtfire reveals the machinations of power that underlie both the crisis of masculinity and the move toward fatherhood. Daniel's economic privilege and his time with his children rely heavily on Miranda's status as breadwinner. When she snaps at him early in the film, "I have no choices, Daniel!" she illustrates the necessary sacrifice that underpins Daniel's survival through fatherhood. Daniel's narrative survival is reliant upon Miranda being displaced. In embracing fatherhood—both as himself and as Mrs. Doubtfire—Daniel is able to appropriate the parental space within the Hillard family and in doing so suggests that paternal salvation must always, on some level, come at the expense of, rather than as a complement to, the mother.

Mrs. Doubtfire is arguably the peak of Williams's fatherhood films in a decade when his star persona became inextricably linked with an image of domestic, redemptive fatherhood. Yet as Hollywood moved into the 2000s, Williams's star persona began to deviate from this paternal model. Films such as *One Hour Photo* (2002), *Insomnia* (2002), and *Death to Smoochy* (2002) demonstrate a conscious shift away from the family man image, suggesting in the process a post-millennial disappointment in the promise of paternal survival. When he does return to on-screen fatherhood, as in *World's Greatest Dad* (2009), it is often with a heavy dose of black comedy. Here, the title levels an ironic swipe at Williams's paternal persona, as he portrays a failed father exploiting the death of his son. Williams remains a significant figure in Hollywood's construction of fatherhood as the answer to the masculine crisis; however, his films also lay bare the limitations of this approach, relying as they do on privilege, performance, and the appropriation of maternal space in a final bid for renewed power.

Williams's on-screen fatherhood is made particularly poignant by his death from suicide in 2014, at the age of sixty-three. Outpourings of sentiment were immediate from a public who had grown up with his cinematic presence. The refrain of Nattie in *Mrs. Doubtfire*—"we're his goddamn kids too!"—took on a wider significance as a generation of adults reflected on Williams's contribution to popular Hollywood cinema. This blurring of the line between Williams's own life and his star persona is further heightened by the comments made in the days following his death by Mara Wilson and Lisa Jakub, his on-screen daughters in *Mrs. Doubtfire*. Both recall Williams as an affable, kind man who took pains to make them comfortable and, in the case of Jakub, campaign for her education. Perhaps inevitably, given their roles in the film, there is a fondness in their public statements that reinforces the wider paternal appeal of Williams, beyond his own biological fatherhood.

Williams's death leaves a finite body of work that reveals an enduring paternal theme. Until the end, his work returns again and again to fatherhood:

to its joys, its disappointments, its potential to "save" the men who embrace it. Reactions to his death only serve to highlight the paternal space Williams occupied on the Hollywood screen, and the fatherhood, however flawed, that would eventually define his legacy.

WORKS CITED

Baskerville, Stephen. "The Politics of Fatherhood." *PS: Political Science and Politics* 35:4 (2002): 695–99. Print.

Blos, Peter. *Son and Father: Before and Beyond the Oedipus Complex*. London: Free Press, 1985. Print.

Bruzzi, Stella. *Bringing Up Daddy: Fatherhood and Masculinity in Post-War Hollywood*. London: British Film Institute, 2005. Print.

Canetti, Elias. *Crowds and Power*. Trans. Carol Stewart. London: Penguin, 1992. Print.

Edelman, Lee. *No Future: Queer Theory and the Death Drive*. Durham: Duke UP, 2004. Print.

Faludi, Susan. *Stiffed*. London: Chatto & Windus, 1999. Print.

Greven, David. *Manhood in Hollywood from Bush to Bush*. Austin: U of Texas P, 2009. Print.

Griswold, Robert L. *Fatherhood in America: A History*. New York: Basic, 1993. Print.

Hamad, Hannah. *Postfeminism and Paternity in Contemporary US Film: Framing Fatherhood*. London: Routledge, 2014. Print.

———. "Hollywood Fatherhood: Paternal Postfeminism in Contemporary Popular Cinema." *Postfeminism and Contemporary Hollywood Cinema*. Ed. Joel Gwynne and Nadine Muller. New York: Palgrave Macmillan, 2013. 99–115. Print.

Jeffords, Susan. *Hard Bodies: Hollywood Masculinity in the Reagan Era*. New Brunswick, NJ: Rutgers UP, 1994. Print.

Kimmel, Michael. *Manhood in America: A Cultural History*. 3rd ed. Oxford: Oxford UP, 2012. Print.

Kord, Susanne, and Elisabeth Krimmer. *Contemporary Hollywood Masculinities: Gender, Genre, and Politics*. New York: Palgrave Macmillan, 2011. Print.

Matthews, Nicole. *Comic Politics: Gender in Hollywood Comedy after the New Right*. Manchester: Manchester UP, 2000. Print.

Modleski, Tania. *Feminism without Women: Culture and Criticism in a "Postfeminist" Age*. London: Routledge, 1991. Print.

Tasker, Yvonne. "Practically Perfect People: Postfeminism, Masculinity and Male Parenting in Contemporary Cinema." *A Family Affair: Cinema Calls Home*. Ed. Murray Pomerance. London: Wallflower, 2008. 175-87. Print.

Rethinking the Nation and the Body Politic: *The Wrestler* and the Demise of American Exceptionalism

John A. Gronbeck-Tedesco

Appearing as a performative interview in his critical exegesis on postmodern cinema and 9/11 in *This Is a Picture and Not the World* (2007), Joseph Natoli presents this reading:

> Americans live in a story of their exceptionalism, and that's been severely challenged. On the neocon end, fear has to be kept on the boil so that a tongue-tied, born again president from Texas can appear to be a laconic, heroic westerner like Gary Cooper "come to bring 'em to justice." We're caught between manufactured fear and not supposing to care, and what shows up on the diagnostic screen looks like cultural post-traumatic shock (2).

Natoli paraphrases the sentiments of many: at the conclusion of George W. Bush's second term, what kind of world had been built (or destroyed) since 2001 and what would be America's role therein? Cultural studies scholars since have channeled their efforts toward understanding how this world has been portrayed in newsreels and political speeches, on pages and in music, and on multiple screens. What Baudrillard memorably called the "mother of all events," or the "pure event that concentrates in itself all events that never took place," was edited, cropped, and instantaneously narrativized via photograph and video (403). Above all, 9/11 was a postmodern catastrophe that was immediately and viscerally experienced as *visual*.

Since the event, film criticism has signaled its commitment to reading American cinema in the context of 9/11, with studies that have probed a cinematic typology consisting of a cornucopia of fear, hyperconsumerism, war fetish, and a range of other representational fields that have reaped harvest out of the sensational (Birkenstein, Froula, and Randell; Markert). The semiotics of post-9/11 trauma has popularized some new and not-so-new genres within American filmmaking including bullet-ridden action-adventure, apocalyptic sci-fi, and biological horror. Together, these narrative conglomerations have served up a potpourri of allegorical meanings ranging from dystopian nihilism to collective planetary resistance, from self-sacrifice of the lone survivor to nationalist chest thumping in an attempt to save the world. In many of these well-known storylines, the plot hails the American masses that once again have been "called into action," as Wheeler Winston Dixon wrote, by "encourag[ing] the warrior spirit" (1). This is the martial cause so central to America's historical fascination with "victory culture," in Tom Engelhardt's apt reading. This obsession has been renewed in post-9/11 films in which America's place in the world is reaffirmed by destroying an evil Other in movies about war, biological epidemics, and zombie takeovers (Engelhardt). Yet unmistakably, the recurring business of victory culture has also come under fire.

While enjoying a long lineage of triumphal narratives, war films, and the like have also revealed cracks in US cultural mythology. Just as mixed tales of 9/11 phantasms prompt episodes of duty, contagion, and invasion, they also envision the spectral horror of modernity culpable for creating the circumstances that made 9/11 possible. This culpability reveals itself in a montage of futurist scenarios in which humankind's undoing is the product of its own making. Modern science made the virus; human curiosity brought the zombie-like existence; capitalist arrangements led to genocidal competition and the conditions for planetary dissolution.

The following discussion enters into this diverse body of film scholarship by situating *The Wrestler* (2008) within the broader lineaments of two "posts": post–9/11 popular culture and post–second wave masculinity. I submit that the filmic text uses varying iterations of the male body as a gendered site of physical and psychic trauma symbolizing the nation. As both biological organism and national community (or the body politic), the wrestling body acts as a repository of 9/11 memory and lingering spiritual pain that masks impulses of self-destruction. That is, the shadow of 9/11 violence that largely was omitted from visual accounts of the event made public reappears in *The Wrestler*. My reading rests on the premise that there was an unusual *lack* of violence in most of the footage from the attacks, as commented on by Mikita Brottman. In Brottman's definition, horror denotes the "visual representations of violence done to the human body" (164). While absence of carnage does not necessarily connote absence of horror, Brottman's argument does raise the problem of where we place the bodily and psychic wounds inflicted by 9/11 and its aftermath. Because of the absence of carnal violence—that is, violence committed to the human body—we are continually forced to reimagine this violence, which arguably has the potential to produce an infinitely longer, more painful, even more "real" scenario, because it can never be contained, resolved, or concluded. This violence without finitude adds an essential ingredient to the ongoing politics of traumatic memory and gives primacy to the male body in service to the nation.

The Wrestler makes visible this flushing out of a violence that relies on impulses of self-destruction—here literally embodied—that mark post-9/11 American nationalism in gendered performances on the screen. Viewing the film as an allegorical text of national anxiety permits us to uncover an ambivalent commentary on American masculinity and nation building in a new landscape of postmodern globalization and the War on Terror. In one way, *The Wrestler* appears to follow a longer lineage of sports films, particularly boxing, that deal with archetypical vicissitudes of the physically tested working-class male hero, often culminating in victory through brutal perseverance (Grindon; Streible). This is the oft-cited American spirit never to give up, to vanquish one's enemies even if it is at the expense of one's body, for that *is* the utility of the fetishized, beaten working-class personhood on display. But *The Wrestler*'s characters are stand-ins for national communities caught in the throes of loss and lack, while their respective performative spaces represent a commodified and crumbling American economic and spiritual geography. The film focuses on the injunction to give up oneself wholly in the name of spectacle, making the politics of the male body enmeshed with systematic physical and psychic abuse, which concludes with the sacrifice of the main character in the name of catharsis. These images of sadomasochism expose an undercurrent of self-loathing that allows for the debasement of bodies on screen, sacrificial tokens of America's postindustrial and imperial malaise.

Like boxing films, the wrestling ring becomes an aspirational place to claim first-class whiteness, which is under threat in our current global, postfeminist world. The withering body exposes its overused materiality that parallels the spiritual or metaphysical lack of the protagonist. This is white masculinity in crisis (Grindon 7). Hamilton Carroll asserts that the contemporary discourse of white masculinity in crisis reconfigures social transformations at the global and national level into "white male injury," which "is a phenomenon that attempts to recoup political, economic, and cultural authority in the face of a destabilized national consensus" (2). The process of reclaiming his preferred place in the nation hinges on the protagonist Ram's recuperation of white masculinity. *The Wrestler* indirectly comments on postfeminist America in that both men and women in the film lack traditional social centers. Men and women of Ram's world are not of the postfeminist, postmodern world, but are its victims.

By weaving a unique thematic combination of gender, class, race, and sexuality, the film presents individual suffering sustained on behalf of performative labor, to earn income and to please a crowd, which direct us to a figurative national pain that threatens the body politic and the status of American masculinity today. *The Wrestler* is a post-9/11 jeremiad that examines the diminishing reservoirs of national purpose by ruefully confronting the possibility of defeat. Rather than staging an uphill battle through which the nation and the workingman emerge victorious, *The Wrestler* centers on individual denial spoken through oscillating scenes of self-flagellation (male) and eroticism (female) in which the weathered body assumes the likeness of the browbeaten and fetishized nation. The disconcerting dual spectacle of pleasure and pain forces us to ponder a national imaginary bereft of its foundational pillars.

THE BODY AS A SITE OF PLEASURE AND PAIN

The Wrestler tells the story of Randy "the Ram" Robinson (Mickey Rourke), an aging professional wrestler attempting to resuscitate his career. Ram's heyday was the 1980s, when he enjoyed star status facing Olympian opponents like Hulk Hogan and Randy "Macho Man" Savage. Though dwindling, his spectators still venture to community centers and elementary schools temporarily transformed into wrestling rings with the trappings of arena flair. The main conflict arises when Randy suffers a heart attack, the moment when he reluctantly realizes that he must retire lest his passion for the ring end his life prematurely. Afraid of dying alone, Randy takes this period of convalescence to build relationships; he tries to make amends with his estranged daughter, Stephanie, a college-age lesbian who has forgotten her neglectful father. Randy also enlists the help of a friend/love interest, "Cassidy" (Marisa Tomei), a stripper and single mother (whose real name is Pam) whose reluctant acceptance of Randy's romantic entreaties solidifies his downfall. The tragedy of the film comes when, after ruining his chances for reconciliation with his daughter, he decides to reenter the ring. Unbeknownst to him, Randy has also won the interest of Pam who has decided to leave stripping and possibly pursue a relationship with him. It is too late; "the world," he tells Pam, "don't give a shit about me." The glimmer of romantic hope fades and the demise of the protagonist is secured.

The dual gendered identities of Randy/Ram and Pam/Cassidy advance bodily expressions that become performative symbols of the nation. As the consummate sport of the American workingman, professional wrestling, a precursor to NASCAR, displays the physical essence of victory and defeat. But it is distinct due to the entertainment value that comes from its reliance on choreographed success. Indeed, part of the disconcerting aura of the film is the intent with which the wrestlers plan their gruesome fights, such as when Ram must endure a torrent of staples inlaid in his skin by fellow wrestler

Necro Butcher. Perhaps what is most disturbing about *The Wrestler* is the methodical sadomasochism employed, the precision of exacting pain from the partner and the self for the sake of paycheck and notoriety. There is no shortage of ghastly scenes that put the viewer in the ring to witness slaps, cuts, and blows, with the wrestlers' steadfast resolve to fulfill their expected duties. It is the practice of real pain and suffering, though it is perceived as fake, that induces fetishization of the male gladiatorial body, which must agonize in order to affect the anticipated spectacle.

Even out of the ring Randy desires to maintain his performative self, Ram. We track the wrestler through work, home, and in the ring, granted access to his life, "behind the scenes" as it were, to catch the wrestler bleaching his hair blonde, injecting steroids, and visiting a tanning bed regularly. Randy lives his life for the maintenance of Ram, which depends on a steady routine of drugs and bandages in his weekly recuperation. Living in a trailer home with no phone and often late with rent, he is the projection of the beaten and commodified working-class male body who wheezes, coughs, and relies on a hearing aid and thick eyeglasses to get by in life. And despite the degree of self-abuse, Randy's imminent downfall cannot be avoided; no matter how much mutilation Ram sustains, his priorities to maintain visibility and to be the star are unalterable.

The issue of visibility is significant here. Randy earns additional money by working in a warehouse that keeps him hidden from society. Prior to the fatal decision to return to the ring, however, he reluctantly takes a second job at the deli counter as another source of income when he is no longer able to wrestle. An explosive plot point arises when Randy, fed up at the counter after a customer recognizes him as Ram the wrestler, punches a cheese slicer that sets blood spewing from his hand. At this moment the internal struggle of Randy/Ram becomes externalized. This instance of self-awareness and embarrassment destabilizes dual identities that are locked in conflict; they are confined to one body but always at odds. Caught in an alter ego tension, Randy eschews his working-class identity by physically rejecting it in the public space of the service industry. What he truly yearns for is a form of performative labor that is glamorous, as Ram the wrestler. Upon slicing his hand (intentionally, the film suggests), Randy returns to his customary psycho-physical space of masochistic indulgence. Tragically, self-mutilation—violence to the self—is the only way that Randy/Ram may feel important.

It is at this point that Randy decides, against his doctor's advice, to return to the ring, having effectively decided that he would rather die in the ring as Ram than live barred from wrestling as Randy.

If there is any lightness palpable in *The Wrestler*, it is brought out by the character, Cassidy/Pam, who works at a local strip club, Randy's social hangout. Here working-class womanhood offers important parallels to American manhood while diverging in certain key ways. Pam is a single parent whose bodily display is also the essence of her labor. Ram's collisional physicality is balanced by the grace of Cassidy's sensual striptease. While she also represents the ogled working body exhibited for popular consumption, her performative labor negates the wrestler's barbarity and violence via a mode of fleshliness that rests on erotic enticement. The film juxtaposes male and female models of bodily display, each of which depends on a kind of identity splitting and performance in the service of mass entertainment. Each gendered working-class labor—wrestling (male) and stripping (female)—necessarily embodies a psychic other to perform the spectacle, Randy as "Ram" and Pam as "Cassidy." But whereas Randy is unable to extricate himself from Ram outside of the ring—thereby creating the primary conflict of the film—Pam *is* able to rid herself of her alter ego. Telling Randy that "the club and the real world don't mix," Pam cannot combine selves, which is why she does not commit to a relationship with Randy ("a customer") until she quits the club. Thus in her working environment, Cassidy is an identity that is nothing but alienated labor, which is clearly distinguished from the "real" Pam. Randy, however, carries Ram wherever he goes and wishes to live life

Figure 3.1.   Cassidy (Marisa Tomei) as Ram's gendered working-class complement. *(The Wrestler)*

as the wrestler at all times. Ultimately Pam decides to leave the stripping profession, her psychic break occurring in a scene while performing on stage, as she suddenly experiences shame. Rushing out of the club, she utters out loud, "Pam," a verbal affirmation of her preferred identity. Whereas Pam's emotional interior is removed from her labor thus allowing her to divest herself from Cassidy, Randy must be Ram to access his desired emotional space.

These contrasting performative displays of Randy/Ram and Pam/Cassidy summon commentary on sexuality, more obviously in the figure of Cassidy/ Pam, but also in the case of Ram/Randy since the staging of semi-clad men engaged in violent ritual invites examination of the erotic economy of wrestling within the overlapping space of voyeurism and spectacle. Inspired by Laura Mulvey's seminal work on gender and film, Steve Neale sees the interplay between voyeurism and spectacle of the male body as part of the semiotic work of phantasy. Here voyeurism involves "sadomasochistic phantasies and themes," so that in Westerns and war films (and perhaps wrestling films), male personae become subjects of "voyeuristic looking" by both viewers and other male characters in scenes that disavow symbolic castration in the service of heteromasculinity. By this token, we become voyeurs as we follow Randy/Ram through his quotidian routines, watching him perform for adoring fans and fellow wrestlers. Our observing is therefore mediated, condoned, and encouraged by other spectators and wrestlers. We in effect emulate other voyeurs on screen, so that part of this voyeuristic pleasure, Neale continues, becomes the indulgence of "fetishistic looking" that contextualizes the male body in pleasing forms of ritualistic spectacle (16-18). *The Wrestler* depends on this transference of fetishized violence into forms of pleasing spectacle in highly ritualized scenes of heterosexual and homosocial bonding. This dynamic structures the film's ambivalent workings of male bodily desire.

The liminal space between homosexuality and homosociality has been explored in numerous works of literary criticism and popular culture. In cinema, "buddy films" are oft-cited examples of male bonding that arrive in the form of crime-fighting partners or military comrades. Cynthia Fuchs notes this kinship "figures a masculine hegemony which appears to subsume [cultural and ideological tensions]" and "typically collapses intramasculine differences by effecting an uncomfortable sameness, a transgression of boundaries between self and other, inside and outside, legitimate and illicit" (194). Such bonding replays Eve Sedgwick's memorable framing of "male homosocial desire," which Fuchs cites in the slippage between homosexuality and homophobia (Fuchs 194). In a similar fashion, Ram exists in a fraternal community of wrestlers that enacts the slippage that Justin Wyatt has identified as homoerotic tension in "male friendship films." Wyatt argues that such movies "virulently attempt to heterosexualize their homosocial protagonists through secondary romantic liaisons," but that "homoerotic tension remains, creating a space for the violent spectacle that ironically sometimes allows key moments of physical contact" (52–53). Such contact is abundant throughout *The Wrestler* locker room and bar scenes where wrestlers establish a heterosexual male domain that may "safely" occasion ambiguous bodily desire. Because of the high visibility of skin and violence, the film presents a topos of hetero/ homoeroticism, where on the one hand heterosexuality is championed amid displays of homosocial bonding in the ring, while on the other is the homoerotic suggestion in scenes of cavorting wrestlers.

In considering different encodings of masculinity, it is worth recalling Linda Williams's likening of emotive filmic junctures to "body genres" in which the "excess" of sexual, violent, or melodramatic content formulates a sensationalist aesthetic. This framework uncovers the nature of gratuitousness itself as it relates to the "body 'beside itself' with sexual pleasure, fear and terror or overpowering sadness." *The Wrestler* displays a violence that yields the "body beside itself," which inheres the excessiveness of such "bodily ecstasy." Borrowing from Williams's analysis of sadomasochistic horror films, the body bashing of wrestlers always concurrently bears the threat of castration, thereby exposing the real of originary sexual difference. Both male and female working-class bodies are belabored and fetishized in settings of male violence (wrestling) and female eroticism (stripping) that privilege a heterosexual male viewership. But while the alternation between violence and erotica intimates a sublation of any homoerotic tension, it ineluctably sparks associations with fluctuating gestures of companionship (3–4, 9–10).

In fact there is a crisis in Randy's manhood since he appears to lack the virility often associated with familiar paragons of masculinity. His worn, aging body imparts an impaired vitality—a suggestion of asexuality or even impotence—that threatens the state of traditional male identity. The desire to elude symbolic castration drives Randy's quest for self-affirmation in scenes of heteromasculinity, such as when he watches Cassidy's strip tease or when he takes a young coed home from a bar. Both Pam and Randy solicit their gendered opposite for self-affirmation. Pam needs Randy's gaze as a striptease viewer not only for money but as an antidote to aging, just as Randy needs the affection of Pam and Stephanie if he is to have any hope for a meaningful life. To return to a psychoanalytical reading, female love would grant Randy an attachment that repels symbolic castration and fulfills his heteromasculine injunction.

Such ambivalence provokes further scrutiny of the American male collective in today's postindustrial malaise. Interrogating the state of traditional heteromasculine identity, the film asks, what is the status of today's buddies? Randy's continued nostalgia for the 1980s (a decade he and Pam long for while charging "the nineties fucking sucked") idealizes the post-Vietnam era when the brawn of a Schwarzenegger or Stallone was celebrated and respected. Randy, while not shorn of brawn, is frustratingly falling short, a broken version of once notable heroes, John Wayne, Chuck Norris, or Clint Eastwood. But unlike the worldly forces that animated these classic luminaries, *The Wrestler* lays out that there is no longer a wild frontier or enemy of the state for the protagonist to combat and vanquish. The proverbial archenemy is now within. The embattled psychic self is the despairing byproduct of a postindustrial, postnational displacement that has wreaked havoc on conventional understandings of heteromasculine identity.

Randy/Ram is a tragic protagonist, and although he is the fetishized male body on display for viewing pleasure, he is also the subject of our voyeurism that forces us to behold his demise and lament his inability to channel the superlative ego of traditional male leads. In the end his aspirations persist unsatisfied, so that Randy can become nothing more than a symbol of broken sociality. This development moves the sexual and gendered politics of the film toward an allegorical narrative of the nation, casting light on America's wounded platonic communality.

THE WRESTLER AS POLITICAL ALLEGORY

At this point we can corral these diverse bodily acts and disclose the ways in which they occupy the terrain of nation and community simultaneously. The (self-)violence Randy/Ram sustains, I assert, is suggestive of a symbolic violence America enacts on itself. The doubling of the body as biology and nation constructs an analogy between the mission that the wrestler must carry out to satisfy his spectators and the national purpose that drives the United States to satiate its publics. This dual reading of corporeality presents the interrelated questions, to what extent and at what expense must the male body endure and for the benefit of whom or what? The protagonist's conflicted identity mirrors America's internal division, so that if Ram represents the victorious nation, Randy is its modern-day belabored enabler, the withered working-class body. As the film comments, the spectacle of supremacy can only be achieved at the necessary expense of the bodily and psychic self with the real cost of global capitalism and empire becoming too great. In this sense, victory is *and can only be* spectacle.

Randy/Ram's self-destruction evinces the proposition that America is on a wayward path of imperial fantasy, where, in the process of saving the world and capitalizing on it, the United States is paving the way for its own downfall. History, in this case, is the unavoidable enabler. The film makes evident that post-9/11 nationalism is written from earlier scripts of empire, with expansion of conflict in the Middle East not only purportedly justified but expected. Triumph is hereby staged ("Mission Accomplished"), relying on a form of masochistic punishment that has enervated the body politic. In its most pessimistic light, the film leaves the viewer wondering if America's heroism has been reduced to mere farce.

Political and wrestling theaters converge, calling forth an assortment of national communities and narratives. Here the ring is an index of nationalist tropes that reimagines an America which is slowly disappearing, much like the wrestlers who are its vocal champions. When in action, Ram combats foes that personify inimical ideas and groups historically threatening to the status quo; they are stand-ins for the anti-American element. Ram faces Tommy Rotten who bears the anarchical encircled "A" tattooed on his back and dons a Goth-Punk style fashioned with black mascara and a Mohawk. Also present is the brutal Necro Butcher, a caricature of an Appalachian bumpkin who is the bloodiest opponent of the film.

However, enemies in the ring are friends backstage. Ram's wrestling co-hort consists of a multiracial and supportive community. Although the inter-racial camaraderie bespeaks an image of American working-class plurality, the focus on Randy/Ram favors a white masculinity to symbolize this particu-lar America, which parallels the history of professional wrestling more gener-ally. Yet the film also makes plain that even Randy's whiteness is rooted in the embattled history of US racial and ethnic discord. We learn that Randy's actual birth name is Robin Ramzinski, suggesting his Polish roots and unveil-ing his choice to hide his ethnicity. The process of renaming not only creates his wrestling persona but also refers to a common experience of Americaniza-tion that historically has stripped names of their racial and ethnic signifiers. The thorough burial of "Robin" further distances Randy/Ram from any origi-nary self, any "I" that is Robin. His subjectivity, then, has always been rooted in alterity, including in his pre-wrestling days as part of the process of cultural acclimatization that has compelled immigrants to remake their national self-hood in accordance with normative American nomenclature.

Whiteness is thus highlighted in America's new community where Ram is searching for membership. As one who lives in a trailer park and fraternizes at a strip club, Randy conforms to a white trash figure whose ethnic white-ness is aspirational. His claim to first-class whiteness can only occur in the ring, another reason Randy prefers being Ram. Writing about the film *Million Dollar Baby*, Carroll draws from the work of Diane Negra to discuss how Irishness becomes "'enriched whiteness' that allows for the celebration of whiteness by casting it as something other than privilege" (131). Similarly, Randy is a "good" white man, not a bigoted WASP of privilege, because he inhabits second-class whiteness. Victory in the ring grants Ram the white privilege he is denied as Randy.

Another key aesthetic that projects working-class male whiteness is the film's music, the soundtrack of this traditional—yet increasingly peripheral—community. Streaming throughout the film is the sonic *jouissance* of heavy metal that blasts standard hair rock anthems like Quiet Riot's "Bang Your Head," Slaughter's "Dangerous," and Rat Attack's "Round and Round." Along with the title track, "The Wrestler," a ballad performed by Bruce Springsteen during the concluding credits, these melodies comprise the lyricism of a New Jersey jeremiad. They attest to an America that clings to recognizable cultural codes in order to grapple with the uncontrollable dynamism of globalization and reworking of postmodern identities. Randy struggles to understand his place in these changing surroundings, for outside of the timeless ring lies a new cultural topography that is more distant and unknowable. Many of the non-wrestling working people Randy encounters, for example, are foreign born, capturing the demographic metamorphosis of the United States in the wake of globalization. There is the South Asian convenience store worker, Iranian doctor, and the Korean hair stylist. The film relays that New Jersey, like the United States, has changed in the postindustrial, transnational age. Randy and his brethren are ambling on the margins of an evolving national landscape not of their making. They are the victims of postmodernity, which makes them unable to form viable relationships. The dissociative conflict within the psychic space of Randy/Ram is the fractured constitution of postmodern America in its blurry global form.

This blurriness is a function of American nationalism that itself has undergone a transformation since 9/11. Numerous images permeate *The Wrestler* that inspire manifold readings of national metaphor. Throughout the film's background lies a striking visual idiom illustrative of the allegorical interpretation I am attempting in this chapter. There is no shortage of scenes, for example, which contain the US flag. We see it prominently displayed in the bar where Pam and Randy go and sing 1980s hard rock classics (and where they both agree that "the nineties fucking sucked"), and we witness it prominently draped above Randy's bed. In one pivotal moment, Randy stands in front of his bathroom mirror removing his surgical dressing. Beneath the bandage appears a massive postoperative vertical scar that hemisects his chest. The large flag hangs in the background but is contained within the mirror's reflection. The illusion is that Randy's foregrounded wound extends back to the flag, so that the union of foreground and background by way of the physical scar conjures speculation about America's scars. Here the correlation between Randy's damaged body and America's is most pronounced. Both bodies are wounded, making America's durability inextricable from

Randy's. In fact, there are several mirror scenes throughout the film where we see Randy looking at himself. Shots of these reflections reinscribe Randy's search for self-affirmation but in the end cannot see (or accept) himself in any loveable way. What he sees in the mirror is not what he imagines in the ring, his desired spectacular self. By extension, we might surmise that this speculative "seeing" now directs the wishful nationalism of today's post–9/11 body politic, with the uncomfortable query: Must the United States now confront a different reflection?

The issue of national reflection is most provocatively conveyed when Randy, disgusted that he has stood up Stephanie and depressed that Pam does not want a relationship, picks up a young girl in bar who wants to "party like a fireman." After a night of alcohol, cocaine, and bathroom sex, Ram wakes up in the girl's room the next morning surrounded by titillating posters of firemen on the wall. Excessive revelations of the quintessential 9/11 American hero might impress ambivalent conclusions. On the one hand, the fireman could be the working subject whose sacrifice is not spectacle, in contrast to the wrestler. Or perhaps the fireman is an icon that has become overly indulged, elevated to superhero-like proportions which helps ensure that 9/11 memory conforms to a certain visual narrative. They are the hyperconsumed male agents of nationalism that have been thoroughly fetishized in today's visual lexicon. The fireman allusion is made acrid amid the confluence of spectacle, desire, and bodily sacrifice, which strengthens the film's tendency toward souring US triumphalism. The sequence of drugs, risqué sex, and fireman imagery establishes addiction and fetish as impoverishing variables in the equation of modern nationalism and the larger choreography of the American mission.

Other visual motifs illuminate the film's proclamation that the United States has been led astray. Religious messages crop up throughout the film, completing the well-known American dyad of "God and country." It is therefore possible to interpret Randy/Ram not as a victim but as a sacrificial character. He is likened to Jesus Christ, the chosen sufferer of a bygone America. This connection is made most apparent when Cassidy, while giving Randy a lap dance, plays with his hair and abruptly quotes lines from *Passion of the Christ*. Randy, she quips, is the "sacrificial Ram." The film revisits this theme when the two are talking outside a vintage clothing store. Behind Randy looms a Spanish-language church displaying the words "pare de sufrir" (suffer no longer). Another comment on the globalization of Elizabeth, New Jersey, the sign also acts as a verbal demand for America to discontinue its present course.

But sacrifice Ram (and America) must. Appropriately, the themes of religion, nation, and the male body come to a head in the climax of the film, when Ram, against his doctor's orders, decides to participate in the twentieth anniversary rematch against the "Ayatollah." The latter turns out to be a used car salesman named Bob, a former wrestling colleague who caringly cautions Randy to take it easy in the match. The figure of the Ayatollah is *the* specter of America's post-9/11 enemy: Islam, Iran, the greater Middle East. In a throwback to Rocky's bout with his great Soviet opponent, Ivan Drago, the frosted-blonde Ram must fight a new foe: the Middle Eastern subject, the phantasm that is post-9/11 America's quintessential Big Other. The final scene is inundated with national symbolism and American whiteness. A giant American flag is unfurled in the background as Ram enters to chants of "USA, USA" and the song, "Sweet Child O' Mine" by Guns N' Roses. In his concluding monologue, Ram discloses to the crowd that he will continue to wrestle for the fans until they no longer cheer. During the course of the match, Ram's health rapidly deteriorates, but he is determined in the end to perform the "Ram Jam" to appease his admirers. He climbs the ropes and, after stabilizing himself in a Christ-like pose, jumps.

POST-9/11 CATHARSIS AND
REIMAGINING THE (MALE) BODY POLITIC

Ram's leap is the final fusion between wrestling and post-9/11 nationalism, both deemed tragic exercises that come with risks of imminent failure. *The Wrestler* presents a reeling national community in a story that treats the inability to forge personal and political relationships in the modern era. For Randy/Ram, there is only the ring, only the choreographed field of battle, a performative space that exacts a bounty on the corporeal and political body (see figure 3.2). Ultimately the spectacle involves real self-sacrifice, the film suggests, by irreducibly charging that the pleasure-through-pain principle could lead the USA to a suicidal body slam. However, not knowing exactly whether Ram lives or dies at the end (though it is presumed the latter) may also indicate an absence of clear direction of where America is headed, an uncertainty as to whether it can or will dismount the ropes. The message is critical of both America's embrace of neoliberalism and of its War on Terror. How then do we rewrite the commonplace narratives of triumphalism and wherein to we locate a new vision of American manhood not predicated on the performance of violence?

By way of conclusion, I would like to recall some of the ways M. Jacqui Alexander has beautifully explored the terrain of the body as a carrier of history and the social and psychic forces of community building. Alexander sees the body not only as a key locus of human pain and suffering but also one of rehabilitation and redirection of selfhood. What she calls "body praxis" is

Figure 3.2.   The sacrificial body in America's politico-theatrical ring. *(The Wrestler)*

"central in our mapping of subjectivity," and, she writes, "is equally central in understanding the structure of healing as well." In her estimation, "healing work" is a "call to remember" and that "remembering is embodied" (316). "Body praxis" signifies "the positioning of the body as a source of knowledge within terms differently modulated than the materiality of the body and its entanglement in the struggle against commodification, as it continues to be summoned in the service of capital." This is a "theory of the flesh" that requires consideration of how "to transmute [the] body and the pain of its dismemberment to a remembering of the body to its existential purpose" (329).

While in this context Alexander is specifically referring to body praxis as a radical possibility for transnational feminism and women of color, I think it is worth applying her formulations to carving out different outcomes for the Randy/Rams of the world and for America's transubstantiation toward a greater bodily self that averts a tragic ending. It is preferable that we harness Alexander's theory of the flesh, the Sacred, and body praxis toward new understandings of the relationship between the body politic the politics of the body, particularly in utterances of post-9/11 gendered evocations of the American nation. For her work directs us to constructions of American nationalism that consist of myriad affective events, performances of cohesive as well as contested alignments of the spiritual and the political which more than ever rest on bodily service to capitalism and country. A theory of the flesh yields the possibility of positioning biopolitical bodies within a new post-9/11 constellation that go beyond mere labor-use and avoid empire building altogether. Finding new ways to build a post-9/11 national community depends on, in Alexander's words, "sacred means through which we come to be at home in the body that supercede its positioning in materiality" (329).

Following this theory of the flesh, Jafari Allen has advocated for an "erotic subjectivity" to revamp the political. Erotic subjectivity "is the deeper understandings and compulsions of the body and soul—simultaneously embodying and invoking sex and death [which] works toward not only transgressing but transcending and finally transforming hegemonies of global capital, the state, and of bourgeois, limited, and limiting notions of gender, sexuality, and blackness, for example (97)."

The body as purely consumed good or alienated labor in the service of spectacle is a perverse and tragic appropriation of the Sacred. It surrenders the political corpus of the nation-state toward a path of self-destruction in service of capitalism and empire, from which no way out emerges. Understanding body praxis means extricating the gendered body from its alienated serviceability and redefining our bodily relation to governmental and social directives. At the very least it requires an assessment of the different ways the body is managed and mismanaged and for whom and what. Searching for alternative manifestations of 9/11 memory offers the possibility for rethinking the "event" as something beyond the justification of empire but rather a legacy with which the body politic must continue to wrestle.

WORKS CITED

Alexander, M. Jacqui. *Pedagogies of Crossing: Meditations on Feminism, Sexual Politics, Memory, and the Sacred.* Durham: Duke UP, 2005. Print.

Allen, Jafari S. *¡Venceremos? The Erotics of Black Self-Making in Cuba.* Durham: Duke UP, 2011. Print.

Baudrillard, Jean. "L'Esprit du Terrorisme." Trans. Michel Valentin. *The South Atlantic Quarterly* 101.2 (2002): 403-15. Print.

Birkenstein, Jeff, Anna Froula, and Karen Randell. *Reframing 9/11: Film, Popular Culture and the "War on Terror."* New York: Continuum, 2010. Print.

Brottman, Mikita. "The Fascination of the Abomination: The Censored Images of 9/11." *Film and Television after 9/11.* Ed. Wheeler Winston Dixon. Carbondale: Southern Illinois UP, 2004. Print.

Carroll, Hamilton. *Affirmative Reaction: New Formations of White Masculinity.* Durham: Duke UP, 2011. Print.

Dixon, Wheeler Winston. "Something Lost—Film after 9/11." *Film and Television after 9/11*. Ed. Wheeler Winston Dixon. Carbondale: Southern Illinois UP, 2004. Print.

Engelhardt, Tom. *The End of Victory Culture: Cold War America and the Disillusioning of a Generation*. 2nd ed. Amherst: U of Massachusetts P, 2007. Print.

Fuchs, Cynthia J. "The Buddy Politic." *Screening the Male, Exploring Masculinities in Hollywood Cinema*. Ed. Steven Cohan and Ina Rae Hark. New York: Routledge, 1993. Print.

Grindon, Leger. *Knockout: The Boxer and Boxing in American Cinema*. Jackson: UP of Mississippi, 2011. Print.

Markert, John. *Post-9/11 Cinema: Through a Lens Darkly*. Lanham, MD: Scarecrow, 2011. Print.

Natoli, Joseph. *This Is a Picture and Not the World: Movies and a Post-9/11 America*. Albany: SUNY Albany P, 2007. Print.

Neale, Steve. "Masculinity as Spectacle: Reflections on Men and Mainstream Cinema." *Screening the Male: Exploring Masculinities in Hollywood Cinema*. Ed. Steven Cohan and Ina Rae Hark. New York: Routledge, 1993. 253–64. Print.

Negra, Diane. *What a Girl Wants? Fantasizing the Reclamation of Self in Postfeminism*. New York: Routledge, 2009. Print.

Streible, Dan. *Fight Pictures: A History of Boxing and Early Cinema*. Berkeley: University of California P, 2008. Print.

Williams, Linda. "Film Bodies: Gender, Genre, and Excess." *Film Quarterly* 44, no. 4 (1991): 2–12. Print.

Wyatt, Justin. "Identity, Queerness, and Homosocial Bonding: The Case of Swingers." *Masculinity: Bodies, Movies, Culture*. Ed. Peter Lehman. New York: Routledge, 2001. Print.

4

The *Bourne* Refusal:
Changing the Rules of the Game?

Mary T. Hartson

As early as 1957 nascent masculinity studies, inaugurated by sociologist Helen Mayer Hacker's pioneering paper, "The New Burdens of Masculinity," indicated that the concept of masculinity was changing: new expressive functions (interpersonal skills) were being added to men's instrumental function as "sturdy oaks." Over fifty years later the destabilization of masculinity has become commonplace and male action heroes walk a fine line between conforming to the codes of an increasingly violent and irrelevant patriarchy, and risking a potentially threatening "feminization" by adopting qualities like compassion, sensitivity, and expressiveness traditionally associated with women. It would appear that this is the primary conflict afoot in the identity crisis undergone by rogue agent Jason Bourne (Matt Damon) in the extremely successful *Bourne* trilogy of films—*The Bourne Identity* (2002); *The Bourne Supremacy* (2004) directed by Doug Liman; and *The Bourne Ultimatum* (2007) directed by Paul Greengrass. Though the expectation that men occupy the role of "sturdy oaks" while also engaging their own sensitivity and compassion has continued, the *Bourne* trilogy suggests that this process is fraught with peril, as the two appear antithetical in nature. Since the patriarchy within the film demands the sacrifice of those "expressive functions" to sustain and reproduce itself, the sturdy and unfeeling "oaks"—"assets" or agents such as Bourne—who serve the organization must perform without emotion.

But despite Bourne's apparent paradigm shift toward a kinder, gentler form of masculinity, his behavior on screen remains essentially that of a violent warrior. The continuing and even intensifying pace of violence throughout the three films suggests that, though a break with the existing patriarchy may have occurred, its logic of force continues to underlie the hero's behavior.

In fact, any potential "feminization" of the protagonist is carefully limited through a variety of techniques, most notably the films' steadfast refusal, through dress and camera work, to specularize the hero, as well as a constant recourse to the use of violence as a marker of unequivocal masculine power. Through the repeated staging of violence and the shame it often elicits in the protagonist, the films also work to absolve any sense of guilt incurred for past violent acts. In this way they provide a comforting vision of powerful yet ethical masculinity that deflects attention from the insecurities projected in the film, allaying fears of objectification or patriarchal abandonment while also absolving the hero from any shame or guilt associated with the violent acts he has committed.

Action hero Jason Bourne rejects his place in the patriarchy that claims him by disobeying his "fathers" and abandoning the organization that trained him, apparently choosing to break with the training that created him as a violent, unfeeling killing machine. Acting in accordance with his feelings, he rejects an assigned kill and attempts to live apart with his newly developed moral code. However, as the power of a corrupt and antiquated patriarchy over him appears to wane, the action hero continues to fight—harder than ever—to assert his power and establish his identity. Not allowed to simply become a feeling, non-violent masculine being, not allowed to opt out (Bourne: "I don't wanna do this anymore"; Conklin [Chris Cooper]: "I don't think that's a decision you can make." *Identity*), this action hero must continue to use his body in the way he was trained.

Susan Faludi's exploration of the concept of "ornamental culture" sheds light on the transformation that prevailing conceptualizations of masculinity have undergone since Hacker's essay appeared. She argues that in the latter half of the twentieth-century man as the self-sufficient "doer" was replaced by man as an object to be consumed, suggesting that masculinity's primary conflict may be more complicated than Hacker puts forth. Masculinity has indeed become feminized, as Faludi argues, though not in becoming more sensitive or more compassionate, but rather by threatening to convert men into objects to be looked at, just as women already were. As Faludi states: "In a culture of ornament, by contrast, manhood is defined by appearance, by youth and attractiveness, by money and aggression . . . objectification, passivity, infantilization. . . . Not only are they losing the society they were once essential to, they are "gaining" the very world women so recently shucked off as demeaning and dehumanizing" (38). Bourne's victory seems not so much based in his incipient emotionalism as it is in the active mastery of his environment despite a lack of support from the patriarchal institution to which he belonged. He is a man who gets things done, who just tries to "do the right thing" (*Identity*), but above all, who is always doing. More than acted upon, he acts. Struggling to convert his body into autonomous actor or agent rather than object or ornament, Bourne's masculinity poses as a return to a manhood defined by character, stoicism, integrity, and so on, as described by Faludi. But ironically, this return takes the form of a spectacular performance and object of consumption in the form of the film itself, and thus serves as a decoy or deflection of attention from the fundamental problem. The performance of the character's ongoing identity crisis and the emotions generated by it provides imaginary relief from objectification as the hero continually faces and masters all challenges.

The fantastic success of the *Bourne* trilogy calls attention to itself, even in a world of blockbuster action films—*The Bourne Ultimatum* outperformed the James Bond film *Casino Royale* (2006) in gross domestic returns by $60 million[1]—and is a testament to the films' relevance and resonance for their American audience and masculinity studies in the United States.[2] The three *Bourne* films provide a privileged vantage point from which to observe how masculinity works given that they achieved an extreme degree of success with such a wide audience. As Anthony Easthope says "men in fact live the dominant myth of masculinity unevenly, often resisting it. But as a social force popular culture cannot be escaped. And it provides a solid base of evidence from which to discuss masculinity" (81). The popularity of the *Bourne* trilogy provides a window through which to observe the way the films' American audience enjoyed seeing masculinity represented—and to speculate about some of the underlying insecurities that may find their phantasmagoric resolution in the actions of their heroic protagonist.

In the three films, Jason Bourne, former CIA operative who as one of his superiors asserts has "gone off the reservation," tries to piece together his past while evading capture or assassination by his former employers. The amnesia-stricken Bourne gradually recalls his identity as a government-trained assassin who finally rebelled against that training in refusing to kill an African politician to whom he had been assigned—all because he encountered the man relaxing among his children. Bourne's humanity interferes with his ability to perform the function for which he was trained, but he is repeatedly drawn back into violent contact with his old world as he struggles not only to escape the grip of the CIA but to answer the question, "who am I?"

While giving up none of the strength and mastery needed to dominate every situation he encounters, Bourne embodies the compassion and sensitivity that threaten his position in the reigning patriarchal power structure—a structure whose power seems to be waning as a result of his transformation. A destabilized, shadowy, far-reaching yet chaotic division of CIA Black-Ops produced Bourne the killing machine. Yet the tug of Bourne's humanity and his rejection of single-minded violence wrests him from his place within this unfeeling, machine-like structure. Nevertheless, the regular if reluctant recourse to violence reasserts his masculine power—and protects against "slippage" into the dangerous "feminine"—represented within this context as allowing feeling to interfere with function. The character's amnesia and questioning of his own identity highlight his alienation from the masculine system of military domination. Within a postmodern, high-tech environment, Bourne consistently dominates every situation, and with tactics ranging from very high to very low tech, he stays one step ahead of his patriarchal "fathers" who would eliminate him as a malfunctioning "asset." His shadowy memory of past assignments reflects a sense of confusion and guilt about his US military involvement, but his character provides the fantasy relief that a strong, capable, heterosexual male will prevail. Bourne's appeal resides in the fact that, in an international, consumerist, and postmodern world where the patriarchy has failed to protect its sons both literally and figuratively, all things are possible for this lone individual.

Though Bourne is clearly a dysfunctional, or perhaps more accurately "malfunctioning" male model within the patriarchal hierarchy presented in these films, his struggle may reflect that of many in this complex, high-tech, postmodern world. It is a condition that Krishan Kumar characterizes as demonstrating a "heightened degree of fragmentation, pluralism and individualism . . . partly related to the changes in work organization and technology" (142). Confusing scenes in international train stations, airports, embassies, and police stations create a sense of displacement and heighten Bourne's own confusion about his identity. In a scene set in a Geneva train station (*Identity*) the camera performs a rapid 360-degree pan encompassing the kinetic movement of the crowd, the scene intercut with shots of the trains' timetable and closeups of Bourne's face. His momentary confusion dissolves into a purposeful stride as his body in motion assures the viewer that he is in control of his surroundings. Throughout the films Bourne appears to follow his instincts, engaging with his constantly changing surroundings, improvising as necessary and never making a mistake. His weakness in not remembering his past makes his version of masculinity accessible to a public who admires his ability to "get the job done" despite his fundamental uncertainty about what the job entails.

Bourne's triumph seems to lie in his ability to manage his environment more than in his ability to act in accordance with his emotions. Though his emotionalism is seen as the primary initial plot motivator, it is his consistent, unemotional ability to manage his surroundings and outwit his pursuers that make him a hero. His thinking appears as action given that he never stops to deliberate or plan, but rather so integrates himself in his surroundings that the world seems an extension of his body. As seen in *Supremacy*, he fashions the most mundane items into powerful tools during his nonstop quest: a rolled-up magazine becomes a club, a pen disables his attacker's grip, a lamp cord strangles his opponent, and a magazine stuck in a toaster combined with an intentional gas leak blows up an entire building. The character is never at a loss as to what to do next and the end result makes his opponents look fumbling and inept.

ALIENATION FROM THE PATRIARCHY

The sense of abandonment—and even hostility—that Bourne feels from his "fathers" in the secret "Treadstone" program causes his further distancing from the organization that "raised him" in a sense. Here Treadstone is a division of CIA Black-Ops that trains military volunteers to work as secret government assassins or "assets" and Bourne was supposed to be their greatest achievement. In *Identity* Conklin, Bourne's immediate superior, tells him "You're US government property . . . a 30 million dollar malfunctioning machine. I don't send you to kill. I send you to be invisible." And Treadstone, we find out in *Ultimatum*, is "an umbrella organization for all Black-Ops," a way to bypass official jurisdiction and commit acts of clandestine violence. An organizational sketch of the fictional sector of the CIA concerned with "Black-Ops" reveals a peculiar division in age and gender reflecting each sector's function within the hierarchy—a division which parallels the post–World War II American context described by Faludi in *Stiffed: The Betrayal of the American Man*. Unlike their fathers who had embraced the nascent corporate culture, their sons felt betrayed and abandoned as the promise of a stable and well-paid career proved illusory: "And finally, as the boy grew older, the institutions that had promised him a masculine honor and pride in exchange for his loyalty, double-crossed him. . . . The institutions that men had identified with no longer identified with them" (29–30). In the Pentagon are those whose hands stay, both literally and figuratively, clean. These men are almost universally older (apparently over the age of fifty-five) and very well dressed, wearing suits and ties. Many from their ranks prove to be corrupt and opportunistic. Beneath them is the "generation" of Bourne and his fellow assets. These men appear to be between the ages of thirty and forty, and, except for Bourne, follow orders slavishly. Their depersonalization is reflected in their designation as "assets" rather than "agents" or "collaborators." Merely functioning as an extension of a larger organization, they renounce their individual identities and at least initially, wholeheartedly embrace the purposes of their superiors. While they resemble those "sturdy oaks" described by Hacker, they perform their duties without emotion, thus lacking the "interpersonal" dimension. When Bourne strays from the path laid out for him and fails to operate in accordance with his training, he is ordered eliminated as a threatening liability. His value to the organization resides in his absolute renunciation of his own personal moral judgment and emotions so that he can serve as an object or tool of the larger organization. The film portrays him literally as a malfunctioning machine. In jarring bursts, Bourne's memory of his first act of rebellion returns to him. On a stormy night he creeps up behind his target, Wombosi (Adewale Akinnuoye-Agbaje), the African dictator he has been ordered to kill. The rough sea and flashes of lightening buffeting the dictator's yacht reflect Bourne's own agitated state and perhaps an even more cosmic disruption as the system is about to break down. As Bourne's vision expands to include not only the back of Wombosi's head, but his three sleeping children as well, Bourne is thrown into a state of confusion.

The extra-diagetic sound of electricity shorting out reflects the misfiring of Bourne's neurons as he struggles to make sense of the situation. Suddenly Bourne employs his own judgment, refusing to kill and thus directly contravening the orders he has been given—and is instantly made a fugitive from the hierarchy to which he belonged. The cost of allegiance to the hierarchy becomes clear as the films progress. In *The Bourne Identity*, it is only upon death that a fellow asset (Clive Owen) says to Bourne, "Look at us. Look at what they make you give"—a recognition of the futile sacrifice demanded by their superiors which is echoed in *The Bourne Supremacy* when Bourne pronounces these identical words to another wounded asset—reflecting the sense of betrayal felt by Bourne and his contemporaries in the face of an incomprehensible corporate/military environment.

The bitter sentiment of the sacrificed "son" resembles that expressed by generations of American soldiers who came back from wars in Korea, Vietnam, Iraq and Afghanistan—wars in which the stakes were never clear and victory never apparent, or by those displaced workers in American corporations and industries who suddenly found themselves abandoned by a system within which they had founded their identity. Soldiering has been seen as a way to perform masculinity and is especially relevant in the Bourne films since the protagonist is cast in a quasi-military role as a fighting tool of the US government. Jon Robert Adams labels as "'soldierly masculinity' the particular brand of traditional male function associated with heroism—courage, suppressed emotion, strength, and clearheaded decisiveness . . . soldier heroes" (9). Though Bourne performs in accordance with the heroic model, he does not accept the label and thus fails to identify with the patriarchal inheritance on offer. This is seen in *Supremacy* when Conklin, Bourne's direct superior in *Identity*, insists on calling him "soldier" even as Bourne rejects the term and says he is not part of the organization. He chooses to walk away from his position as their number one asset and to embrace a retired life with his newfound love, Marie (Franka Potente). He elects to live in peace, respecting his autonomous moral sense and "interpersonal" dictates.

The division between the masculine ideal of manhood as represented by the soldier, and the reality of those men who served and returned from service as "broken" or emasculated mirrors Bourne's early idealism in committing his life to a purpose, and later on, his disillusionment upon understanding what he is being asked to do: "War provides society with definitions of manhood, while, simultaneously, men experience war as the antithesis of society's definition. Something has to break somewhere and it's usually the men" (Adams 2). Just as many soldiers in real wars suffer from PTSD,[3] Bourne and the other assets experience a variety of symptoms. Nicky, the young woman in *The Bourne Supremacy* who is charged with overseeing the health of the assets reports: [that these men suffer from] "depression, anger, compulsive behaviors. They had physical symptoms—sensitivity to light" and in Bourne's case, amnesia as well.

In his fragmented memory of the first assassination he performed, in Berlin, he hears Conklin's voice reminding him repeatedly, "this is war soldier," and "this is a live operation." But because of his recognition of

Figure 4.1. The *Bourne* trilogy's insistence on violence attempts to anchor an uncertain masculinity, as Jason Bourne (Matt Damon) continues to fight without a clear enemy. *(The Bourne Ultimatum)*

his own compassion, Bourne no longer sees himself as Conklin does. He no longer thinks of himself as an "asset," or functioning part of the military machine, and therefore expresses only confusion when Conklin repeatedly addresses him as "soldier." Bourne believes he has broken free of this patriarchal structure and no longer identifies with his former self. Bourne's amnesia and constant questioning of his own identity highlight his alienation from his former position in a hierarchical organization. It seems a break with the dominant patriarchal masculinity that has been foisted on men in the past, "insofar as men live the dominant version of masculinity . . . they are themselves trapped in structures that fix and limit masculine identity. They do what they *have* to do" (Easthope 82). But Bourne opens himself to his own sensitivity and compassion and thus loses his place in the hierarchical military organization. As he insists to a doubtful Marie, who has just discovered that he is a trained killer, "I'm just trying to do the right thing here." Bourne no longer does what *he has to do*, he does what he thinks is right, guided largely by his emotions.

Bourne does not seem concerned about being guided by his emotions. He is seen cutting Marie's hair, expressing his weakness and confusion, and refusing to kill in the presence of children. His version of masculinity seems to embrace his "feminine" side. The level of sympathy Bourne establishes with the three women represented in the films demonstrates a more emotional approach that is represented as antithetical to the functionality of his CIA Black-Ops training. Nicky, the CIA agent assigned to monitor the health and well-being of the assets in the field as seen in *Supremacy*, becomes sympathetic with Bourne's plight (having previously been linked to him romantically) and assists him in his escape—in effect defecting from the organization herself at the moment she allows her feelings to guide her actions. And Pamela Landy, the CIA agent who is being set up to take the fall in case the wrongdoings of the agency are exposed, is ridiculed by colleagues and superiors for being out of her depth and unable to use the sort of clear rational thinking necessary in the management of the situation with Bourne. Marie, Bourne's love interest in *Identity* who is killed off at the beginning of *Supremacy*, consistently (naively?) underestimates the violence they face and tells Bourne immediately before she is shot: "it doesn't have to be this way," meaning that perhaps the man Bourne eludes may not be out to kill him and they may not be in grave danger.

Her assassination shortly after uttering these words seems to prove that it most certainly does have to be this way. Bourne appears as an outcast of a decaying and corrupt system that seems at odds with the gentler ethos represented by the free-spirited, vagabond, Marie.[4] The casting of the star of the internationally successful German thriller *Run Lola Run*, Franka Potente, emphasizes international mobility while providing a striking ideological contrast between Bourne's formation and her own. His military demeanor and appearance contrast markedly with Marie's euro-hippie bright red hair (a warm and lively color that is repeatedly associated with her in contrast to the tans, browns, and cool blues that surround Bourne), unconventional clothing, and relaxed disposition. This woman's innocence, something that she consistently demonstrates even up to a moment before her death (Bourne: "We don't have a choice." Marie: "Yes, we do."), is cited by Bourne later in the film as motivation for his behavior when he doesn't kill Ward Abbott, a corrupt superior ("she wouldn't want me to").

Despite the disintegration of the patriarchal social system as represented in the film by the military "fathers" will to destroy their "son," the alternative—an irrelevant "feminized" or decorative masculinity does not come to pass. The character of Jason Bourne is not presented primarily to be ogled or admired for his physical beauty. He frequently wears worn and shapeless sweaters. And even when he is shown exercising, his body is covered—doing pull-ups in a sweater, for example, or running on the beach in shorts down to his knees. The sole sex scene in the trilogy occurs in *Identity* and, though Marie helps Bourne remove his tank top, the camera quickly pulls away and shows only a part of his bare back. Such treatment presents a marked contrast to the Rambo series in which an oiled and pumped up Sylvester Stallone spends much of the movie flexing his abs and biceps, and the Bond films in which the hero is known as much for his personal style, elegance, and sex appeal as he is for his talents as an action hero. Bourne's non-focus on the male body seems a return to old-style protection of masculinity from the "wrong" kind of looking—what Mark Simpson calls a "crisis of looking" or look-at-ness. There is no whiff of homosexuality that could cause slippage of the heterosexual hero (94). The films' extreme focus on Bourne the "doer," or performing body, also allays any anxiety the viewer may have about the irrelevance a man may feel in a culture that focuses on physical display rather than on functionality. As Faludi states:

> Ornamental culture has proved the ultimate expression of the American Century, sweeping away institutions in which men felt some sense of belonging and replacing them with visual spectacles that they can only watch and that benefit global commercial forces they cannot fathom. . . . The internal qualities once said to embody manhood—surefootedness, inner strength, confidence of purpose—are merchandised to men to enhance their manliness. (35)

And of course these films are one more way to merchandise manliness to men. Bourne the action hero becomes both the threatening object and the antidote to being perceived as an object.

THE FUNCTION OF VIOLENCE

Despite his repeated attempts to leave his old life of violence behind him, Bourne is drawn back in by the need to defend himself and discover the culprit behind Marie's death. Like the reluctant killer heroes in a long tradition including *Rambo* (1982, 1985, 1988, 2008), *Robocop* (1987, 2014), Clint Eastwood's character in *Unforgiven* (1992), or more recently, Matt Damon's character in *Elysium* (2013) and Kevin Costner's character in the 2014 film *3 Days to Kill*, the protagonist is not looking for trouble, but wants only to live a peaceful life. Circumstances demand they return to their violent past in an attempt to right some wrong that is being foisted upon them or someone they love, but their very reluctance serves as a sort of absolution for the killing that ensues.

The apparent justification for further violence constituted by Marie's murder ensures that, despite Bourne's initial refusal to kill, each film is as violent as the last. Bourne's body continues to perform the violence for which it was trained and ultimately his transition is incomplete: "it is through the training of the body that the most fundamental dispositions are imposed" (118), according to Pierre Bourdieu. Furthermore, it is through violence that Bourne's transition is made safe for the films' viewing public. As R. W. Connell notes "with gradually increasing pressure for gender equality, it seems a market was created for representations of power in the arena men could still claim as distinctly their own, plain violence" (215). Though Bourne deploys violence in a purely utilitarian fashion, it is a constant throughout the three films and as such, constantly reaffirms the masculinity of the protagonist. Bourne's physical prowess and super-human endurance provide a defense against any erosion of masculinity as he begins to act in accordance with his own emotions and sense of compassion rather than with the orders of his superiors. Bourne's experience of his impotence threatens to reveal the abject within—a prospect that is successfully suppressed time and again as he proves himself capable of mastering every threat and defeating every foe. In these films, the character of Bourne seems part of a dying social structure and the assets are seen as a sort of endangered species: "We're the last ones, you and I," says a Treadstone product in Berlin shortly before Bourne is "forced" to kill him.

Still, more assets appear as needed: in Paris, Madrid, Tangier, New York. In every situation, their behavior is understated, efficient, and unemotional, and their importance is that they are there to do a job, no questions asked. As the ultimate example of this efficiency and purposefulness, Bourne does nothing but act. He does not hesitate; he is not there to be looked at; he is there to do. As Nicky says, "they don't do random." Everything he does seems a logical extension of an instantaneous and thorough thought process.

It is a reassuring model of self-sufficiency and preparedness despite the fact that the character is completely cut off from society in the attempt to keep his identity secret. On the contrary, his complete independence adds to his mystique:

> The man controlling his environment is today the prevailing American image of masculinity. A man is expected to prove himself not by being part of society but by being untouched by it, soaring above it. He's a man because he won't be stopped. He'll fight attempts to tamp him down; if he has to, he'll use his gun (Faludi 10).

Thus Bourne's isolation increases his heroic stature rather than diminishing it. In a very real sense, Bourne is a decoy masculinity, a fantasy created to provide the reassurance that, though it has been modified and displaced, it is still very much in charge.

THE PERFORMANCE OF CRISIS

The performance of crisis in these films is not a mere consequence of traumatic circumstances. Instead it plays an important part in the embodied social and political domain that is masculinity. Following Fintan Walsh, I would like to draw attention to crisis' constitutive—and often re-constitutive—power. As he asserts: "In place of this presumption of stasis, or failure . . . crisis is not an end in itself but a period of disorder that precedes and precipitates a longer period of productivity, restructuring, and redevelopment, which may even lead to the reestablishment of the temporarily agitated norm" (8). The representation, or deliberate staging, of crisis and the emotions associated with it in this film may perform the psychological function of protecting the subject from a prolonged encounter with the abject, promoting heteronormative masculine subjectivity in the face of a destabilized patriarchal hierarchy; and, on a larger scale, providing absolution from the sense of shame that accompanies the use of violence.

Bourne's intense ambivalence in the face of his own violent acts seems to indicate that he is struggling with the logic of his dominators. He has been softened through his resistance to killing and, perhaps even more so, through contact with Marie, yet he continues to engage in violent encounters as others try to subdue or destroy him. Interestingly, his behavior in many of these encounters exhibits those characteristics of shame as outlined by Sara Ahmed:

> The subject may seek to hide from that other; she or he may turn away from the other's gaze, or drop the head in a sensation more acute and intense than

embarrassment. In other words, shame feels like an exposure—another sees what I have done that is bad and hence shameful—but also involves an attempt to hide, a hiding that requires the subject turn away from the other and towards itself . . . To be witnessed in one's failure is to be ashamed: to have one's shame witnessed is even more shaming (103).

He continues to perform violence, but appears to have a sense of shame about it as demonstrated through his facial expressions and demeanor when he looks up at Marie or Nicky immediately after brutally defeating his attackers. After a grueling fight scene in *Ultimatum* with a Morrocan asset in which he finally kills his opponent in a bathroom, Bourne glances as Nicky and then looks away guiltily as if to protest that he did not want things to be this way and regrets the need for such force. The experience of shame itself implies that the subject "knows better" or "is better than that," internalizing the standard of goodness, and thus returning to the subject the possibility of salvation: "shame collapses the 'I' with the 'we' in the failure to transform the social ideal into action, a failure which, when witnessed, confirms the ideal, and makes possible a return to pride . . . (the fact that we are shamed by this past 'shows' that we are now good and caring subjects)" (Ahmed 109–10). The mechanism of a sense of shame functions to reconcile the hero's brutality (and the audience's enjoyment of the display) with the maintenance of perception of oneself as a good and caring person.

Remorse, shame, and disgust, among other emotions, can be read as potent performatives in themselves. Ahmed offers an analysis of "affective economies" in which feelings are seen not as emanations of individual, interior states, but as "effects of circulation" (8)—social and cultural practices that are repeated and which generate effects through their repetition. The staging of Bourne's crisis, along with its management and resolution, works to bolster heteronormative masculinity as the hero's encounter with the abject is successfully contained. The films' logic that maintains that violence is a necessary means to resolving one's differences is never seriously interrogated despite the hero's apparent conversion to non-violence. Furthermore, the experience of his emotions works to absolve him—and by extension, the viewer—of any guilt or shame that may have been incurred by participating in or supporting violent acts. Ahmed maintains that the public performance of shame can act to restore the individual's relationship to a higher ideal. In these films Bourne is seemingly restored in this way through the expression of shame, but the repeated enactment of his crisis necessitates the continued use of force. As Ahmed points out: "it is through announcing a crisis in security that new forms of security, border policing and surveillance become justified" (76). Ultimately a masculinity predicated on violence is upheld, though the hero's sense of shame and reformation remove any taint of accompanying guilt.

In the *Bourne* trilogy, male trouble is performed repeatedly in order that it may be successfully managed and overcome. The hero faces his own weakness and confusion, not as the terminal result of being psychologically or physically dominated, but rather as a platform upon which to assert his individual strength and emerge victorious in the face of adversity. Bourne's body drops from great heights, suffers gunshots, car crashes, blows, knife wounds, and drowning so that he can be shown emerging whole and strong.

Through the repeated encounter with the abject in the form of his own weakness, Bourne performs a containment of the non-heteronormative masculine subject positioning. By overcoming his weakness, he recovers his position in the patriarchal system despite its apparent compromise posed by his betrayal by corrupt military "fathers." The spectacularization of crisis works to reconstitute a phallic masculinity by way of what Walsh refers to as a "performative politics of suffering" (182) betraying an underlying fear of feminization. The films' obsessive insistence on violent encounter and the hero's capability in this arena protects against any potential "feminization" represented by his reluctance to kill in certain circumstances, and also by his sensitive and close relationships with the women in the film. The victim-hero's initial encounter with his own impotence both heightens his valor by humanizing him and, like the severe physical wounding from which he invariable recovers, demonstrates the magnitude of his feat.

Thus the *Bourne* trilogy works as one more attempt to prop up an inadequate paradigm or, as I have explained earlier, as setting up a decoy masculinity. Rather than confronting and accepting a sense of powerlessness, Bourne insists through his heroic actions that he is not the victim but rather the master of his own fate. In Faludi's view it is just this sort of delusional thinking that prevents men from addressing their real situation: "If men are the masters of their fate what do they do about the unspoken sense that they are being mastered, in the marketplace and at home, by forces that seem to be sweeping away the soil from beneath their feet? If men are mythologized as the ones that *make things happen*, then how can they begin to analyze what is *happening to them*" (13)? Watching the character of Jason Bourne affords the viewer pleasure and provides imaginary relief for millions of viewers who want to see a decent, resourceful, capable man consistently outwit those powers that would deprive him of his independence and power. The logic of violence is not refuted through the action portrayed, ensuring that this traditional prop or defense of heteronormative masculinity continues to work to contain the threat of the abject and to maintain a societal status quo. The apparent ethos of non-violence is maintained through the employment of the representation of shame, an emotion which serves to exonerate the hero for the extreme acts of violence he commits—and the viewer for enjoying such displays of violence.

Through the figure of the soldier-hero who claims to renounce violence while continually employing it, the *Bourne* trilogy also works to redefine masculinity as outside the existing patriarchal hierarchy, yet safely distant from objectivity or any association with "ornamental culture" that might threaten it. Bourne, the eminently capable hero, proves time and again he is ready for anything and only wants "to do the right thing."

NOTES

1. Box Office Mojo. http://boxofficemojo.com/movies/?id=bourneultimatum.htm.

2. The *Bourne* franchise continued beyond the Damon trilogy with the release of a fourth film, *The Bourne Legacy* (directed by Tony Gilroy) in 2012. Starring Jeremy Renner, Rachel Weisz, and Edward Norton, it is cast as a separate project but has many repeating characters (though without Jason Bourne/Matt Damon). This film is set in the world created by Robert Ludlum but is based on the novel *The Bourne Legacy* (2004) by Eric Van Lustbader. Related plot elements, including the extreme government agent gone rogue, can also be seen in other popular films such as *Knight and Day* with Tom Cruise (2010) and *Safe House* with Denzel Washington (2012).

3. With over one million soldiers serving or having served in present-day conflicts in Iraq and Afghanistan, estimates are that as many as one in six will suffer PTSD (Armor 5).

4. It is interesting to note that the choice of a female lead character who doesn't work, doesn't compete, and has no money replaced the PhD economist Marie in the original book *The Bourne Identity* (1980) by Robert Ludlum. The character Marie of the first two films (she is killed early in the second of the three) poses no threat to Bourne in terms of ability or economic and social status; thus her love can be considered the transformative influence that Michael Kimmel identified as a resilient cultural trope before feminism (39).

WORKS CITED

Adams, Jon Robert. *Male Armor: The Soldier-Hero in Contemporary American Culture*. Charlottesville: U of Virginia P, 2008. Print.

Ahmed, Sara. *The Cultural Politics of Emotion*. New York: Routledge, 2004. Print.

Bourdieu, Pierre. *Masculine Domination*. Trans. Richard Nice. Cambridge: Polity, 2001. Print.

Connell, R.W. *Masculinities*. Berkeley: U of California P, 2005. Print.

Easthope, Anthony. *What a Man's Gotta Do: The Masculinity Myth in Popular Culture*. London: Paladin, 1986. Print.

Faludi, Susan. *Stiffed: The Betrayal of the American Male*. New York: Harper, 2000. Print.

Hacker, Helen Mayer. "The New Burdens of Masculinity." *Marriage and Family Living* 19 (1957): 227–33. Print.

Kimmel, Michael S. *The Gender of Desire: Essays on Male Sexuality.* Albany: SUNY P, 2005. Print.

Lehman, Peter. *Running Scared: Masculinity and the Representation of the Male Body.* Philadelphia: Temple UP, 1993. Print.

MacKinnon, Kenneth. *Representing Men: Maleness and Masculinity in the Media.* London: Arnold, 2003. Print.

Simpson, Mark. *Male Impersonators: Men Performing Masculinity.* London: Cassell, 1994. Print.

Trice, Ashton D., and Samuel A. Holland. *Heroes Antiheroes and Dolts: Portrayals of Masculinity in American Popular Films, 1921–1999.* Jefferson, NC: McFarland, 2001. Print.

Walsh, Fintan. *Male Trouble: Masculinity and the Performance of Crisis.* London: Palgrave MacMillan, 2010. Print.

MASCULINITIES FOR MEN AND WOMEN

5

Subverting the Master's Hero: *Firefly*'s Malcolm Reynolds as a Feminist-Inflected Space Cowboy

Laura L. Beadling

In looking for evidence of feminism's influence on popular culture, science fiction with its traditionally male audience may not be the first place that critics look. Calling for expanding feminist critical territory, Yvonne Tasker and Diane Negra note that "existing scholarship on postfeminist media culture tilts heavily toward analysis of the romantic comedies and female-centered sitcoms and dramas that have been so strongly associated with female audiences since the 1990s. Our hope is to dismantle any tendency we might have to assume that postfeminist effects are felt only in recognizably, reliably 'female-centered' genres. . . . The starting point for these postfeminist debates is a recognition that by the late 1990s representational verisimilitude required an acknowledgment of feminism as a feature of the cultural milieu." Likewise feminism is not merely evident in strong female protagonists, but as part of the cultural milieu is likewise evident in the construction of male protagonists, who likewise are influenced and changed by feminism's work. Feminist explorations of such characters remain infrequent, especially in science fiction and action genres, including the Western.

Producer/director Joss Whedon's television series *Firefly* (2002–2003) creatively blended the genres of the Western and science fiction. Through the figure of Malcolm Reynolds (Nathan Fillion), the ship's captain in *Firefly* (2002–2003), Whedon fashions a new form of masculinity, blending both the warrior's aggression and ruthlesssness with characteristics more in tune with feminism. These characteristics of Malcolm Reynolds include a willingness to change, an acceptance of women as individuals, an ethics of community, and a nonaggressive sexuality that avoids conquest in favor of egalitarian relationships.

Analysis of male characters like Malcolm Reynolds in terms of postfeminism is *as* necessary as examinations of strong female characters in that "men
have a necessary relationship to feminism—the point after all is that it should
change them too, that it involves learning new ways of being women *and men*
against and as an end to the reality of women's oppression" (Heath 1). This
is what makes Mal a specifically postfeminist male character: he has been
changed by the women he works with and the community they have created.
Rather than take postfeminist at its most common definitions—either the
regressive idea á la Katie Rophie that feminism is no longer needed because
all of its worthy goals have been achieved, or the more academic definition
that posits that feminism can no longer be theorized separately from other
strands of postmodern thought—I use it here to indicate Whedon's creation
of a world and characters who have been genuinely changed by feminism.
Whedon's vision is one that allows us to see what kinds of masculinities and
femininities might be created, on screen and in society at large.

Through his repeated avowal of feminism and his stated belief that media
can send needed social messages of change, Whedon has himself set the
terms for evaluation of his work. While much of the critical discussion of
both his earlier television show *Buffy the Vampire Slayer* (1997–2003) and
his later show *Dollhouse* (2009–2010) has focused on his creation of female
characters, Whedon demonstrates in his short-lived show *Firefly* and its
follow-up movie *Serenity* (2005) that he is also committed to exploring forms
of masculinity. Elyce Rae Helford aptly observes that science fiction is of
particular value to feminist thought: "No other genres so actively invite representations of the ultimate goals of feminism: worlds free of sexism, worlds in
which women's contributions (to science) are recognized and valued, worlds
in which the diversity of women's desire and sexuality, and worlds that move
beyond gender" (291). Whedon's vision of such a world makes him a postfeminist media activist who offers appealing visions of what men who have
responded to feminist discourse and ideals might turn out to be. Since moving
to film direction, Joss Whedon has continued to explore evolving twentieth-
century masculinities in the Marvel Universe in *The Avengers* (2012) and
Avengers: Age of Ultron (2015), as well as overseeing the development of
the mixed-gender team on television's *Agents of S.H.I.E.L.D* (2013–). (See
Derek McGrath's discussion in chapter 9.)

Overall, Whedon has consistently embraced media-making as a form of
activist pedagogy and, despite *Firefly*'s abrupt cancellation, its elevation to
cult classic status indicates at least a partially successful intervention into a
science fiction mediascape, a mediascape that has succeeded in promoting
strong female characters but has yet to update versions of masculinity as
successfully. Science fiction, fantasy, and action genres are valuable territory

to plant progressive gender elements since they can provide an avenue to communicate feminist ideals to men and boys, who are often the consumers of these genres (though, of course, not the only ones). Regardless of gender, a generation of teenagers and young adults are growing up on Whedon's ensemble, following idiosyncratic leaders like Mal Reynolds.

For those who may not have seen the show, a very brief explanation will be useful. Whedon pitched *Firefly* as "nine people looking into the blackness of space and seeing nine different things" and, indeed, the crew is diverse, although they do form a family of choice, one of Whedon's trademarks. The show follows these nine characters aboard the ship Serenity, a Firefly class transport vessel, and through their adventures smuggling, thieving, and avoiding the Alliance, a goal made all the more difficult once they pick up two wanted fugitives. The show blends conventions of both the Western and the science fiction genres while simultaneously showcasing Whedon's trademark witty dialogue and well-rounded characters. Along with Mal, the crew is made up of four women—Zoe (Gina Torres), Kaylee (Jewel Staite), Inara (Morena Baccarin), and River (Summer Glau)—and four men—Book (Ron Glass), Wash (Alan Tudyk), Jayne (Adam Baldwin), and Simon (Sean Maher), who represent a spectrum of masculinities and femininities.

In particular, Whedon's interest in expanding the range of masculinities can be seen in the wide range of gender expression in *Firefly*'s male characters. While both Simon and Book are intellectual men of education, they are quite different from each other, with Simon's fastidiousness and inept bumblings with most social situations (in particular, with Kaylee), contrasting with Book's pacifism tempered with a pragmatic capacity for violence. Likewise, Mal's authoritative stance is contrasted with Jayne, who is both tough and capable of ruthless action, but who is also sexually aggressive and blatantly mercenary in his ethos. Wash rarely fights but instead pilots the ship capably. His version of masculinity is also exhibited in his marriage to Zoe, who he characterizes gleefully as a "warrior woman." Nevertheless, he is quite capable of standing up to her and making his own desires known when needed. Whedon surrounds Mal with diverse male characters to demonstrate the range of masculine options, while setting off Mal's own, unusual gender performance.

Whedon has indicated not only his support of feminism and its goals, but also the need for media messages that embrace feminism while actually reaching large audiences. After all, he has said in interviews about *Buffy the Vampire Slayer*, "I wasn't trying to make Buffy the Lesbian Separatist because I didn't think anyone would show up" (Said 140). I believe that Mal as a Whedon character serves a similar pedagogical purpose, with Mal's ability to appeal to a wide range of viewers. While both *Buffy the Vampire Slayer*

Figure 5.1. Mal (Nathan Fillion), the captain of the Serenity, is flanked by Zoe (Gia Torres) and Jayne (Adam Baldwin). Mal mediates his crew's versions of masculinity. *(Firefly)*

and *Firefly* have been interpreted as conveying deliberate social messages about gender and equality, the two shows take different paths to this goal. Lorna Jowett argues that in *Buffy the Vampire Slayer*, "'good' new masculinity contrasts with 'bad' tough-guy masculinity by being 'feminized,' passive, sensitive, weak, and emotional" (199). This is very different from the path taken in *Firefly*, in which Mal, a tough-guy character, unlearns some of the aspects of the code of rugged individualism and instead learns to value cooperation, community, connection, and trust.

Although the show was unceremoniously canceled after a brief run, perhaps partly because of its unconventional gender roles, it has nevertheless attracted a large and diverse cult following that stands as testimony to the appeal of Whedon's vision; *SFX Magazine* voted Malcolm Reynolds number one on their list of "top 100 Sci-Fi Icons of the Century" in 2011, suggesting the enduring populist appeal of the character among a variety of fans. Fillion's fan base from both *Desperate Housewives* (2004–2012) and especially from *Firefly* helped launch his current series, *Castle* (2009–), which, like *Firefly*, experienced early genre and rating troubles although, unlike *Firefly*, it was able to survive them (Dawn). Like Mal, Rick Castle willingly partners with a woman who may display more traditionally masculine traits than himself. Fillion's depiction of Mal Reynolds on *Firefly* has been foundational to his career, remaining a touchpoint for his fans.

Significantly, Whedon created a leading character who appeals to a wide range of fans; Mike Russell notes in his interview with Whedon, "in terms of both gender and personal politics, *Firefly* and *Serenity* have one of the more diverse fan bases I've ever seen. The show's been written up in both progressive and conservative journals" (112). Yet Mal's character continually subverts several precepts that are typically folded into the Western hero, providing a model of masculinity in the wake of feminist gains that engages men and women, liberals, conservatives, and others.

MAL, MASCULINITY, AND MOVING TOWARD COMMUNITY

Despite his stoic silence, willingness to take lethal action, and his total control of his crew, Mal nevertheless espouses a feminist-inflected rhetoric of communality, rejects the demands for sexual conquest and virility typical of hegemonic masculinity, treats female colleagues (and enemies) respectfully, and accepts women as individuals who may or may not want his protection. By making Mal a warrior who reflects feminism's ideals and goals, Whedon offers viewers a vision of what one version of postfeminist masculinity might look like. Linda Wight asserts that "one of the oldest and most persistent hegemonic ideals is the warrior narrative of masculinity," which is also one of the first identities that young boys are taught to desire (5). Masculinity theorists R. W. Connell and James W. Messerschmidt caution that it "is desirable to eliminate any usage of hegemonic masculinity as a fixed, transhistorical model. This usage violates the historicity of gender and ignores the massive evidence of change in social definitions of masculinity" (838). While Wight acknowledges critical work that documents how men and masculinities vary culturally and historically, she remarks that "they identify violence, physical strength, lack of emotion, rationality, and sexual virility as some of the common markers of this current idealized construction" (5), traits that generally Mal does in fact exhibit.

Indeed, the primacy of these stereotypically masculine traits to Mal's character is established during the original pilot episode "Serenity" (1.11). Viewers quickly learn that Mal prefers to avoid killing but will do so if there is no other option (he spares Patience but kills Dobson because he lacks the time for anything more subtle). He rules over his ship and crew, noting "We do not vote on my ship because my ship is not the gorram town hall." As he acts, he does not show or even acknowledge his feelings, as he appears impassive to Inara's threat to leave with Simon and River if they're kicked off the ship. Furthermore, while Lynne Segal notes that hegemonic masculinity is also "defined through a series of hierarchical relations: rejection and suppression of femininity and homosexual desire, command and control over the 'weak' and 'inferior,'" Mal resists some of these hierarchical moves (qtd. in Wight 5).

In addition to maintaining an authoritative control of his ship while working with a nontraditional, gender-inclusive community, Mal surprisingly lacks one frequent characteristic of the warrior version of hegemonic masculinity: the staunch and often aggressive heterosexuality that is focused primarily on promiscuity and conquest. In her article on the construction of hegemonic masculinity in popular culture, Heather Schell notes that the "popularity of 'alpha male' in common parlance suggests that men are seen as sharing the canine genetic imperative for dominance behaviors . . . [alpha male masculinity] is also aggressively heterosexual" and often in ways that were "antithetical to women's best interests" (113–14). Schell goes on to note that, in many paranormal romances and other popular culture texts, the "alpha male" character "is the dominant, aggressive, controlling, powerful, passionate seducer whose very masculinity makes the heroine weak in the knees, all the better for him to sweep her off her feet and carry her to his bed" (118). In contrast to this, Whedon offers a different kind of hero who embraces feminist ideals and yet is not a caricature of the "Sensitive New Age Man" of 1980s and 1990s television who talked about his feelings and helped with the housework and kids.

That is not to say that Malcolm Reynolds is an easy-to-define, one-dimensional, or caricatured feminist character; Whedon has said of his own creation that "Mal is somebody that I knew, as I created him, I would not get along with. I don't think we have the same politics" (Russell 110), which he describes as "very reactionary and 'Big government is bad' and 'Don't interfere with my life'" (Nussbaum 68). Such characterizations of Mal as individualistic and reactionary resonate with the idea of the traditional Western hero, who also tends to be conceived of as a solitary, rugged individual. However, while Mal may start there as a character, he evolves into someone who understands the importance of connection, trust, and allies for survival in the wilderness. Emma Bull argues that Whedon presents Mal as a character in process, whose outlook on life significantly changes as he struggles to survive on the frontier. Bull delineates the myth of the Old West, which emphasized rugged individualism and a lone wolf ethic, in contrast to the reality: "those who can, help those who can't" (195).

Yet Mal does not fit neatly within this position. Bull points out that it is precisely those characters in *Firefly* who embody the lone wolf mentality of the Old West mythos who die alone—notably Jubal Early and Rance

Burgess—while Mal and his crew survive through trust and cooperation. Whedon has Mal explicitly articulate this outlook at the end of "Our Mrs. Reynolds" (1.03): once he's caught up to Saffron, another advocate of the lone wolf mentality, he tells her, "You got all kinds of learnin' and you made me look the fool without tryin', and yet here I am with a gun to your head. That's 'cause I got people with me. People who trust each other, who do for each other, and ain't always looking for the advantage." While Saffron is manifestly uninterested in this lesson, Mal has clearly embraced the need for cooperation.

Not despite, but because of the Western setting, Whedon rewrites the Western genre as one of necessarily communal action, a lesson Mal has learned well and which viewers may also learn from. Whedon makes Mal open to change and development, much as he hopes his viewers might also find themselves more open to change through Mal's evolving focus on the need for connection certainly resonates with feminist theory and activism, which has long stressed that the personal is political in order to spur collective empowerment and action. Feminist theorists and activists have sought to find connections between individual and groups of women's experience in order to articulate the structural and systemic workings of oppression. Catharine A. MacKinnon asserts that consciousness-raising is an act that encourages recognition of "women's consciousness, not as individual or subjective ideas, but as a collective social being" (450). Miriam Liss similarly notes in "What Makes a Feminist" that "belief in collective action is probably very important in developing a feminist identity" (125).

This is exactly the trajectory on which Whedon has put Mal: from a belief in the hierarchical ideologies based on individual adherence to authority—whether to a religion or an army, both of which Mal embraces in the pilot episode—Mal comes to the understanding that, while philosophies and outlooks may differ depending on one's standpoint, connection, and trust is necessary for survival. Witness, for example, that Mal will stand up for any member of his crew, despite his sharing politics with almost no one on board: Book is a preacher while Mal has become an atheist; Inara is a Companion, a job that Mal seems to despise; River and Simon both come from wealth and high culture while Mal lives on the edge and appears unmoved by the arts. The crew's final member Jayne follows the path of a true mercenary in maintaining no stable connections to or love for anyone, which puts him in clear conflict with Mal's ethos of crew solidarity [a subtext that is worked out fully in "Ariel" (1.08)].

Mal's crew represents neither identity nor coalition politics but is instead a family of choice that Mal has created. While Mal begins the series as a man who is committed to the army and its leaders, kissing his cross before taking dangerous action, he becomes a man who retains close connections only to those who he determines are "on his crew." Those connections, though, are paramount to him and represent people that he would risk his life for; he does for them and expects them to do for him. Throughout the show and Mal's character arc in particular, Whedon stresses the need for masculinity to change to be more inclusive and more accepting of communal action. Whedon creates Mal as a character who is able to change, representing a new style of feminist-inflected masculinity that nevertheless appeals to a wide range of viewers. Featuring a male character who evolves into his communitarian stance, as opposed to one who begins the series committed to community, provides an important model for society. Such a model is especially crucial in popular culture that appeals to various viewers, including boys and men who must continue to interact in a world in which some of feminism's gains seem immutable, but a world which nevertheless retains a palpable hostility to feminism and women.

MAL AND THE *FIREFLY* 'VERSE'S WOMEN

Furthermore, Whedon uses Mal's relationships with the various women on the crew to demonstrate his difference from a traditional Western hero with his choice of a form of masculinity that treats women as individuals and in an egalitarian way, while remaining tough and aggressive. Mal's relationship with Kaylee demonstrates how the show could make Mal a stereotypical Western character but refuses to do so. There is an almost sibling-like relationship between Mal and Kaylee; Mal teases Kaylee, encourages her, looks out for her, praises her, and sometimes hurts her feelings with his insensitivity. He calls her "little Kaylee" and *meimei*, "little sister" in Chinese. Such a stance could easily slip into Mal making decisions for Kaylee, discounting her opinion, or attempting to control or advise her. While Mal does defend Kaylee—for instance against Jayne's crude sexual jokes—he nevertheless respects and values her.

In much popular culture and, all too often, in real life, little sisters frequently have their sexuality denied or controlled by older brothers and other male relations. Mal, however, accepts Kaylee's sexual choices and desires as normal. Although he does not want any details, he acknowledges that women are sexual beings and does not judge them for having or wanting sex. Mal is (or perhaps pretends to be?) horrified by Kaylee's forlorn comment in *Serenity* that "goin' on a year now I ain't had nothin' twixt my nethers weren't run on batteries!" but, despite this, he does not seem bothered in the least that she has a high sex drive and voices her desires freely.

Even more tellingly, Mal does not discount her professional competence because of her sexual activity, as clearly shown in "Out of Gas" (1.05), which depicts how Kaylee became Serenity's mechanic. As Mal enters the engine room to demand why the ship isn't space-worthy yet, he walks in on his original, male mechanic Bester having sex with Kaylee, who is unknown to Mal at that time. Mal continues to question and berate Bester, telling him to get his "prairie harpy" off the ship and fix the engine. When Bester makes excuses and claims that the "gravboot is shot," Kaylee perkily interjects "no it ain't. Ain't nothing wrong with your grav boot." As she continues getting dressed, she goes on to say, "I seen the trouble plain as day when I's down there on my back. Your reg couple's bad." While Bester's sexuality interferes with his judgment, Kaylee remains clear.

Kaylee now has Mal's full attention as she demonstrates her knowledge of the engine and how to make it run properly. When she's finished, he offers her Bester's job on the spot, much to Bester's dismay. Although he is annoyed with his mechanic for having sex when he should have been working on the engine, Mal nevertheless is undeterred and unphased by Kaylee's sexual activity when he sees her competence. She has earned his respect for her ability and her confidence. In scenes like this, Whedon both creates fully sexual (without being sexualized) female characters as well as, more unusually, male characters like Mal who present a model of workplace respect and acceptance.

Whedon is also careful to demonstrate through Mal that respect for women does not translate to lack of conflict or humor. This is the same point that Whedon makes through Mal's interactions with Inara in "Shindig" (1.06), when Mal says that, while he himself may not respect her job as a Companion, it is unacceptable to Mal that her client Atherton Wing fails to respect her. Mal draws a clear line between disrespecting Inara's profession, as he himself does with his disparaging remarks, and disrespecting her as a person, which is what Wing does with his presumption of control over Inara's person. In one of his shows of high-handedness—for which Inara calls him out several times—he attacks Wing on Inara's behalf, despite the fact that she proves more capable than Mal of handling this social realm. When Wing again blusters and threatens Inara at the end of the episode, Mal exhorts Inara, "See how I'm not punching him? I think I've grown." While this is clearly meant to be humorous, it also appears to be true since Mal does not attempt to be chivalric toward Inara after this. His trust in Inara to handle business is seen in his relying on her to be the fail-safe in "trash" (1.13). Inara performs beautifully and saves the day.

Furthermore, Whedon is also careful to show that this older brother stance is not Mal's only way to relate to women; he is able to create relationships with very different women, seeing each woman as an individual and adjusting himself to her. For example, he does not insist on protecting or looking out for Zoe, who is quite capable of looking out for herself, even looking after Mal on occasion. Likewise, while he takes a captain's interest in both Simon and River, rescuing them both from the villagers who kidnapped them in "Safe" (1.07) and from Jayne in "Ariel" (1.08), he does not have the same easy affection for them that he has for Kaylee. Whedon uses Mal to show that men, even strong and authoritative characters like Mal, can learn from women and develop into better people and more effective leaders; to be strong is not the same as being rigid or self-contained in all circumstances.

MAL, SEXUALITY, AND HETERONORMATIVITY

Another way that Mal marks his difference from the typical Western hero is through his sexuality. Unlike Jayne, Kaylee, and Wash, all of whom are quite upfront about their sexual needs and desires (although Wash confines his to Zoe, his passion and devotion are quite apparent), Mal is reserved in his expressions of sexuality. While some critics have noted that, in *Buffy the Vampire Slayer*, Buffy's sexuality was quite conservative, they have only occasionally observed that Mal seems to share this trait, even though the trait is more rare for a male protagonist, especially a leader like Mal. Buffy was sexually conservative in a way that didn't overtly challenge social norms of (especially teenage) femininity while Mal's sexual conservativism challenges the ethos of sexual conquest that often goes hand in hand with warrior masculinity.

Mal's sexual conservatism separates him from his colleagues: Kaylee openly bemoans her lack of available sexual partners, Wash enthusiastically describes what he loves about his wife's body to an Alliance interrogator, and Jayne helps himself to as many willing women as happen to be about (for instance, in both "Jaynestown" (1.04) and "Heart of Gold" (1.12)). Yet Mal is reticent about his desires and reserved in his approach to potential sexual partners. He has only two sexual encounters over the course of the show and the film, and during each of these he acknowledges without embarrassment that he hasn't had sex in quite a while. This decoupling of masculinity and strength from libido and sexual conquest again can serve as a role model for young male viewers; in *Firefly*, an ethos of sexual conquest has nothing to do with being a hero or a "real man."

Other than Mal's love for Inara, which he never expresses physically, the viewer sees Mal in two sexual situations: one with Saffron in "Our Mrs. Reynolds" (1.03) and one with Nandi in "Heart of Gold." In neither situation is Mal the initiator. Mal indicates from the very beginning of "Our Mrs. Reynolds" his lack of desire to have a wife or to engage in sex with Saffron, saying early on "We'll be together on the ship, not in any." to which Saffron accedes. Even when he is initially flummoxed and upset at Saffron's sudden appearance and claim, he tries to be considerate of her feelings (despite Kaylee's assurance to Saffron, "he makes everyone cry. He's like a monster"). He assures Saffron, "You don't shame me, and you have very nice qualities but I didn't ever marry you." Later, after she has insisted on making him a meal, he compliments the food and her cooking but leaves most of it uneaten so as to not encourage her in what he perceives to be her hopes of making him change his mind. Mal also seems genuinely shocked and indignant at the multiple suggestions that he, like Jayne, has immediate designs to take sexual advantage of Saffron; huffily, he exclaims, "Preacher, you got a smutty mind" when Book threatens him with a "special level of hell" if he takes sexual advantage of Saffron.

Likewise, in "Heart of Gold" (1.12), the episode in which Mal has his second sexual encounter, he again marks his difference from the other male and female characters on the show who have a high sex drive. Unlike Jayne, it appears that Mal is interested in helping the women of the Heart of Gold not because they're prostitutes, but because they are not Alliance-approved, regulated companions but are instead independents—a word that clearly has much resonance for Mal—working on their own. When Nandi voices her determination to stand her ground even without Mal's help, he tells her admiringly, "Lady, you're my kind of stupid." He clearly feels a kinship with her as another tough and stubborn leader of a crew of ragtag misfits, who nevertheless believes in an individual's right to determine the course of his or her own life.

Like Saffron, Nandi must initiate the sexual encounter with Mal, who seems reluctant to impose on her. Nandi frankly addresses the question of whether Mal plans on taking payment for helping them in trade, remarking that if he's sly (apparently a colloquial term for gay) she has male prostitutes that could service him. Rather than engaging in a moment of homosexual panic or violently affirming his heterosexuality, Mal simply responds that he's not sly, with no horror involved. Clearly, his sexual identity is not threatened by the suggestion of homosexuality, a common theme running through much American popular culture. When Mal claims he'll trade after the job is done, she remarks that he hasn't looked at any of her prostitutes as long or as lovingly as he's looked at her pistols. Relying on her companion training to read his discomfort and find a way to continue the encounter, she engages him in conversation and drinks with him, working to put him at his ease. Nandi continues to make her availability known so, when Mal tells her,

"If I'm overstepping my bounds, you let me know," she becomes impatient and tells him she's been waiting for him to kiss her since she showed him her guns. After they kiss, it is she who frankly states, "I want you to bed me," to which he replies, "I guess I mean to." As with Saffron, Mal is careful not to be coercive, and giving each woman opportunities to back out of the encounter.

Finally, Mal also demonstrates comfort with non-heteronormativity in several ways, although this aspect is not as developed in the series as it might have been. Whedon's attempts to open room for other sexualities can be seen in Mal's lack of homosexual panic, as noted earlier, as well as his adoption of drag as a pragmatic strategy in "Our Mrs. Reynolds" (1.03). Mal disguises himself as a woman in order to surprise the thieves they've been hired to rout. As Meredith King asserts about this episode, it not only shows that Mal "is not tied down to traditional gender roles" but, more importantly, that he "uses his false-femininity as a set-up to entrap those who would otherwise be doing him harm" (7). Whedon makes it especially clear in this episode that Mal is comfortable playing with and deconstructing gender when needed. Zoe, as the best shot, had to be in the back of the wagon rather than in front, so Mal pragmatically took the woman's role in order to gain an advantage over their adversaries, who are momentarily taken by surprise by the revelation of Mal's gender performance. With Mal, Whedon decouples aggressive sexuality from toughness by creating a character who is unquestionably cold-blooded and pragmatic as needed, without carrying that attitude into relationships, whether personal or professional, with women.

CONCLUSION

In each of his shows, Whedon attempts to craft needed social messages of equality and gender critique while making the narratives and characters compelling enough to succeed on American television. While only *Buffy* and its spin-off *Angel* (1999–2004) lasted more than two seasons, both *Firefly* and *Dollhouse* have found devoted cult audiences who have helped enable Whedon's continued work as well as Nathan Fillion's. The Sensitive New Age Guy of the 1970s and 1980s have been one early attempt to answer the question of how feminism would or should change masculinity. However, as Susan Moore notes, he was rarely found outside media representations. On the other hand, Malcolm Reynolds's version of a hard-as-nails and uncompromising captain who is respectful of women provides a more appealing version of new masculinity that accepts feminism's ideals without sacrificing toughness or action, essential qualities in the captain of a smuggling vessel.

As Connell and Messerschmidt assert that "a considerable body of research shows that masculinities are not simply different but also subject to change" (835), Whedon integrates this concept into his work as he continues to create shows and characters that challenge the gender status quo of our time, entertaining *and* educating viewers. Furthermore, as Thomas Newkirk argues, "popular culture [can act as] a powerful alternative literacy that attracts boys," and thus media activists like Whedon who revise older forms of still-valued masculine identities, like the cowboy, offers boys an appealing character who also is testimony that masculinity can change and there are other "cool" possibilities for a masculine, tough identity that doesn't also embrace homophobia, sexism, or racism (7).

While the demographics of the science fiction fan community have changed dramatically over the last few decades, there are still many male fans, young and old alike. Camille Bacon-Smith notes that while male science fiction fans have long claimed to comprise an open-minded and inclusive community, there are actually a number of ways that while male fans have resisted the incursion of women, gays and lesbians, and people of color, among others. In Malcolm Reynolds, Joss Whedon offers an exemplar of a hero who not only accepts the presence of women, gays, and people of color, but who actively supports and engages with feminist ideals. And still kicks ass.

WORKS CITED

Bacon-Smith, Camille. *Science Fiction Culture*. Philadelphia: U of Pennsylvania P, 1999. Print.

Bull, Emma. "Malcom Reynolds, the Myth of the West, and Me." *Whedonistas: A Celebration of the Worlds of Joss Whedon by the Women Who Love Them*. Ed. Lynne M. Thomas and Deborah Stanish. Des Moines: Mad Norwegian, 2011. 190–96. Print.

Connell, R. W., and James W. Messerschmidt. "Hegemonic Masculinity: Rethinking the Concept." *Gender and Society* 19 (6): 829–59. Print.

Dawn, Randee. 'Castle' Thrives on Romance, Nathan Fillion's Dedicated Fans." *Variety*. 1 Apr. 2013: n. page. Web. 4. Sept. 2013.

Heath, Stephen. "Male Feminism." *Men in Feminism*. Ed. Alice Jardine and Paul Smith. New York: Routledge, 1989. 1–32. Print.

Helford, Elyce Rae. "Feminism." *The Greenwood Encyclopedia of Science Fiction and Fantasy*. Westport, CT: Greenwood, 2005. Print.

Jowett, Lorna. *Sex and the Slayer: A Gender Studies Primer for the Buffy Fan*. Middleton, CT: Wesleyan UP, 2005. Print.

King, Meredith. "Mad about Saffron: Identity Construction in 'Our Mrs. Reynolds.'" *Academia.edu*. Web. 5 Sept. 2013.

Liss, Miriam, Christy O'Connor, Elena Morosky, and Mary Crawford. "What Makes a Feminist? Predictors and Correlates of Feminist Social Identity in College Women." *Psychology of Women Quarterly* 25 (2001). 124–33. Print.

MacKinnon, Catherine A. "Feminism, Marxism, Method, and the State: An Agenda for Theory." *Feminist Legal Theory: Foundations.* Ed. D. Kelly Weisberg. Philadelphia: Temple UP, 1993. 437–53. Print.

Newkirk, Thomas. *Misreading Masculinity: Boys, Literacy, and Popular Culture.* Portsmouth, NH: Heinemann, 2002. Print.

Nussbaum, Emily. "Must-See Metaphysics." *Joss Whedon: Conversations.* Television Conversation Series. Ed. David Lavery and Cynthia Burkhead. Jackson: UP of Mississippi, 2011. 64–70. Print.

Porter, Lynette. *Tarnished Heroes, Charming Villains, and Modern Monsters: Science Fiction in Shades of Gray on 21st Century Television.* Jefferson, NC: McFarland, 2010. Print.

Russell, Mike. "The CulturePulp Q&A: Joss Whedon." *Joss Whedon: Conversations.* Television Conversation Series. Ed. David Lavery and Cynthia Burkhead. Jackson: UP of Mississippi, 2011. 107–28. Print.

Said, S. F. "About *Buffy, Alien,* and *Firefly*: The Shebytches.com Interview." *Joss Whedon: Conversations.* Television Conversation Series. Ed. David Lavery and Cynthia Burkhead. Jackson: U of Mississippi P, 2011. 138–42. Print.

Schell, Heather. "The Big Bad Wolf: Masculinity and Genetics in Popular Culture." *Literature and Medicine* 26.1 (2007): 109–25. Web. 10 Sept. 2013.

Smith, Jason, and Ximena C. Gallardo. *Alien Woman: The Making of Lt. Ellen Ripley.* NY: Continuum, 2006. Print.

Tasker, Yvonne, and Diane Negra. "In Focus: Postfeminism and Contemporary Media Studies." *Cinema Journal* 44, no. 2 (2005): 107–10. Print.

Wight, Linda. *Talking about Men: Conversations about Masculinities in Recent "Gender-Bending" Science Fiction.* Diss. James Cook University, 2009. Web. 3 Sept. 2013.

Wright, John C. "Just Shove Him in the Engine, or the Role of Chivalry in Joss Whedon's Firefly." *Finding Serenity: Anti-Heroes, Lost Shepherds and Space Hookers in Joss Whedon's Firefly.* Ed. Jane Espenson. Dallas: BenBella, 2004. 155–68. Print.

6

When Eleven-Year-Old Girls *Kick-Ass*:
The Gender Politics of Hit-Girl

Keith Friedlander

As a child reading comics during the first years of the superhero boom, a young Gloria Steinem was confronted with a dearth of strong female characters that she could identify with and look up to: "The only option for a girl reader is to identify with the male characters—pretty difficult, even in the androgynous years of childhood. If she can't do that, she faces limited prospects: an ideal life of sitting around like a Technicolor clothes horse getting into jams with villains, and saying things like, 'Oh Superman, I'll always be grateful to you'" (203–204).

Superhero comics were a predominantly male genre, with the phenomenal success of Superman spawning countless carbon-copy imitations. One could reasonably draw a connection between Steinem's predicament in the 1930s and the current situation facing girls growing up during the modern boom of superhero movies.

Despite the growing commercial success of film adaptations based on Marvel and DC superheroes, the companies' vast catalogues of superheroines have remained largely overlooked. While there are some notable exceptions, such as Scarlett Johansson's fan-favorite performance as super-spy Black Widow in *The Avengers* (2012) and *Captain America: Winter Soldier* (2014), even these characters are routinely relegated to secondary roles in films starring their male counterparts. Whereas Steinem describes how she was rescued from her limited prospects by the arrival of Wonder Woman in 1941, a character whose combination of strength and wisdom inspired her as a child, today Wonder Woman's big screen debut in the upcoming *Batman v Superman: Dawn of Justice* (2016) will see her name left off the marquee.

One factor contributing to this general disregard for female viewers and characters is the genre's concern with exploring models of modern masculinity. As Susanne Kord and Elisabeth Krimmer note in *Contemporary Hollywood Masculinities: Gender, Genre, and Politics*, superhero films form one facet of a broader reconceptualization of masculinity taking place throughout modern Hollywood blockbusters. For Kord and Krimmer, superhero films are visually coded to endorse a meritorious concept of masculinity, where leaders are defined by their ability to make stark moral choices and the strength of the individual is promoted over the contributions of groups (89). Given this focus on self-assertive manliness, it is perhaps not surprising that the studios producing these films are hesitant to target a female demographic.[1] Yet, to dismiss the potential appeal these movies may have for female viewers (as the studios appear to have done) requires making the problematic assumption that this brand of aggressive individualism does not relate to them. Rather than focus on criticizing the male gender roles in superhero movies, this chapter will examine the popularity of one of Hollywood's rare superheroines. Specifically, this chapter will consider how Hit-Girl, the pre-teen superheroine from the comic series *Kick-Ass* and its 2010 movie adaptation, serves as a postfeminist action heroine that manages to both harness and subvert superhero masculinity.[2] Before discussing the film itself, however, it is important to define postfeminism as a critical concept and explain how it will be applied.

SITUATING THE POSTFEMINIST HEROINE

The female action hero is a polarizing character in feminist discourse. Enthusiasts celebrate her as a liberating figure, capable of undermining gender distinctions by taking on the violent, adventurous roles traditionally played by male actors. More skeptical feminists question the subversive potential of adopting masculine roles, suggesting instead that these female heroes are simply male archetypes dressed up as women. While characters such as Sarah Conner from *Terminator 2* (1991) or Beatrix Kiddo from *Kill Bill* (2003) may show that a woman can be as deadly and aggressive as any man, in doing so they only serve to reinforce such phallocentric standards of heroism. Thus the growing prevalence and box-office success of these femme brutales gives rise to mixed feelings: we take pleasure in watching them break gender barriers and out-muscle their male counterparts, but we fear this pleasure is contingent on their ultimate subordination to the traditional values of a male-dominated culture. These fears are exacerbated when we consider how many of these female stars simultaneously serve as sexual objects primarily designed to titillate male consumers rather than empower female ones.

These different interpretations of the female hero can be related to an underlying disconnect in feminist discourse that divides traditional, second-wave feminism from the more recent third-wave development of postfeminism. As a theoretical school of thought, postfeminism is difficult to define since it encompasses a number of concerns and objectives within feminist discourse. Two key objectives are shedding the partisan approach to gender politics associated with traditional feminism and prioritizing the freedom of individuals to define their own gender roles in accordance with Judith Butler's concept of gender performativity. No longer interested in perpetuating a gender binary by which female empowerment is continually defined by its opposition to male control, postfeminism views gender as a social construct and promotes the individual's freedom to actively define their own identity. However, critics of postfeminism focus on its tendency to obscure and ignore relevant social issues pertaining to gender equality. In positing the a priori nature of equality, postfeminist interpretations fail to address factors that contribute to the persistence of inequality, drawing attention away from the contemporary consequences of misogyny such as date rape, income disparity, and honor killings. Similarly, hesitancy to glorify female action heroes stems from this concern that celebrating gender equality means willfully ignoring gender disparity.

Nonetheless, from a postfeminist perspective, the action heroine *is* a figure to be celebrated. Her ability to take on traditional male roles need not be condemned as a glorification of masculine traits, but rather should be enjoyed as a liberating act of self-determination. After all, to dismiss these figures for appearing too similar to their male counterparts would be rather reductive. As Jeffrey Brown rightly points out in *Dangerous Curves: Action Heroines, Gender, Fetishism and Popular Culture*, "If a female character seen as kicking ass must be read as masculine, then women are systematically denied as a gender capable of behaving in any way other than passive" (33). While Brown is careful to outline his reservations regarding postfeminism, his conviction that the increasing popularity of these characters represents a positive development, "push[ing] the envelope of culturally appropriate gender traits," clearly places him in the enthusiast camp (42). Despite his measured stance regarding postfeminism, Brown is still susceptible to the kinds of criticism described earlier. In her book *Super Bitches and Action Babes*, Rikke Schubart suggests that Brown is too optimistic, claiming that he exemplifies a "postfeminist tendency to read the female hero as a gender bender and a subversive figure" and, as a result, overlooks factors that compromise the progressive potential of many action heroines (198).[3] Schubart identifies her own approach as a more pragmatic form of postfeminism, standing, as she puts it, in-between endorsement and skepticism to remain sensitive to how these ass-kicking women are both empowered and objectified.

This chapter will follow Schubart in applying a balanced approach to consider the appeal of Hit-Girl, interpreting her as a model of postfeminist empowerment. Identifying her within a specific tradition of action heroines—women trained to be deadly assassins and agents by patriarchal figures—I shall argue that the movie version of Hit-Girl presents a radically optimistic example of such empowerment, one that elides many of the compromising factors identified by Schubart. However, this optimism is achieved only by excluding many of the more troubling aspects of her character as she appears in the original comic. These problematic qualities help raise important questions regarding Hit-Girl's commitment to masculine values, but simultaneously diminish her potency as an example of female autonomy. Applying Schubart's notion of an "in-between" stance, I will endeavor to show how each version of Hit-Girl respectively addresses feminist and postfeminist concerns. Before qualifying her radical potential though, it is important to appreciate its efficacy. First and foremost, Hit-Girl is a subversive figure whose entrance into the adult world of R-rated movie violence pushes at the limits of acceptable gender and age roles. The sacrosanct nature of the standards she challenges is evident from the indignant responses of the film critics who rejected her.

CRITICAL RECEPTION OF HIT-GIRL

While director Matthew Vaughn's movie adaptation of the comic series *Kick-Ass* received mixed critical reactions, the reviews all shared a fixation upon Hit-Girl, the ultra-violent, foul-mouthed, eleven-year-old superheroine played by Chloë Grace Moretz. While many critics praised Moretz's performance, there was a split between those who enjoyed the unabashed brutality and cynical overtones of Hit-Girl's bloody avenger and those who found the entire character to be in poor taste, if not morally wrong. As Roger Ebert wrote in his review:

> Let's say you're a big fan of the original comic book, and you think the movie does it justice. You know what? You inhabit a world I am so very not interested in. A movie camera makes a record of whatever is placed in front of it, and in this case, it shows deadly carnage dished out by an 11-year-old girl, after which an adult man brutally hammers her to within an inch of her life. Blood everywhere. Now tell me all about the context.

Ebert was among the most vocal of the film's detractors, refusing to give any consideration to a movie that would involve an eleven-year-old girl in graphic scenes of violence ranging from shoot outs to knife fights to blood-soaked brawls. The fact that Ebert was unwilling to examine the movie on any level beyond the empirical evidence of that violence suggests the severity of the taboo being tested here.

According to *The New Yorker*'s reviewer Anthony Lane, such a movie is designed to provoke reactions like Ebert's. For Lane, *Kick-Ass* comes off as a confused attempt to challenge its audience's comfort levels. Casting the sweet schoolgirl as a violent figure threatening mobsters not only satirizes the roles of traditional action movies, it plays upon cultural anxieties concerning the vulnerability of the young to violence. The end result would presumably be an unnervingly fetishistic depiction of R-rated entertainment that makes the viewer question his or her own desensitization. However, Lane is no more forgiving in his review than Ebert, writing that any claim *Kick-Ass* may have had toward humanizing movie/comic book violence is sacrificed as the movie becomes lost in its own indulgent sensationalism. After Hit-Girl's stylized fight scenes and the over-the-top finale (complete with an execution via bazooka) it is not clear "whether we have witnessed a silly mismatch of innocence and experience, to be relished for its gross-out verve, or a formidable exercise in cynicism" (Lane). Thus, *Kick-Ass* fails because it cannot reconcile its pretensions to critical insight with its less reflective, action movie sensibilities.

It seems that *Kick-Ass* must be disregarded either for completely overstepping the bounds of good taste or, perhaps more pardonably, for glossing over its discomforting subject matter with its inundating pop aesthetic. And yet, despite Ebert's and Lane's respective misgivings toward Moretz's Hit-Girl, the majority of critics recommended the movie based on the strength of her performance. While many of these critics note the potential perversity of Hit-Girl's character, they still do not hesitate to endorse the film. Unlike Lane, *The Toronto Star*'s Peter Howell does not seem to consider the movie's willingness to depict disturbing images with levity as a flaw, awarding a perfect four-star review while describing it as a mixture of Looney Tunes, Quentin Tarantino, and torture porn. This popular acceptance suggests that Hit-Girl's violent (pre)mature persona carries an appeal that does not require a validating interpretation as socially conscious satire. On the contrary, Hit-Girl's appeal may very well rest in her blurring of innocence and experience.

That is to suggest that Hit-Girl engages viewers by conflating the classic archetypes of masculine warrior and innocent girl. Hit-Girl provokes both interest and admiration because she fills the role of action hero commonly associated with male adults: she is confident, aggressive, forthright, and, of course, deadly. Moreover, her position within the story is that of a typical male action movie protagonist: to avenge her family's murder she must overcome overwhelming odds and wipe out an entire crime syndicate. This impression of Hit-Girl as action hero is only further emphasized when she

Figure 6.1. Chloë Grace Moretz's Hit-Girl dons an impish smile as she dispatches drug dealers in the film adaptation of *Kick-Ass.*

is viewed alongside Dave Lizewski (Aaron Johnson), the film's eponymous hero. Dave is a normal teenaged boy who, aspiring to emulate the heroes from his comic books, dons a costume and begins an ill-conceived career as Kick-Ass, a crime fighter. Whereas Hit-Girl successfully embodies a hero's strength, Dave does not. Inept, insecure, and ill-equipped to combat criminals, he is a vulnerable figure who must be repeatedly saved by the domineering Hit-Girl. In the film's climactic scene, Hit-Girl's brutal fight with the central villain is made to seem more impressive when interrupted by shots of Kick-Ass's incompetent duel with the villain's son.

Claiming the heroic mantle from the more customary figure of the older male, Hit-Girl subverts the audience's perception of what constitutes appropriate female behavior, while simultaneously challenging ageist attitudes. To borrow a description of a similar character (La Femme Nikita) from Jeffrey Brown, the enjoyment in watching Hit-Girl rests in her "pleasurable appropriation of masculine power" ("Gender" 61). The satisfaction brought on by such a role reversal would only be undermined if the film were to offset it by highlighting the moral uncertainty of sensationalizing a violent young girl, as Hale seems to think it should. In fact, it is because the movie is so unconcerned with exploring such problematic concerns that Hit-Girl provides a more radical, uncompromising model of autonomy than the similar heroines who came before her.

BREAKING DOWN THE DAUGHTER TROPE

Despite Hit-Girl's ability to shock critics, she is certainly not the first character of her kind and can readily be identified as a clear-cut example of the "daughter archetype" of action heroine. Schubart defines this subset of heroine by a few key traits. First, the daughter undergoes an education at the hands of a controlling father figure who takes the young, inexperienced girl and shapes her into a masculine warrior. Filling the void left by an absent mother, this father figure often exerts a strong influence over the daughter's actions: supervising her training, assigning her missions, and controlling her movements. Charly (Geena Davis) from *The Long Kiss Goodnight* (1996), Beatrix (Uma Thurman) from *Kill Bill* (2003), and Lara Croft (Angelina Jolie) from *Tomb Raider* (2001) are all examples of deadly women who are influenced by the older men who trained them (195). In Hit-Girl's case, this father figure is literally her father: Big Daddy (Nicolas Cage), an ex-cop who trained his young daughter to help him wage a personal war against the mob. Depicted as a loving (if not dangerously unfit) parent, Big Daddy is shown introducing Hit-Girl to bulletproof vests, planning out her missions, and watching over her while she is combating criminals.

A second characteristic of the daughter archetype is her tendency to masquerade in a variety of disguises as part of her missions. Having acquired the combat skills of a male hero, the daughter figure can utilize her feminine appearance to fool her enemies and gain the upper hand when infiltrating a stronghold or facing off against an unsuspecting opponent. These disguises often exaggerate the daughter's artificial femininity as a way of emphasizing the reversal of gender roles. The audience derives an added pleasure knowing that the apparently submissive female is actually the dominant figure and that the villain who underestimates her is in for a rude awakening. Sydney Bristow (Jennifer Garner), the main character from the television series *Alias* (2001–2006), is a perfect example of the masquerading daughter figure, as she assumes a new faux feminine identity in each episode to carry out missions for the CIA. As a superhero, Hit-Girl's entire persona is an act of masquerade as she dons the costume her father made for her to fight crime. In the movie version this masquerade is taken a step further, as Hit-Girl dresses as a lost schoolgirl so that she can gain access to the crime lord's penthouse.

Hit-Girl is clearly grounded in a distinct tradition of female action heroes. Thus, she shares in the positive and negative implications of these characters.

These aspects can best be illustrated with reference to the character that helped establish this trope: Nikita from Luc Besson's 1990 film *La Femme Nikita*. Nikita (Anne Parillaud) begins her story as a young, almost feral criminal. After being arrested for the murder of a police officer, Nikita undergoes a staged execution, waking up as a prisoner in a government training facility. Under the tutelage of her overseer, Nikita undergoes a diverse training regimen as she is transformed into an undercover assassin. This includes learning not only to fight and shoot (skills she is already adept at), but also to dress seductively and smile demurely. It is only once she has mastered both masculine and feminine behavior that she is ready to become an agent. According to Brown, this education teaches Nikita that gender roles are nothing more than social constructs that can be controlled by anyone who understands them. Far from being a woman standing in for the male action hero, Nikita exposes the arbitrary basis of such distinctions as she illustrates the performative nature of gender.

In *Super Bitches and Action Babes*, Schubart provides an alternative perspective on *La Femme Nikita*, complicating Brown's optimistic interpretation by drawing attention to the problematic implications of Nikita's male relationships. First, there are obvious questions raised by her servitude to an abusive, mysterious body of male authority. For all her formidable abilities, it is possible that the daughter figure's ultimate role is to serve as an object for male desire. As a result, the true appeal of the daughter figure for male viewers may have less to do with her ability to defy gender distinctions and more to do with the voyeuristic pleasure of watching the exploitation of a powerful woman. The fetishistic nature of this pleasure is again exaggerated by the variety of provocative disguises the daughter must use in her missions.[4] Rather than confound gender roles, daughter characters such as Nikita "acquire an essence, a gendered 'I' which is every cliché of a 'woman'" (Schubart 208). Thus, Nikita's potential as a model of postfeminist self-definition is undermined by the film's focus on persistent gender roles. In the end, her masculine behavior as an international assassin becomes an obstacle to her achieving happiness as a married woman. It is the absence of such complications and misgivings that makes Hit-Girl an exceptionally radical example of the daughter archetype. Hit-Girl presents none of Nikita's indecision regarding her role as a heroine. She is unwavering in her dedication to costumed crime fighting. There is no clash between the behavior that identifies her as a typical young girl (such as asking to be rewarded with ice cream for completing a task or pestering her father to pay attention to her) and the behavior that identifies her as an action hero (the casual swearing or the acts of violence). Rather than shift between one kind of performative mode and another, Hit-Girl combines the contrasting aspects of her personality into the singular identity of the warrior girl, seamlessly blending ebullience and savagery.

Moreover, the disconcerting tendency to transform the daughter figure into a sexual fetish does not apply to Hit-Girl. In *La Femme Nikita*, her overseer's conflicted feelings toward Nikita, which oscillate between fatherly protection and romantic infatuation, underscore her dual roles as heroine and sex object. By contrast, Vaughan gives no indication of an incestuous undercurrent existing between Hit-Girl and her father. While Big Daddy's decision to train her certainly calls his parenting into question (an issue that figures more prominently in the comic, as will be thoroughly discussed in the following sections), their partnership as crime fighters is rooted in their mutual affection rather than an abusive power dynamic. Accordingly, Hit-Girl's appeal as an action heroine lies in her charismatic nature and subversion of character tropes, rather than her objectification. When the film does use Hit-Girl to reference the traditional eroticization of the female hero, it presents her as that figure's derisive parody. Hit-Girl's costume lampoons the leather-clad, hyper-sexualized Bad Girl comic book heroines of the 1990s, such as Barb Wire or Witchblade, and her masquerade as a schoolgirl, à la Alias, comes to a quick, predictable, and violent end. Rather than provoke male fantasies, Hit-Girl takes the wind out of them.

Vaughn's *Kick-Ass* is so single-minded in portraying Hit-Girl as an empowered figure that it succeeds in avoiding the many problematic associations that have plagued similar characters. However, in this regard the *Kick-Ass* movie not only differs from previous examples of the daughter trope, but from its source material as well.

MATTERS OF ADAPTATION: MILLAR'S HIT-GIRL AS VICTIM

Kick-Ass presents the radical possibility of viewing the prepubescent female vigilante as a potential role model, a rare example of a young girl more than capable of filling a masculine model of heroism. Such a possibility is denied by Roger Ebert's blanket judgment of the movie as "morally reprehensible" based solely on its inclusion of a young girl in gratuitous acts of violence. In doing so, Ebert implies that, regardless of her consistent role as an aggressor throughout the movie, Hit-Girl must necessarily be viewed as the victim of that violence due to her age and gender. Such exploitive depictions remain an appropriate venue for the countless examples of male leads of all ages (there was little mention in the reviews of Nicolas Cage being set on fire or Aaron Johnson's numerous beatings), and an increasingly popular vehicle for adult female actors, from Sigourney Weaver in *Aliens* (1986) to Gina Carano in *Haywire* (2012). Yet, Ebert evokes a moral imperative excluding young females. The abrupt finality of his opinion is indicative of the kind of predisposed perceptions of age and gender that are undermined by Hit-Girl's performance. However, before committing to an interpretation of Hit-Girl as an empowering role model, it is important to note that the movie's source material, the Marvel comic series written by Mark Millar, does not present the same uncomplicated, empowering depiction of her character.

It is ironic that Ebert refuses to consider the movie's source material, as Millar's original comic presents a much more critical depiction of the vigilante figures and the acts of violence they commit, one that shares Ebert's misgivings. Utilizing a much darker aesthetic than the brightly colored movie, the comic's action sequences emphasize the disturbing nature of the bloodshed, incorporating the cynical self-consciousness Hale felt was lacking in the movie. Hit-Girl's introductory fight scene against a small gang of drug dealers offers a clear distinction between the film's frenetic style and the comic's focus on gore. In the movie, Hit-Girl's cocksure smile and quips emit a playful attitude amidst the chaos and gore. This playful nature is further emphasized by Hit-Girl's garish purple costume, as well as Vaughn's choice of music for the scene: the innocuous theme song from the children's variety show *The Banana Splits*. In the comic, however, there is something disturbing about Hit-Girl's appearance and demeanor. John Romita Jr.'s art draws attention to the sheer amount of bloodshed, covering Hit-Girl in such large

Figure 6.2. John Romita Jr.'s renderings of Hit-Girl in the original comic *Kick-Ass*.

splotches of red that it becomes the most prominent color on her otherwise drab uniform. Instead of donning a smile, Hit-Girl's face is expressionless, suggesting neither excitement nor remorse at her actions. Her most striking features are her large doe eyes that stare at her enemies unflinchingly as she advances upon them, undeterred by their missiles. The overall impression is that of an unfeeling, robotic killer, not unlike Arnold Schwarzenegger's Terminator. Whereas the film's Hit-Girl is intended to amuse and charm the audience, the version from the comic seems intended to unsettle the readership. Introduced as an emotionally alienated killing machine, her youth only serves to render her actions more disturbing.

This is not to suggest that the comic version of Hit-Girl is depicted as a monster. As the story continues, Millar invests Hit-Girl with the same humor and humanity that characterizes her in the movie. What this offsetting first impression does suggest, however, is that the reader is meant to perceive something unnatural and inappropriate about her character. The significance of this difference becomes evident upon consideration of the most radical change made when adapting the comic into the movie: the origin of Big Daddy. An ex-cop whose wife was killed by gangsters working for mob boss John Genovese, Big Daddy escaped with his daughter and trained her in the deadly arts so that she could fight alongside him in their quest for revenge.[5] In both versions there is a strong bond of friendship and affection between father and daughter. They share interests in firearms and action movies and have clearly been brought closer together by their escapades. It is only in the comic, however, that Big Daddy reveals that he is not actually an ex-cop. Instead he is an ex-accountant and comic book nerd who kidnapped his own daughter and retreated from a hollow career and failing marriage so that he could build a more exciting life. His entire backstory as a cop is an elaborate lie told to ensure his daughter's cooperation; her entire superhero identity is founded upon a deception that robbed her of a family and a safe childhood. Once this secret is disclosed, Hit-Girl's deadly skills and cold, assured attitude cease to appear empowering and instead become evidence of abuse resulting from her father's selfish desires for glory and virility.

Thus, Millar's original concept of Hit-Girl is much more in line with Ebert's interpretation, where the inclusion of a young girl into the dangerous world of adult violence necessarily renders her a victim. Forced into filling an inappropriate role, her function is no longer to serve as a subversion of traditional young female roles but rather to emphasize the innate perversity of deviating from those roles. This marked difference in the significance of her heroic identity can be seen in the contrast between Hit-Girl's demeanor during the climactic scenes of the comic and the movie. In the comic, Hit-Girl's moment of triumph sees her finally transform into a more natural, vulnerable state. Having just gunned down the final room of mobsters, Hit-Girl stands motionless, with her arms limp, perhaps in a state of shock or simply exhaustion, before removing her mask and tearfully seeking consolation in Kick-Ass's arms. Relieved of the obligation to her father that had forced her to become an adult before her time, her tone takes on the innocence and vulnerability of a child as she expresses the grief she had previously stifled to maintain her heroic persona. Meanwhile, at the conclusion of the movie, Hit-Girl successfully exacts revenge upon the criminals who were responsible for the deaths of her parents, fulfilling her father's (legitimate) quest for revenge. Escaping with Kick-Ass to a distant rooftop, Hit-Girl takes solace in the thought that her father would be proud of them both and shares her true identity with Kick-Ass/Dave in a gesture of mutual friendship and trust. In this latter case, Hit-Girl appears filled with a sense of genuine accomplishment from having achieved her heroic objective and, maintaining her mature poise, reaches out to Dave as an equal (a coup for Dave). In the comic, the completion of her father's erroneous objective brings only a sense of loss as her mature façade is cast away to expose the authentic, fragile child underneath.

Thus, it could be argued that by eschewing the details that change Hit-Girl from an empowered heroine into a deceived child, Vaughn's movie offers a more radical, postfeminist interpretation of her character. In doing so however, it is important not to discount Millar's graphic novel as anti-feminist. A close reading of the comic version of *Kick-Ass* reveals critical insights linking the anxieties surrounding masculine identity and the appeal of the superhero fantasy.

"THE PERFECT COMBINATION OF LONELINESS AND DESPAIR": THE MALE SUPERHERO FANTASY

In an interview conducted around the release of the *Kick-Ass* movie, Mark Millar admitted that he was surprised that so many readers considered the comic to be more cynical than the movie:

> And what I'm finding out, almost by accident, is that people want three-dimensional superheroes. Each generational shift is slightly more realistic and radical than the previous. So Dave Lizewski, the hero of *Kick-Ass*, follows that lineage back through Peter Parker to Clark Kent. Clark was envisioned as an amazing guy with superpowers, who pretended to be a bit of a nerd. Peter Parker was a bit of a nerd, who then got superpowers. Dave Lizewski . . . is just a nerd! (qtd in Hunt).

According to Millar, the dark, gritty tone of the comic was not intended to undermine the appeal of the superhero fantasy, as in such deconstructionist works as Alan Moore's *Watchmen*. Instead it was intended to make it more realistic. Millar describes *Kick-Ass* as an attempt to add an extra layer of depth to the traditional superhero by grounding his stories in a realist world where violence has consequences and characters are naturally flawed. In doing so, he did not intend to sacrifice the romantic moralism inherent to the genre: "the story is, at its core, about a wee guy who wants to help people. . . . There's a 'Good Samaritan' charm to the high concept" (qtd in Hunt). Although Millar's intent was to render his superheroes more relevant and identifiable while preserving their essential idealism, in doing so he exposes the underlying insecurities that motivate his characters to adopt their heroic personas. Specifically, he identifies superheroism as a means of obtaining an outwardly stable, masculine identity.

Describing himself as a normal teenaged boy, Dave Lizewski perceives himself as being rather nondescript: "I wasn't the class clown or class genius or class anything, really. Like most people my age I merely existed" (Millar, issue 1). Dave does not appear to be particularly concerned with meeting a preconceived notion of identity, but he is also not satisfied with his lack of identity. His description of his impetus as a "perfect combination of loneliness and despair" implies that he is driven by the insecurities common to most isolated, sexually frustrated teenaged boys. David Coughlan explains how the hero's costumed self often represents a transition from childhood to the public world of adult labor: "the comic book hero's costume, therefore, constructs him as a man exactly because it marks him as a public figure. In this way, comics suggest that strength in the masculine public sphere is the truest sign of manhood" (238). Implicit in Dave's anonymity as just another teenager is a sense of emasculating insignificance.

As Coughlan suggests, donning a superhero costume has a transformative effect essential to Dave's efforts to take control of and redefine his public identity. By putting on the costume, he achieves a new identity and with it a new sense of self-worth, instantly changing from awkward uncertainty to complete confidence. This new self-possession allows Dave to project an idealized masculine persona in other public settings. Returning to school, he describes how wearing his costume under his clothes "empowers" him as he approaches girls with a new sense of assuredness. Even when hidden from sight, the costume provides Dave with perhaps the most essential manly quality: autonomy. It shields him from feeling beholden to social pressure that would reinforce his feelings of inadequacy and anonymity, and it sustains the identity he has created for himself as a tough, confident hero.

Millar's realist approach not only makes plain how the superhero fantasy derives its appeal from anxiety surrounding male self-image, it also highlights the unhealthy consequences and ultimate futility of its escapist solution. Describing the impracticality of male models of identity, Lynne Segal has suggested that the pursuit of ideal manhood is a perpetual, unachievable endeavor, claiming, "Men will fail, and fail again, to measure up to its promise. Masculinity is always in crisis" (239). Millar seems to share this view of manly power as an unrealistic and misleading goal, consistently depicting the unfortunate disparity between Dave's expectations and his reality. Despite Dave's newfound confidence, his increasing popularity with his love interest is not a result of his heroic persona; on the contrary, it is due to her misled belief that he is homosexual, a misconception that only serves to further aggravate his identity crisis. His career as a crime fighter is often equally dissatisfying. After being brutally assaulted multiple times, Dave continually berates himself for persisting in his heroic activities, acknowledging the foolishness of his actions even as he continues to repeat them. He describes his recidivism in terms of an addiction, presenting superheroism as a dangerous habit perpetually reinforced by its delusive appeal to his sense of manhood.

Certainly the most cautionary example of male power fantasies is that of Big Daddy endangering his daughter for a self-affirming but meaningless quest against crime. Coughlan explains how the masculine persona achieved through superheroism is incompatible with family life and often serves as an alternative to domesticity (241). Frequently superheroes will have to choose between the two, only managing to commit to a private life when they withdraw completely from their public, costumed existence (Peter Parker giving up his identity as Spiderman so that he can be with Mary Jane or Bruce Banner seeking a cure to his becoming The Hulk so that he can be with Betty Ross). In such stories, domestic life often serves as an impediment to the hero's more important public responsibilities and must be continually deferred so that he can meet his manly obligations. In *Kick-Ass* the implicit antagonism between the virile hero and the domesticated male is not only made explicit, but the traditional priority granted to the hero's public duties is destabilized. Big Daddy's decision to become a hero has nothing to do with civic responsibility. He admits that his battle against Genovese's crime syndicate is entirely arbitrary: "We needed a villain" (Millar, issue 7). Stripped of its social utility, the superhero ceases to serve as a legitimating model of powerful male identity. Instead, it serves as an escape from the more realistic responsibilities of the family man, a duty that "requires a different kind of bravery because it means replacing the armored shell with a naked emotional vulnerability" (Coughlan 244). It is Big Daddy's failure in the domestic aspects of his life (the job he hated, the wife who hated him) that drives him to superheroism as a means of reasserting his fragile manhood (much as Dave does). His transformation from a dangerous vigilante to a delusional, negligent parent in the moments before his death redefines the proper criteria of manliness.

Far from reinforcing traditional gender roles, the *Kick-Ass* comic series presents a number of critical insights that force the reader to reevaluate the significance of those roles. These insights are largely glossed over by the movie adaptation in favor of telling a more upbeat, sensationalistic story. In the movie, Dave eventually succeeds in gaining a girlfriend who comes to validate his manliness as a sex object and Big Daddy actually is an ex-cop with a legitimate vendetta who dies a noble death in his daughter's arms. More willing to explore the realistic, unpleasant consequences of its characters' actions than the movie, Millar's story certainly offers a more complex and thoughtful consideration of its subject matter. Yet, it is noteworthy that in doing so he causes *Kick-Ass*'s most intriguing character to fill a more traditional role. Serving less as an empowering example of a female hero and more as a symbol of male guilt, Hit-Girl's significance to the story becomes subordinated to an examination of male identity crises, conforming to a longstanding trope of the female superhero as largely a sounding board for their male counterparts. Hit-Girl falls into a tradition of female heroes like Sue Storm, the Invisible Girl, whose first decade with the Fantastic Four was spent serving as a prize for male figures like Mr. Fantatsic and Namor to fight over, "the morale-boosting beauty who was usually welcome to tag along for the ride, even if she could not be of any real use" (D'Amore). While Hit-Girl is certainly more assertive than the Invisible Girl, her final function as a victim of parental abuse shows that Millar's three-dimensional superheroes may have inherited some two-dimensional gender dynamics.

CONCLUSION: FEMINIST AND
POSTFEMINIST READINGS OF HIT-GIRL

It seems that the progressive postfeminist emphasis of the movie must come at the cost of sacrificing the comic's sensitivity to feminist concerns regarding the abusive potential of male wish fulfillment. It would be a mistake to attempt to determine whether the movie or the comic version of *Kick-Ass* presents a more appropriate feminist message. Each has strengths and shortfalls. The comic, while presenting a number of pertinent insights, perpetuates the priority of male characters in the superhero genre. However, the movie version of Hit-Girl should not necessarily be promoted as a more positive feminist character simply because she manifests the masculine qualities that are so effectively scrutinized and deflated in the comic. In this situation, it is useful to return to Schubart's notion of an "in-between" stance regarding postfeminism, a critical approach that remains open to both the progressive and the problematic aspects of the action heroine. Rather than attempt to rank or reconcile these two versions of Hit-Girl into a uniform feminist view, it is important to consider the value of examining both in conjunction. A more rounded discussion of the action heroine's feminist implications results from observing how Hit-Girl can fill dual roles: the uncompromising action heroine who exposes the arbitrary nature of gender distinctions and the victimized daughter who exposes the danger of male power fantasies.

The resulting juxtaposition allows us to at once celebrate gender equality without ignoring the persistent reality of gender disparity. In doing so, the question that these two versions of Hit-Girl force us to consider is whether the appropriation of masculinity by the action heroine is a pleasure worth indulging. Fan outcry for superheroine movies has begun to gain traction as the popularity of the superhero genre raises the demand for women in lead action roles. With DC and Marvel's first female-led properties scheduled to hit theaters in 2017 and 2018, respectively, it is important to examine the consequences of conflating depictions of strong women with the glorification of traditionally masculine notions of strength. If the ideal of the self-assertive, autonomous hero is a fantasy born out of male insecurities and pursued as an alternative to the complex responsibilities of adulthood, what does it mean to apply such a model as a measure of gender equality? Should we be concerned that such a model could entirely eclipse alternative conceptions of strength, conceptions that promote emotional or social attributes?

An in-between interpretation of Hit-Girl is valuable because it helps articulate these important concerns, but it also raises a more radical possibility. Despite the potential problems associated with the postfeminist action heroine, Chloë Grace Moretz's transgressive performance as Hit-Girl uproots the associations linking assertive, aggressive models of strength from the gendered terms of masculinity. Shedding the baggage of over-compensation and the misogynistic tropes common to her forerunners, she is an eleven-year-old ass-kicker that looks forward to a more diverse generation of heroines whose identities are not reflexive shadows of their male counterparts.

NOTES

1. There are, of course, exceptions to this argument. Kord and Krimmer acknowledge the variations of his aesthetic by examining a wide range of films, each of which depict the relationship between individual self-reliance and dependence upon communities in a distinct manner.

2. For the purposes of this chapter, I will be limiting my discussion to the first volume of *Kick-Ass* and its corresponding film adaptation.

3. It is important to point out that Schubart is actually referring to an earlier article by Brown, rather than his recent book, though material from the article is incorpo-

rated into his book. Brown's caution in analyzing postfeminism and qualifying the subversive potential of female heroes in *Dangerous Curves* may well be a response to Schubart's criticism, though this is merely conjecture on my part.

4. While Brown does not fully explore this issue in relation to Nikita, he does offer a very insightful examination of this fetishistic voyeurism regarding the female spy's disguises in his discussion of the television show *Alias* in chapter 3 of *Dangerous Curves*.

5. John Genovese is the name of the central villain in the comic. In the movie, his name is changed to Frank D'Amico.

WORKS CITED

Brown, Jeffrey A. *Dangerous Curves: Action Heroines, Gender, Fetishism, and Popular Culture*. Jackson: UP of Mississippi, 2011. Print.

———. "Gender and the Action Heroine: Hardbodies and the Point of No Return." *Cinema Journal* 35.3 (1996): 52–71. Print.

Butler, Judith. *Gender Trouble*. New York: Routledge, 1990. Print.

Coughlan, David. "The Naked Hero and Model Man: Costumed Identity in Comic Book Narratives." *Heroes of Film, Comics and American Culture*. Ed. Lisa M. Detora. Jefferson, NC: McFarland, 2009. Print.

D'Amore, Laura Mattoon. "Invisible Girl's Quest for Visibility: Early Second Wave Feminism and the Comic Book Superheroine." *Americana: The Journal of American Popular Culture* 7.2 (2008). Web. 26 Apr. 2013.

Ebert, Roger. "Kick-Ass." Rev. of *Kick-Ass*, dir. Matthew Vaughn. *The Chicago Sun* 14 Apr. 2010. *rogerebert.com*. Web. 14 Feb. 2011.

Halberstam, Judith. *Female Masculinity*. Durham: Duke UP, 1998. Print.

Howell, Peter. "Kick-Ass: A Violent, Five-Alarm, Four-Star Fantasy." Rev. of *Kick-Ass*, dir. Matthew Vaughn. *The Toronto Star* 15 Apr. 2010. *thestar.com*. Web. 14 Feb. 2011.

Hunt, James. "Mark Millar Interview: *Kick-Ass*, Marvel, *Avengers* and More . . ." *Den of Geek*. 10 Feb. 2010. Web. 17 Feb. 2011.

Kord, Susanne and Elisabeth Krimmer. *Contemporary Hollywood Masculinities: Gender, Genre, and Politics*. New York: Palgrave, 2011. Print.

Lane, Anthony. "Street Justice: 'Kick-Ass' and 'Exit through the Giftshop.'" *The New Yorker* 26 Apr. 2010. Web. 14 Feb. 2011.

Millar, Mark, John Romita Jr., et al. *Kick-Ass*. New York: Marvel Comics, 2010. Print.

Schubart, Rikke. *Super Bitches and Action Babes: The Female Hero in Popular Cinema, 1970–2006*. Jefferson, NC: McFarland, 2007. Print.

Segal, Lynne. "Back to the Boys? Temptations of the Good Gender Theorist." *Textual Practice* 15, no. 2 (2001): 231–50. Print.

Steinem, Gloria. "Wonder Woman." *The Superhero Reader*. Ed. Charles Hatfield, Jeet Heer, and Kent Worcester. Jackson: UP of Mississippi, 2013. 203-10. Print.

NEGOTIATED MASCULINITIES

7

"I'm Listening": Analyzing the Masculine Example of Frasier Crane

Dustin Gann

Frasier (1993–2004), a sitcom depicting both the public and private life of an educated, single man surrounded by accomplished and independent women, highlights the impacts of second-wave feminism and the possibilities of post-feminist masculinity. Joanne Morreale connects popular culture with societal evolution when she argues "television, like all forms of social discourse, helps to shape not only beliefs, values, and attitudes, but also subjectivities, people's sense of themselves and their place in the world" (xi). In particular, shows such as *The Mary Tyler Moore Show* (1970–1977) and *Murphy Brown* (1988–1998) paralleled the expanding role of women in the workplace. Similarly, the popularity of *Ellen* (1994–1998) and *Will and Grace* (1998–2006) mirrored society's growing acceptance of homosexuality. Numerous scholars also trace the evolution of twentieth-century American masculinity through sit-com characters such as Ward Cleaver, Archie Bunker, and Al Bundy. Morreale argues "sitcoms address significant ideas and issues within seemingly innocuous narrative frames, and analyzing them can help us account for the complexity and complications involved in the . . . reception contexts of popular culture" (xi). Too often, however, a show's focus on a single character or demographic profile obscures the relationships between diverse individuals.

As a spinoff of *Cheers*, *Frasier* features a multigenerational cast of both male and female leading characters. At the show's center is a recently divorced psychiatrist, Frasier Crane (Kelsey Grammar) who leaves a successful private practice in Boston to begin hosting a radio call-in show on Seattle radio station KACL. The character of Roz Doyle (Peri Gilpin) represents the show's female counterpoint. She is Frasier's constant coworker, close personal friend, and a potential lover. Frasier's brother, Niles (David Hyde Pierce), is a psychiatrist with his own private practice and a constant source of companionship and antagonism. Frasier's father Martin (John Mahoney) and home healthcare worker Daphne Moon (Jane Leeves) also share Frasier's apartment. The show's complexity reveals Frasier's struggle to balance platonic professionalism and sexual chemistry with female coworkers, compete with other men for occupational and romantic success, and grapple with questions of homosexuality.

MASCULINITY IN TRANSITION

During the eleven seasons *Frasier* aired on NBC, American men found themselves facing evolving professional and personal circumstances. In the workplace, intellectual and collaborative skills became more important than brute physical strength. Female coworkers and potential romantic partners, as a result of second-wave feminism, increasingly earned equal education and career credentials. Expanding opportunities for women altered masculine expectations because, as R. W. Connell observes, "gender is not fixed in advance of social interaction, but is constructed in interaction" (35). David Buchbinder observes that "as historical and social circumstances change, it is likely that new forms of the masculine will come into being." This process, however, occurs "slowly and tentatively, and in competition with residual and dominant forms" (177). The ongoing renegotiation of gender roles leads to an uneven evolution of masculine expectations that reflect the new egalitarian reality.

Understanding postfeminist masculinity requires acknowledging the success of feminism. Yvonne Tasker and Diane Negra assert in *Interrogating Postfeminism* that "postfeminist culture works in part to incorporate, assume, or naturalize aspects of feminism" (2). They argue that the impact on contemporary masculinity has been a deepening appreciation for the inherent variability present within male behavior and an array of culture phenomena aimed at reasserting and maintaining traditional notions of manhood (14–15). Thus, postfeminist masculinity allows men to recognize gender equality and display an array of personality traits previously considered taboo due to their association with femininity. Expanding the range of acceptable traits, however, creates an internal struggle that often leads to conflict between men striving to display disparate notions of masculinity. Benjamin Brabon posits that "the compound nature of contemporary masculinity has developed out of a series of competing social and economic hybrid scripts that have become enmeshed to form conflicting and conflicted identities—postfeminist masculinities" (117). While current masculinity represents an evolution, it involves the negotiation and integration of these multiple strains.

In many ways, the character of Frasier Crane dramatically encapsulates the tension within postfeminist masculinity. His success stems from his nimble mind and specialized psychiatric knowledge. He largely eschews the autonomy, competition, and dominance that American men have been conditioned for generations to value as ideal. Moreover, he actively seeks out accomplished women in both his professional and personal life. At the same time, his lack of traditional masculine traits leaves him vulnerable to ridicule and insecure in his relationships with others. Moreover, his tendency to over analyze everyday minutiae rather than take decisive action—an outgrowth of his cerebral nature and intelligence—often sabotages his relationships with family, friends, and potential lovers.

NAVIGATING RELATIONSHIPS WITH THE NEW WOMAN

Frasier's professional and personal interactions with a range of female characters vividly illustrate the evolving gender landscape. Amanda Lotz argues in *Redesigning Women* that during the last two decades of the twentieth century "narratives decreasingly emphasized women in the public sphere as [an] exception, a shift that corresponds to second-wave feminism's investment in expanding professional opportunities for women" (9–10). In particular, Anthea Taylor asserts that working single women can be seen as "often embodying precisely the types of feminine subjectivity for which feminism fought (independent, financially autonomous, ambitious, sexually fulfilled)" and as a result they represent "a key nodal point in the increasingly complex interactions between feminism and popular culture" (33). As this description makes clear, the rise of the working single woman represents a shift in workplace representations, as women take their place beside their male colleagues.

Roz Doyle is the most visible female character on *Frasier,* and her relationship with Frasier underscores the complicated nature of workplace interactions via postfeminist masculinity. Despite offering a scathing assessment of Frasier's initial KACL broadcast, Roz serves as his producer for the duration of his radio career. On numerous occasions he explicitly credits her skill for his success and multiple episodes demonstrate the intersection of their careers.

Over eleven seasons the relationship between Frasier and Roz deepens to the point that they confide in one another about a wide range of professional and personal issues. In season two, for example, Roz tells Frasier that she skipped her family reunion because "every year . . . My relatives crowd around me and I answer the same questions. No, I'm not married. No, I don't have any kids. Yes, I still have that tattoo. No, you can't see it. It would just be so nice if I could at least say I have a great career" ("Dark Victory" 2.24*)*. Sensing Roz's despair, Frasier praises her career achievements and commends her for breaking new ground. He says "You know, Roz—ten years ago KACL didn't have any women producers? You're a pioneer. You've won awards. You help people." On the other hand, however, he suggests that part of her unhappiness might be resolved by focusing on her personal life. He says, "Maybe you're just looking for too much from your job. Start exploring other areas of your life. Interests. Maybe a serious relationship" (2.24). Frasier's response demonstrates the tension present within postfeminist masculinity as men began to value the contributions of autonomous female coworkers while also continuing to view women in their traditional roles as wives and mothers.

The workplace dynamic between Frasier and Roz also provides the primary story arc of a season eight episode titled "Docu.Drama." In the opening scene, after learning Roz received the green light for a documentary exploring the space race, Frasier immediately begins campaigning for the narrator's role. Initially skeptical of Frasier's involvement, Roz cautions that "it might be kind of awkward, you working for me. I mean, you've been my boss for eight years." Frasier, however, presses his case by assuring her that "I welcome a little role reversal. I think it'll do our relationship a lot of good" ("Docu.Drama" 8.16). During the remainder of the episode Frasier repeatedly tries to influence the direction of the project and the pair quarrel over issues ranging from structural content and major themes to the program's musical accompaniment. At one juncture, as Frasier lectures her on how to be an effective manager, Roz erupts: "I've been listening to you for eight years, and I would like for you to listen to me for a change!" (8.16). Unwilling and unable to become just another member of the project team, Frasier reluctantly relinquishes the narrator's role instead of acknowledging Roz's authority.

Two primary factors prevent Frasier from serving as an effective narrator. First, he seeks dominance in all aspects of his life and he prides himself on possessing deeper intellectual and cultural knowledge than those around him. Second, he has little experience working within a collaborative environment. Thus, the transition to working on a team, not to mention in tandem with someone he has long supervised, proves difficult. By the end of the episode Frasier admits that "maybe I was being a little too assertive" and Roz concedes that her desire "to prove that I could do this on my own" led her to reject his involvement. Tension stemming from the space documentary reveals the closeness of Frasier and Roz within the workplace as well as her growing responsibility at KACL. Moreover, the evolving nature of their professional relationship highlights the ongoing renegotiation of gender roles as women gained increasingly influential positions within the American workplace.

Perpetually single, Frasier's search for a mate provides a majority of the show's comedy and conflicts. Dating smart and sexy women frequently presents Frasier with a dilemma that previous generations never faced: what happens when the woman has more power and a higher salary? For example, Frasier finds himself in the submissive role during his relationship with a lawyer named Samantha Pierce. After meeting Samantha at the mall, Frasier egotistically tells Niles that "when I asked her out, I sensed a bit of shyness which made me wonder if she was perhaps intimidated by my fame" ("My Fair Frasier" 5.07). This sentiment vanishes, however, when Niles points out that Samantha is currently appearing on Larry King Live. Frasier watches in awe as King quizzes Samantha about her current case and rumors linking her to famous men like Kevin Costner, George Stephanopoulos, and Brad Pitt. The unequal prestige and affluence between Frasier and Samantha repeatedly surfaces within the relationship as she showers him with expensive gifts, breaks their dates due to work, and leaves him with her coworkers' wives at a dinner party. Samantha's prestige, power, and success make her in many ways the more masculine half of the couple and, ultimately, this causes her to end the relationship. Frasier's involvement with Samantha highlights the challenges of dating in post second-wave feminism America as women increasingly attain levels of education and occupational success that exceed their male counterparts.

Like Samantha, Frasier's other relationships demonstrate his desire to find a partner that provides both mental and physical stimulation. In contrast to a character like Bulldog (Dan Butler), Frasier actively resists a purely physical relationship. When Niles asks Frasier about his tryst with a woman named Caitlin, Frasier attempts to defend the liaison as full of potential. Niles, however, remains skeptical and presses Frasier for details. Stumbling to recall anything of note, Frasier finds he cannot remember much of anything about Caitlin's background or identify any interests they share. As a result, Niles quips that "the only thing you two in have in common is the faint impression of Sealy on your backsides" ("Frasier Gotta Have It" 5.19).

In the episode's concluding scene Frasier attempts to breakup with Caitlin, telling her that "I'm basically your stuffy, buttoned-up kind of guy! You're, well, you're a free-spirited, adventurous, mouse-painting, moon-howling sort of girl. Is even the most satisfying sexual relationship enough to bridge the gap?" In response, Caitlin whispers "I think so" and drops her robe; Frasier's resolve crumbles yet again (5.19). Caitlin's character does not appear in any subsequent episodes, however, and the audience is left to imagine how the relationship finally ended. Despite the fact that Frasier gave in to his physical desire, his overall approach to dating reflects a quest to find an intellectual connection within a lasting relationship. This approach differentiates Frasier and postfeminist masculinity from traditional versions of manhood that seek physical fulfillment and sexual conquest. Ultimately, it also reflects the success of second-wave feminism because without a large pool of educated, successful, and independent women he could not have hoped to find such a mate.

The hilarious banter and social commentary of *Frasier* also stems from the show's exploration of Roz's romantic relationships. On frequent occasions male characters tease Roz about her active sex life and the ease at which she gains male attention. *Frasier* juxtaposes Roz's promiscuity with Frasier's often unintentional celibacy in order to invert the woman seeking love and man seeking sex trope. Further, Frasier's friendly involvement in Roz's dating life illustrates the increasing complexity of male-female relationships. When Roz complains about a dating drought in an episode titled "Frasier loves Roz" (3.22), Frasier responds by suggesting that "I think your whole problem stems from . . . the men you date. Always flashy and superficial, offering no prospect of a lasting relationship." As a remedy, he urges her to consider "different kinds of men. You know, men who are more settled, a little less flash and more substance." Frasier's well-intentioned advice, however, becomes worrisome when he learns that the man Roz credits him for helping her find— "I'm so glad you gave me that advice, Frasier, because without it, I would never have given him a second look"—is Niles' former patient and a chronic womanizer. The episode draws heavily on the hilarity that ensues as Frasier frantically tries to keep Roz from getting hurt without violating professional ethics preventing him from telling her what he knows about her boyfriend. Frasier finally breaks down and tells Roz that she should avoid getting too attached or letting herself fall in love, only to have Roz think him to be jealous and too protective. Further, she misinterprets his concern for romantic affection (3.22). The interplay between Frasier and Roz demonstrates how the increasing status of women and emergence of postfeminist masculinity leads to the formation of male-female friendships on both a professional and personal level. Simultaneously, however, their interactions also illustrate how these relationships commonly lead to misunderstandings which rarely occur within platonic relationships between two individuals of the same gender.[1]

In many ways, Roz possesses all of the qualities Frasier desires in an ideal partner. She has a successful career, is compatible with his family, and they share many common and complementary interests. In fact, in an episode titled "The Guilt Trippers" (9.23), their mutual loneliness and long simmering attraction causes the relationship to turn sexual. After breaking up with her most recent boyfriend, Roger, Roz tells Frasier that "ever since this whole Roger thing happened, you've really come through for me. It means a lot. Why can't more men be like you? I mean, you are exactly what women are looking for." The following morning, however, both Roz and Frasier immediately recognize the ramifications of their actions. Roz rushes out of the apartment, despite Frasier's suggestion that they discuss what had happened. Frasier, for his part, laments to his father that "I have probably destroyed our friendship. I don't even know how this happened. She probably thinks I took advantage of her, I mean, that's why she ran out of here." Despite Martin's assurance that Roz was fully capable of making her own decisions, Frasier worries that his platonic relationship with Roz may be over because she will see him as "someone who betrayed her trust."

After failing to reach Roz before she left for a family reunion, Frasier's decides to follow her to Wisconsin. Upon arriving, Roz's family assumes Frasier is Roz's boyfriend, Roger, whom they had been expecting. Thus, Frasier is thrust into the position of pretending to be Roz's boyfriend—a charade he continues once Roz arrives—not because he wants the role but because it is easier than offering an actual explanation. After hours of watching her family fawn over her "boyfriend," Roz and Frasier sit on the front porch for a heart to heart conversation. She enthusiastically tells him "That was the best half hour I have ever spent with my family! Thank you! But what are you doing here?" In reply, Frasier explains his concern that their sexual encounter will negatively affect their working relationship and cost him her close personal friendship. Importantly, he does not attempt to woo Roz or express any romantic love for her. Instead, he confesses that "I just had to make sure we were okay."

Roz responds by acknowledging that "I should have stayed and talked to you. It's just, usually when I'm freaked out I turn to you, and this time I just didn't feel like I could." She goes on, however, to assure him that "I'm a grownup, and I make my own decisions . . . we'll always be friends, Frasier, nothing is ever going to change that." Frasier's relief at hearing Roz express a commitment to their friendship confirms that despite her having many of the qualities he sought in a dating partner, he values her friendship, support, and their cooperative professional relationship above any potential romantic involvement (9.22). Thus, their multifaceted friendship illustrates how contemporary male-female relationships balance competing priorities in ways unfathomable to previous generations of Americans.

RESPECTING SINGLE MOTHERS

The growing independence of American women contributes to an increasing number of television characters who enjoy unprecedented independence. Consequently, Lotz observes that "by the late 1990s, series depicted marriage more as an option than a necessity" (95). A continued emphasis on motherhood, however, simultaneously highlights women's autonomy and generates controversy.[2] Lilly Goren argues in *You've Come a Long Way Baby* that the outrage surrounding the title character's pregnancy on *Murphy Brown* "pointed out some of the absurdities that have revolved around the discussion of single motherhood." Further, she connects Murphy Brown to "a rise of single mothers by choice" and a reoccurrence of characters that are "wealthy enough and established enough to support a child; they have supportive and attentive friends (aside from the plotline demands of new mom and old friends working out the parameters of their friendship); and they are generally white, straight, and older than thirty" (160).

Frasier reflects the shifting views toward single women and motherhood in two ways. First, Roz's character becomes a single mother during season five. *Frasier* approaches the development seriously and without stigmatizing Roz's pregnancy; instead the show emphasizes her transition to motherhood and struggle to balance professional and personal responsibilities after giving birth. Unlike Murphy Brown, Roz is not the primary character on *Frasier*.[3] Further, though plotlines directly examine her pregnancy, *Frasier* emphasizes the supportive reaction of coworkers and friends rather than Roz's personal politics or her explicit desire to challenge convention. A series of episodes also addresses the unique circumstances causing her to choose single motherhood—the father was in his early twenties—and indicates that she has both the support of the baby's father and the father's parents. Finally, Roz's dating behavior remains a show staple following her pregnancy through plotlines emphasizing the parental potential of her suitors.

Frasier also examines the issue of single motherhood through Frasier's ex-wife, Lilith, who remained in Boston after Frasier moved to Seattle. Lilith periodically appears on the show through various plotlines: she travels to Seattle for a psychiatry convention; she coauthors a book with Frasier; and she and Frasier work to secure their son, Frederick, admission into a prestigious school. Moreover, in an episode titled "Lilith Needs a Favor" (10.13), Lilith indicates a desire to have another child with Frasier. There was only one catch; she wants his sperm rather than his presence. This offer presents Frasier with an existential question—one that women have faced throughout history—am I only desirable and valuable because of my body? As Frasier considers Lilith's request, he asks Niles if it would be "right to create a human being with a woman to whom you couldn't stand being married?" (10.13).

Ultimately, Frasier concludes that while he adores Frederick, and looks forward to becoming a father again, he cannot agree to having another child with Lilith. He wants to find a woman with whom he can start a family and share his life, not a compatible biological match. He explains to Lilith that "This was a very difficult decision for me and I am touched and flattered that you came to me, but I'm not sure I'd be doing it for the right reason." Despite the easy answer being yes, the rejection of Lilith's request further distances Frasier from the male stereotype because it demonstrates his commitment to finding a lasting relationship and to emotionally embracing fatherhood (10.13). At no point does Frasier suggest that either Roz or Lilith are inferior mothers due to their marital status. Both Roz and Lilith's role as single mothers reinforces the commitment of Frasier to even-handedly depicting a range of female characters embracing the increased freedoms women won through second-wave feminism.

COMPETING MASCULINITIES

The success of second-wave feminism and the simultaneous shift toward white collar careers contributes to increasing tension between men grappling with how to respond to societal expectations. Connell identifies "an important division between forms of masculinity organized around direct domination (e.g., corporate management, military command) and forms organized around technical knowledge (e.g., professions, science)." He argues that, as a result of the increasing value placed upon specialized types of knowledge, "the latter have challenged the former for hegemony in the gender order of advanced capitalist societies, without complete success. They currently coexist as inflections of alternative emphases within hegemonic masculinity" (165). Professional success, by men or women, challenge the more traditional, hierarchical masculine behaviors.

Frasier's radio show, which depends on his unique educational background and specialized skill set, epitomizes this shift. When listeners call into his show, Frasier diagnoses their problem and offers psychological advice to help alleviate their suffering. Far from the historically idealized male qualities of brute strength and dominance, Frasier's famous on air greeting—"Hello caller, I'm listening"—emphasizes empathy and compassion. While this earns him popularity as a radio host, it also opens him up to criticism. In the show's fourth episode, newspaper columnist Derek Mann criticizes Frasier via a column titled "I Hate Frasier Crane." In response, Frasier sarcastically mocks Mann on air: "Move aside Voltaire, step back in the shadows H. L. Menken, there's a new kid in town" ("I Hate Frasier Crane" 1.04). Later, when Derek calls into Frasier's show suggesting that they settle their quarrel "like men," Frasier hesitates. He tells Roz that "I just don't think civilized people behave that way." Even after his listeners goad him into accepting the challenge, Frasier attempts to back out. He tells his father that "I have been to medical school, I hold a certain position in this city, I do not settle my differences with brawling" (1.04). By responding to a physical challenge with an intellectual argument, Frasier tries to present himself as more evolved and more refined than the common man.

Subsequent episodes further emphasize Frasier's lack of traditional masculine markers by revealing that he is unable to ride a bicycle, cannot perform minor home repairs, and once employed a butler. Frasier's disconnect from traditional masculinity separates him from male coworkers and his own family. Most notably, Frasier's fellow radio host Bulldog Briscoe serves as a contrasting masculine archetype. Hyper-competitive and flamboyantly heterosexual, Bulldog hosts a sports call-in show at KACL. In contrast to Frasier's empathetic approach, Bulldog encourages his callers to engage in rancorous criticism of athletes, coaches, and each other. Moreover, Bulldog's approach to women also represents a much more stereotypical attitude. For example, when he sees Roz's bridesmaid dress, he tells her "Oh, I love weddings. Never been to a wedding where I didn't bag at least one bridesmaid. And the uglier the dress, the quicker they want to get out of them" (3.22). Additionally, in the fourth season he jokes that the reason that he allows another coworker to play second base on the company softball team instead of Roz is because of "what she will do that you won't" ("The Unnatural" 4.16). Though

Figure 7.1. Frasier Crane (Kelsey Grammer) and his KACL coworkers represent the increasingly diverse postfeminist American workplace. *(Frasier)*

a colleague, Bulldog represents that other masculinities can exist within the same co-ed workplace.

An episode titled "Love Bites Dog" (4.02) contrasts Frasier's postfeminist embrace of gender equality with Bulldog's traditional view of women as conquests. Roz sets Frasier up on a blind date with her friend, Sharon, telling him she is an "incredible person . . . smart, funny, and a former pro-golfer." When he expresses reluctance, Roz appeals to his sense of superiority by telling him she "plays chess, loves your show, and I know this sort of thing isn't supposed to matter to people like you, but I've seen her in the shower at the gym and she has a body that makes Bo Derek look like Bo Diddley." Thus, Frasier "randomly" bumps into Roz and Sharon at Café Nervosa and the initial moments of the setup proceed flawlessly. After a few moments Bulldog walks into the café. He immediately exclaims, "Whoa! Hello, gorgeous!" and forces an introduction. Much to Frasier's chagrin, his attempts to engage Sharon in intellectual banter fail as she becomes locked in conversation with Bulldog. As the pair argue about whether or not women's golf is a sport, Frasier makes lame attempts to reintegrate himself into the conversation. For example, when Bulldog mentions Sharon won a tournament in 1992, Frasier adds that he particularly enjoys a wine vintage from that year. Later, as the argument continues, Frasier comments that "You know, this reminds me of a debate I had with my brother, Niles, about whether Steven Sondheim is really light opera." Ultimately, Frasier is unable to draw Sharon's attention away from the more aggressive Bulldog and is left sitting alone when the pair leaves for the golf course.

Through encounters like this one *Frasier* challenges popular assumptions about male-female relationships and also highlights the impact of female autonomy. On the one hand, Frasier's losing Sharon to Bulldog highlights the limitations of a cerebral dating approach centering on mutual respect. While Frasier's intellectual expertise earns him workplace dominance, it fails to draw Sharon's attention away from Bulldog's brashness. Frasier explains to Roz that "the whole thing catapulted me back to high school . . . jocks were the bane of my existence. They would always call me a 'weenie' and steal all the girls I wanted." Moreover, he recalls that girls only noticed him when "they wanted a sensitive shoulder to cry on, until some blond-pillar of testosterone would come by" (4.02).

On the other hand, Bulldog's reaction to his encounter with Sharon belies his reputation as a lothario. He focuses on emotion and love, telling Frasier and Roz that he was "crazy about her!" and that "I have never felt this way before . . . last night for the first time in my life I actually says those three little words—'stay for breakfast.'" Ultimately, it turns out to be Sharon who favors a physical encounter more than a relationship and her rejection of future dates devastates Bulldog. The final scenes of the episode feature Frasier helping Bulldog embrace his inner maleness. After Bulldog rebuffs Frasier's initial therapy efforts—"stop being a shrink and just be like a guy"—Frasier delivers a rousing pep talk. He begins by observing that "she wasn't that hot," and "all she did was save you the trouble of having to dump her!" Further, growing in volume and intensity, he adds that "tomorrow you're going to find someone even hotter . . . and you're going to have your fun with her and then dump her just for the hell of it . . . and you're not going to feel bad about it, you know why? Because we're guys and that's what guys do." While Frasier's speech restores Bulldog's confidence, it stands in contrast to his refined persona. Thus, when Frasier uses the same locker room rhetoric on his brother, Niles slaps him back into reality (4.02).

Characters like Derek Mann and Bulldog, who exude exaggerated physicality and heterosexuality, remind *Frasier* viewers that traditional masculinity continues to exist within contemporary society. As Kimmel observes, "when masculinity is perceived as in crisis, there are those who defend a nostalgic traditional vision of gender relations that would return men to their 'rightful' position of dominance" (233). Postfeminist masculinity allows for a wider range of acceptable behaviors within American men, but this variation exacerbates competition and leads to insecurity as men judge themselves alongside other men and prior notions of idealized manhood. Thus, postfeminist man "is a melting post of masculinities, blending a variety of contested subject positions, as well as a chameleon figure still negotiating the ongoing impact of feminism on his identity" (Genz 143). The universe of *Frasier* allows these masculinities to interact, between characters as well as within a specific character, demonstrating these negotiations for comic effect.

NOT THAT THERE'S ANYTHING WRONG WITH THAT . . .

The increasing openness of American society to homosexuality, long regarded as a threat to successful male identity, complicates postfeminist masculinity. Pamela Demory and Christopher Pullen in *Queer Love* connect real world advocacy to fictional plotlines by noting that "cross-relationships between art and life may, in fact, determine that fictional narratives of same-sex couples shown on our television and movie screens may be normalizing those relationships" (3–4). *Will and Grace* (1998–2006), an NBC series overlapping with *Frasier,* establishes commonality between homosexual male protagonists and heterosexual female companion characters (Streitmatter 115–26). Whereas *Will and Grace* emphasizes homosexual coupling and the search for longlasting love, *Frasier* explores the possibility of homosexual behavior within straight characters and the relationship between hetero and homosexual men.[4] Despite no regularly appearing homosexual characters, plotlines on *Frasier* routinely highlight the mutability of gender roles, the fallibility of common homosexual stereotypes, and broadening acceptance of homosexual lifestyles.[5]

Moreover, *Frasier* explores the title character's possible homosexuality on multiple occasions. Frasier displays several of the most common homosexual stereotypes: he is single and middle aged, he prefers intellectual pursuits over physical endeavors, his elite education separates him from the masses, and his knowledge of fashion and décor heightens the value he places on appearance. Steven Cohen's essay "Queer Eye for the Straight Guise" argues that postfeminist masculinity features a permeable divide across which contemporary men can display characteristics previously indicative of femininity without turning away from heterosexuality. Drawing upon the example of the reality show *Queer Eye for the Straight Guy* (2003–2007), Cohen asserts that "straight masculinity is identified as problematic more than oppressive, and it can be remedied through a male's consumption of the same kind of products that enhance in order to regulate femininity (181). The result is a "metrosexual" which Cohen connects to "an earlier representation of what was termed the New Man." According to Cohen, "the meterosexual reimagines masculinity from a postfeminist perspective, but the price remains this new man's sexual ambiguity" (182).[6] Kimmel cautions, however, that "metrosexuality is not for every man, let alone Everyman. Many younger men remain insecure about their sexuality and are unwilling to be mistaken for gay (226).[7] Through the Crane men, *Frasier* frequently explores the anxiety caused by metrosexual male characters who blur the expectations of straight and gay masculinity.

A season two episode titled "Matchmaker" (2.03) uses homosexual stereotypes as the basis for a hilarious case of mistaken sexual identity. In an attempt to set Daphne up with Tom, the handsome new station manager at KACL, Frasier invites him over for dinner. Unbeknownst to Frasier, but revealed to the audience early on, Tom interprets Frasier's invitation as a date. Thus, Tom arrives at Frasier's apartment expecting romance and the resulting scene is ripe for unintended double entendre. For example, Tom compliments the view out Frasier's living room window, and Frasier innocently replies that it is even "better from the bedroom."

Critic Louis Peitzman notes that "Matchmaker" foreshadowed later depictions of homosexuality on television: "The truly amazing thing about 'The Matchmaker' is how casually everyone handles the confusion. OK, Frasier's not thrilled about coming across gay, but he's not horrified either. And while Tom's advances are played for laughs, he's not the butt of the jokes. Instead, Frasier's the idiot for ignoring the obvious and leading his guest on"

(Peitzman). In addition, a similar balance and humor characterizes cases of mistaken sexual identity involving both Martin and Niles ("Out with Dad" 7.15; "Ski Lodge" 5.14). According to Cohen "so-called normative masculinity is a performance, frequently multiple in its signifying effects; that it achieves an impression of stability by maintaining the perceived boundaries strictly differentiating between and culturally locating hetero- and homosexual male identities" (191). Frasier's frequent consideration of the possible homosexuality of major characters reflects an emerging acceptance of homosexuality on television and the overall loosening of previously rigid gender expectations within American society.

A more direct exploration of Frasier's potential homosexuality stems from a reoccurring dream featured in "The Impossible Dream" (4.03). The dream takes place in a seedy motel room and stars Gil Chesterton, a fellow KACL talk show host and rumored homosexual. Each time the dream occurs, Frasier wakes up just prior to Gil emerging from the bathroom and crawling into bed. After his own deductive reasoning, and later Niles' psychiatric advice, fail to end the dream, Frasier tries to engage his father in a late night discussion. He explains the dream in detail—as Martin fidgets and nervously seeks any possible way to avoid the subject—and finally confesses "I've exhausted every other possible interpretation of this dream. Is it possible my subconscious is trying to tell me something about my sexuality?" Martin dismisses the idea out hand, but Frasier persists: "I was sensitive as a child; I didn't go in for sports. God, it's every cliche in the book. Surely it must have occurred to you at some point." Martin's response reinforces the evenhandedness and humor that characterizes *Frasier*. He acknowledges that "okay, yeah, I thought about it. But no, Frasier, no . . . I don't believe that. And you know why? Because you would have known by now. Your unconscious or whatever the hell you call it could no more have kept its yap shut than the rest of you" (4.03).

By de-stigmatizing homosexuality, Frasier is able to fully consider the extent to which Frasier will go in pursuing cultural prestige, material comforts, and companionship. When Niles and Frasier meet Alistair Burke (Patrick Stewart), in an episode titled "The Doctor Is Out" (11.03), both become ecstatic. Frasier explains to Martin that "He is only the head of the Seattle Opera Guild, and one of the finest directors in the world." Both Niles and Frasier enthusiastically introduce themselves, praise Alistair for his past work, and tell him how much they look forward to his upcoming performances. Alistair represents the upper echelon of Seattle society and, more importantly, the type of elite man that Niles and Frasier hope accepts them as equals. After Alistair leaves, the conversation turns toward the sexuality of Roz's new boyfriend, Barry. Both Niles and Frasier believe him to be gay, while Martin expresses disbelief "because of the muscles." Later, Niles and Frasier follow Barry into a gay bar hoping to find proof of their theory. Ironically, a patron who recognizes Frasier calls into his radio show the next day and "outs" him on air.[8] Word of mouth among Frasier's audience, along with other station's reporting, broadcast news of Frasier's "homosexuality" throughout Seattle.

As a result, when Frasier next bumps into Alistair, the conductor offers commiseration. He says that "If it is of any comfort, I went through the same thing once." Moreover, as a way to lift Frasier's spirits he invites him to "a small party after the premiere of my opera next week." The invitation and his developing friendship with Alistair make Frasier the envy of his social circle. Moreover, as Alistair showers Frasier with gifts, a seat on the opera board, the promise of trips to exotic locations and the opportunity to meet celebrities, the relationship provides Frasier with a level of cultural status he has long craved. Instead of being "outed" injuring Frasier professional and personally, as most would fear, it enhances his position in Seattle.

A close male friendship did not undermine Frasier's masculine identity, but as the episode progresses it becomes clear that Alistair regards Frasier as more than a platonic friend. When Niles points out that everyone at Alistair's party believes Frasier to be gay, Frasier defiantly retorts that "all of my life, I have dreamed of being half of a power couple, and I finally am. Is it perfect? No. But it is fun, and I don't want it to end." Thus, Frasier recognizes his own heterosexuality and wrestles with the extent to which he can sacrifice his sexual identity in pursuit of status and prestige. After a bit of introspection, he ends the charade with Alistair for the same reasons that he had broken things off with Caitlyn; a successful relationship requires finding a mate that offers both physical and intellectual companionship (11.03). When only one or the other is present, the relationship cannot survive. The repetitive exploration of Frasier's sexuality allows Frasier to demonstrate the expanding possibilities available to men within contemporary America and suggests that self-expression and individualism are important parts of postfeminist masculinity.

CONCLUSION

As Michael Kimmel explains, "masculinity has become a test by which we prove to other men, to women, and ultimately to ourselves, that we have successfully mastered the part" (41). During *Frasier*'s eleven seasons American television viewers witness the character of Frasier Crane as he faces these tests, struggling with many of the same issues they face in their own lives.

After moving across the country to start a new career and live closer to his family, Frasier endures seemingly endless professional and personal foibles in his new home. Frasier's work at KACL earns him significant financial reward and helps him forge relationships with a variety of colleagues. In particular, his relationship with Roz Doyle reflects the multifaceted male-female relationships that are increasingly common in the wake of second-wave feminism. Roz provides Frasier a valuable colleague, a romantic interest, and, ultimately, a close personal friend. In contrast, misunderstanding and a constant need to win acceptance mark Frasier's familial relationships and interactions with other men. In the workplace Frasier uses a much different occupational skillset than previous generations and his radio call-in show illustrates an American workplace that increasingly rewarded intellectual ability over physical strength. Moreover, Frasier's snobbish elitism and condescending attitude toward traditional markers of masculinity leave him vulnerable to questions of sexual identity.

As a result, Frasier Crane reflects the wide range of professional and personal pressures felt by white educated American men during the late twentieth and early twenty-first centuries.

NOTES

1. Importantly, Julia Wood notes in *Gendered Lives* that "even when cross-sex friends are not sexually involved, an undertone of sexuality often permeates their friendship" (215).

2. Diane Negra argues in *What a Girl Wants* that emphasizing cultural milestones, such as marriage and motherhood, limits the realization of true female autonomy (4). In contrast, Drucialla Cornell argues in *At the Heart of Freedom* that a woman's ability to choose when and how to parent represents a vital component of true independence (41–42).

3. For a thorough examination of *Murphy Brown* see Bonnie J. Dow's *Prime-Time Feminism: Television, Media Culture, and the Women's Movement since 1970.*

4. Multiple essays contained within *Queer Love* explore how homosexual relationships and couples have been portrayed in recent television series. In particular, Ben Aslinger's "'It's Not So Easy for Two Men to Be a Couple': Revisiting Gay Dating in *Will and Grace* and *Queer as Folk.*"

5. *Frasier* prominently featured homosexual actors playing heterosexual characters, including David Hyde Pierce as Niles, Dan Butler as Bulldog, and Edward Hibbert as Gil Chesterton.

6. Michael Kimmel and Amy Aronson specifically identify Crane as the apex of television's "well-bred and well-read 'New Man'" in *Men and Masculinities: A Social, Cultural, and Historical Encyclopedia.*

7. Both Kimmel and Cohen use *Queer Eye for the Straight Guy* as an entry point for consideration of metrosexuality and the thin line separating hetero and homosexuality within postfeminist masculinity.

8. While in the club, Frasier recognizes the bartender as his "furniture polisher." Importantly, this is not only a double entendre but rather a further indication of the luxurious life that Frasier has crafted for himself.

WORKS CITED

Brabon, Benjamin A. "'Chuck Flick': A Genealogy of the Postfeminist Male Singleton." Ed. Joel Gwynne and Nadine Muller. *Postfeminism and Contemporary Hollywood Cinema.* Houndsmills, UK: Palgrave Macmillan, 2013. Print.

Buchbinder, David. *Studying Men and Masculinities.* New York: Routledge, 2012. Print.

Cohen, Steven. "Queer Eye for the Straight Guise." *Interrogating Postfeminism: Gender and the Politics of Popular Culture.* Ed. Yvonne Tasker and Diane Negra. Durham: Duke UP, 2007. Print.

Connell, R. W. *Masculinities.* 2nd ed. Cambridge: Polity Press, 2005. Print.

Cornell, Drucilla. *At the Heart of Freedom: Feminism, Sex and Equality.* Princeton: Princeton UP, 1998. Print.

Dow, Bonnie J. *Prime-Time Feminism: Television, Media Culture, and the Women's Movement since 1970.* Philadelphia: U of Pennsylvania P, 1992. Print.

Genz, Stephanie and Benjamin A. Brabon. *Postfeminism: Cultural Texts and Theories.* Edinburgh, Scotland: Edinburgh UP, 2009. Print.

Goren, Lilly J. "Supermom: The Age of the Pregnant Assassin." Ed. Lilly J. Goren. *You've Come a Long Way, Baby: Women, Politics, and Popular Culture.* Lexington: U of Kentucky P, 2009. Print.

Kimmel, Michael S. *Manhood in America.* New York: Oxford UP, 2006. Print.

Kimmel, Michael S., and Amy Aronson. *Men and Masculinities: A Social, Cultural, and Historical Encyclopedia.* Santa Barbara, CA: ABC-CLIO, 2004. Print.

Kutulas, Judy. "Liberated Women and New Sensitive Men: Reconstructing Gender in the 1970s Workplace Comedies." *The Sitcom Reader: America Viewed and Skewed.* Ed. Mary M. Dalton and Laura R. Linder. Albany: SUNY P, 2005. 217–27. Print.

Lotz, Amanda D. *Redesigning Women: Television after the Network Era.* Urbana: U of Illinois P, 2006. Print.

Morreale, Joanne, ed. *Critiquing the Sitcom: A Reader.* Syracuse: Syracuse UP, 2003. Print.

Peitzman, Louis. "Classic Gay TV: Frasier, 'The Matchmaker.'" *NewNowNext.com* 2 Nov. 2012: n.pag. Logo. Web. 5 July 2013.

Streitmatter, Rodger. *From 'Perverts' to 'Fab Five': The Media's Changing Depiction of Gay Men and Lesbians.* New York: Routledge, 2009. Print.

Tasker, Yvonne, and Diane Negra., eds. *Interrogating Postfeminism: Gender and the Politics of Popular Culture.* Durham: Duke UP, 2007. Print.

Taylor, Anthea. *Single Women in Popular Culture.* Houndsmills: Palgrave Macmillan, 2012. Print.

Wood, Julia. *Gendered Lives: Communication, Gender, and Culture.* Boston: Wadsworth Cengage Learning, 2011. Print.

8

Hanging with the Boys: Homosocial Bonding and Heterosexual Bromance Coupling in *Nip/Tuck* and *Boston Legal*

Pamela Hill Nettleton

They sleep together (with pajamas buttoned up to the collar), slow dance, hold hands, wear matching outfits, cross dress, and profess their love for one another. They live together, work together, vacation together, tell each other everything, and have each other on speed dial.

Yet heteronormativity is preserved—it's a bromance.

The central couples in two long-lived television series, one network and one cable, *Boston Legal* (ABC, 2004–2008) and *Nip/Tuck* (FX, 2003–2010), enact the concept of bromance, defined by Michael DeAngelis as "an emotionally intense bond between presumably straight males who demonstrate an openness to intimacy that they neither regard, acknowledge, avow, nor express sexually" (1). Amanda Lotz identifies these two programs, among others, as possessing "dyadic hetero intimacy" that moves beyond that of buddy films and that is akin to heterosexual relationships (146). Denny Crane (William Shatner) and Alan Shore (James Spader) of *Boston Legal* and Sean McNamara (Dylan Walsh) and Christian Troy (Julian McMahon) of *Nip/Tuck* present intimate views into devoted man-man friendship bonds at the precise cultural moment when gay marriage is in the courts and postfeminism and postfeminist masculinity is in the air. This chapter looks specifically at the attitudes and behaviors embodied in the narratives of these two television bromances because they both occurred during the early years of the new millennium and were at the leading edge of the emergence of male-centered television narratives organized around bromance, and because these two programs conflate heterosexual bromance with homosexual erotic attraction. These programs also offer notable presentations of the problematic interactions between the bromantic experience, the men's avowed heterosexuality, their implied homosexual attraction, and their simultaneous relationships with women, while situating these television bromances in their historical and cultural contexts of postfeminism and national discussions of same-sex marriage.

As Hannah Hamad locates her exploration of cinematic fatherhood contemporaneously with cultural discourses of postfeminist masculinity, these early millennial discourses of television masculinity may be usefully culturally and historically positioned as occurring in a period of postfeminism and postfeminist masculinity (5). In naming historical or cultural moments, use of the prefix "post" might seem to indicate a restful time following some tumultuous period, but it would be incorrect to characterize postfeminism as a state of equanimity following a brief, fruitful struggle for human rights during the second-wave women's movement. Along with other feminist media scholars, I define postfeminism as a sensibility that dismisses feminism entirely, claiming that all its goals have been reached and that feminism is no longer necessary or useful.¹ Postfeminist culture "simultaneously evokes and rejects" feminism, writes Hannah Hamad, "preempting and deflecting feminist criticism" (11). In this way, postfeminism works to advance patriarchy. As Vavrus argues, "The mainstream media's perspective on women's lives is informed by postfeminism to such an extent that it virtually omits even a brief consideration of the possible benefits of feminism" (9–10).

In the FX drama, *Nip/Tuck*, Sean McNamara and Christian Troy are plastic surgeons in practice together in South Beach, Miami, where how one looks in a bikini is essential social collateral. Friends since college and medical school, they set up practice together and perform professional tasks together as if they are joined at the hip. Sean is married for part of the series, but when he's single, the two men live together. At work, they interview patients together, operate on them together (a highly unlikely, and pricey, medical event in uncomplicated cosmetic procedures such as liposuction and blepharoplasty), eat lunch together, and call on recovering patients together.

Repeatedly, scenes include the two men interacting with one woman, be she patient, girlfriend, or wife. Flashbacks over several seasons reveal their original *ménage a trois*: they were both in love with the same woman, Julia (Joely Richardson), in college. Sean married her, Christian impregnated her, they call the resulting son and subsequent children "our family," and the son, Matt, calls them "my two dads." The surgeons share a second virtual *ménage a trois* with Christian's fiancée Kimber (Kelly Carlson); they take turns dating her, Sean becomes addicted to sex with a blow-up doll based on her, and eventually, the son Christian fathered but Sean raised marries her.

In exploring the triangle of two men competing for and sharing the same woman, Eve Kosofsky Sedgwick builds on René Girard in seeing that relationship as homosocial bonding between men through a woman. Sedgwick

Figure 8.1.   In *Nip/Tuck,* plastic surgeons Christian Troy (Julian McMahon) and Sean McNamara (Dylan Walsh) do almost everything together, including interviewing patients side-by-side.

writes, "In any erotic rivalry, the bond that links the two rivals is as intense and potent as the bond that links either of the rivals to the beloved . . . the choice of the beloved is determined . . . by the beloved's already being the choice of the person who has been chosen as a rival" (21).

Nip/Tuck contains many moments of tenderness between Sean and Christian. The men are the central couple of the narrative. Female romantic interests come and go with much less drama than is afforded the moments when the men are feuding. When Sean discovers his son was fathered by Christian years ago, Sean hits Christian in the face, then cries and hugs him and says, "I loved you most." Not "why did you sleep with my wife?" or even "I trusted you" but "I loved you most." Series creator Ryan Murphy is unequivocal in his description of the program's premise, saying it's "a love story between two heterosexual men" (qtd. in Lotz 163).

Denny Crane is a founding partner and legal superstar in ABC's *Boston Legal* law practice Crane, Poole & Schmidt. Alan Shore is a younger, middle-aged lawyer at the firm who is known for bizarre yet successful tactics in the courtroom. The two men bond over their courtroom successes, mutual womanizing, and shared social peculiarities. Denny occasionally asks total strangers to have sex with him, dresses as a flamingo, cowboy, or Lennon Sister for holidays, parties, and vacations, and claims to be suffering from mad cow disease (he has Alzheimer's). Alan rates the sexiness of his secretary's sweaters each day (to her face), sleeps with many clients and colleagues, and concludes most trials with lengthy diatribes against the then-Republican administration and conservative politics. Their relentless womanizing, shameless harassment of women in the office, and constant referencing their own sexual needs and conquests may work to shore up their status as heterosexual and position their friendship and love affair as being firmly platonic. The pair's performance of masculinity, separately and together, is outrageous and over-the-top—they perform heterosexual camp. In doing so, they create a kind of interstitial space between straight-up straightness and romantic homosexual love, and in that space, their pair bond can dwell.

The pair vacation together at dude ranches (in matching sequined cowboy shirts) and at a swank fishing resort in Canada (in coordinated waders and wicker creels), and simultaneously join the volunteer Coast Guard so they can wear matching white uniforms and motor around the bay chatting up bikini-clad women on boats. They attend parties in identical or coordinated masquerade, and sometimes appear in drag as their mutual love and law firm partner Shirley or as female celebrities, such as the Lennon Sisters. Sometimes they have sleepovers, sharing the same bed but dressed in pajamas that cover them, Adam's apples to toes.

Their appearance in costumes—some are drag and some are just silly, as when they dress as pink flamingos—is frequent. It underscores the immaturity of some of their behaviors, as well as their mutual playfulness: they literally play dress-up, as if they were young boys. It reinforces the mirroring quality of their attraction to each other: they do the same professional work, they demonstrate the same sexually cavalier attitudes toward women, they see themselves in each other. And, it reinforces their couple-hood: they match. There is a feminine quality here, expressed in the self-absorbed, metrosexual grooming and display at work. And, there is frank and unapologetic cross-dressing, which the pair exhibit in professional settings without embarrassment or concern. In a profession in which dressing for success is taken literally, executed conservatively, and practiced self-consciously, this seems a particularly provocative claim. Yet, when they get into bed together, literally, they are buttoned up to their chins, and covered to their ankles.

They conclude each episode of the five-season series sitting on a balcony outside the firm's skyscraper offices, smoking cigars, drinking scotch, and occasionally, holding hands. One evening, after Alan's girlfriend has left him and he is newly single, they lift a glass. "You still have me," Denny says.

Alan says, "It's not quite the same. But you know what, Denny? Sometimes it comes remarkably close." He chokes up: "I don't know what I'd do without you." Denny puffs on his cigar and responds, "I especially can't imagine being alone now" ("True Love" 5.4). Another evening on the terrace, Denny tells Alan, "A person only has one true love in his life. Like it or not, your true love—tada-dada!—is me. We may not have sex, but ours is an affair of the heart. And we do spoon well. And I make you smile." Alan says, "Yes, you do." Denny laughs, and Alan suggests, "Sleepover?" ("True Love" 5.4).

This is not the love that dare not speak its name: this is love that speaks openly and constantly, every episode. In television and film bromances, the affection between the characters is observable, but not necessarily expressed with eloquence and frequency. Here, in a sacred, gendered, protected space, armed with the signifiers of masculinity and privilege (the club chairs, the Scotch, the cigars), heterosexual men speak of their love for each other—and with more dignity and respect than they deliver in conversations about their heterosexual love affairs.

Postfeminist masculinity is anchored in the early millennial moment, and is thus distinct and differentiated from masculinities that existed during second-wave feminism and even before. Postfeminist masculinity must negotiate certain feminist expectations of men—treating women more or less equally at work, shouldering household and childrearing duties, refraining from public displays of harassment—while also negotiating the degree of comfort (and discomfort) that popular culture has with homosexuality.

Postfeminist masculinity in media takes into account and renders visible what DeAngelis calls the "discomforts of compulsory heteronormativity and the pleasures of boundary crossings" (24). Forster suggests that film bromances of this period exist as "a self-conscious push back against this trend to bisexualize/homosexualize/metrosexualize the contemporary Western male" (192). Ron Becker terms this "straight panic": "the growing anxiety of a heterosexual culture and straight individuals confronting this shifting social landscape where categories of sexual identity were repeatedly scrutinized and traditional moral hierarchies regulating sexuality were challenged" (4).

At the moment when same-sex marriage is foregrounded politically and culturally, these television bromances may help "progressive straight men can figure out a way to be straight in a culture where being gay isn't reprehensible" (Becker 224). These challenges that work to form postfeminist masculinity arise, in part, out of post-9/11 culture; the aftermath of 9/11 created a cultural climate in which troubling retrograde masculinities could be resurrected and reinscribed.[2] The occasional nod to feminism in the narratives and by the characters in these programs cast these masculinities as newly minted "postfeminist masculinity," rather than as misogynist.

What underpins both of these television bromances is that they not only celebrate homosocial bonding, but elevate it to a status exclusive of women—and do so under the postfeminist aegis, without acknowledging the misogyny present in such a move. The bromancers of *Boston Legal* and *Nip/Tuck* exist somewhat schizophrenically in a postfeminist historical moment that is, itself, schizophrenic in its attitudes toward women and feminism. These men operate within narratives of caring deeply for and working alongside women, but also subjugate them. Initially appearing to honor the women in their lives, both sets of men also objectify, harass, and, in the case of *Nip/Tuck*'s plastics surgeons, do violence to women's bodies together on the operating table. Surgeries appear as vicious and violent, with blood splattering, suctioned fat spewing, and surgeons ramming liposuction rods into exposed buttocks and hammering away on noses with mallets. In a sense, the two doctors "gang bang" each patient, operating on her together while she is prone and inert, incapable of defending herself. They rank women on numeric scales, make sexist jokes during surgeries, and tell women to their faces that their asses are sagging or their breasts need perking up.

Each episode of *Nip/Tuck* opens with a necrophiliac display of naked white manikins with closed eyes, posed with and without arms, dismembered and stored in boxes. In the song "A Perfect Lie" (performed by The Engine Room), a woman sings in a breathy voice, to "make be beautiful," asking for a perfect soul, mind and face, before admitting that what she is asking for is in fact "a perfect lie," not beauty. At the end of a line of lyrics, one manikin twitches; at the end of another, one opens a blue eye. The song ends on a close-up of the lower half of a white-on-white manikin face; its lips begin to pink. Across the images, a surgical marking pen draws a dotted red line where the men plan to improve on nature. It is difficult to read this as anything but an objectification of female bodies; here, the female body becomes malleable clay for men to fashion into any shape they find temporarily pleasing.

In *Boston Legal*, Denny and Alan are mutually attracted to and genuinely fond of one of their law firm's founders, Shirley Schmidt (Candice Bergen). Denny and Alan discuss Shirley's body and debate having sex with her. Denny has fashioned a life-sized blow-up doll to look like her and Alan hoards a collection of naked photographs of her ("Can't We All Get A-Lung?" 3.1). In *Nip/Tuck*, Sean and Christian are mutually in love with the same woman, Kimber, but Christian tells her she requires surgery to become the "perfect 10" ("Pilot" 1.1) and Sean develops a relationship with a life-sized blow-up doll made to look like Kimber.

Such rendering of women as inanimate objects works to reposition them, moving women out of the category of "human" and into the category of "thing." As "thing," women can be shared, rejected, and even rebuilt into an rubber doll or redesigned on an operating table, and the emotional connection to her can be elided and placed onto a male partner. The rejection of the female body—the replacement of the body, the person, by an object—makes way for homosexual, or at least homosocial, desire to be expressed. A doll requires no emotional commitment, leaving the men free to make those commitments to each other while simultaneously performing heterosexual desire on a "female." By uncoupling the erotic so thoroughly from the emotional, these bromances present something decidedly distinct from postfeminist masculinity; they move to foreclose possibilities for heterosexual partnering for their characters and position homosocial bromance as more deeply satisfying for heterosexual men than is heterosexual romance.

To celebrate their five thousandth surgery together, Sean gives Christian a golden scalpel with a note "Get over here, I'm lonely." They lift a champagne toast to "five thousand more" and Christian quips, "and they said it wouldn't last." Sean asks Christian for "some alone time with you this week," and Christian says he would rather celebrate with a nice "slice of hair pie" ("Willy Ward" 4.14). To celebrate this anniversary, Christian picks up a mother-daughter duo and takes them home to the hot tub for disappointing sex. Sean goes home to attempt sex with his pregnant wife, but is frustrated when her swollen abdomen gets in the way. The two men end their evenings unhappy and moody; their women have not satisfied them.

In *Boston Legal*, Shirley is not only replaced by a blow-up doll, but also by Alan, who dresses in drag as her and then slow dances with Denny. Here, a man literally stands in for a woman; Shirley is useful only as an iconic image of an ideal. Shirley, a founding partner of the firm and a formidable, powerful woman, is easily replaced by a doll and perhaps more satisfyingly replaced by a man. Denny and Shirley were once young lovers, and his prior "claim" is challenged by Alan, who continually requests Denny's "permission" to court Shirley. Alan repeatedly asks if he can hit on Shirley, and Denny repeatedly denies Alan. To these men, what appears as an honorable "bro code" of leaving each other's women alone also positions Shirley as property, rather than as a person with free will to choose her own partner. Peter Forster characterizes this triangulation as "crucial to the bromance. The woman . . . may be an object, an obstacle, an excuse, a diversion, or a mediator in the homosocial relationships, but as the institutionalized object of normative male desire, she offers bros the opportunity to have a level of intimacy and liberty with each other" (208). Sharing a common object of erotic desire creates a conduit between the two men that is, in these television bromances, more highly valued than is the heterosexual relationship.

In these two programs, bromantic intimacy and male exclusivity is enabled and assisted by the design of the physical spaces of the sets, which incorporate "boys' clubs" that are male-only spaces denied to women. In *Nip/Tuck*, Christian and Sean inhabit boys' clubs both at home and work. Their office and operating room are sleek, modern spaces with low-slung leather chairs, big screen televisions, glass tables, and dim lighting, resembling a bachelor pad more than a medical office. Although their office caters mainly to women, the spaces are relentlessly masculine: hard-edged, Spartan, crisp, and minimalist. Sometimes, they live together in a bachelor pad beach house that their anesthesiologist, Liz, calls the "male bonding clubhouse." Liz (Roma Maffia) only occasionally appears—some surgeries seem to mysteriously occur without benefit of an anesthesiologist—she introduces a female presence to the clubhouse, but it is a particularly and distinctly bounded one: she is nonwhite and is a lesbian, thus occupying an interstitial space between heterosexual male and heterosexual female that appears far from accidental.

In *Boston Legal*, only Denny and Alan occupy the office tower balcony space that is their boys' club. There is no third chair for Shirley Schmidt, a partner in the firm and their close friend; the balcony is exclusively Denny's and Alan's domain. On the rare occasion that a woman appears on the balcony, she is swiftly escorted back into the building, in an evocation of the "no women allowed" policies of men's clubs. Kimmel suggests that historically, private men's clubs and fraternal organizations offered men solace from the threats of a modern world—threats that included industrialization, modernization, and increased legal rights and earning power of women (*Manhood in America*).

Sitting in postmodern interpretations of men's club armchairs rendered in plastic, Denny and Alan engage in a kind of postmodern masculinity, exchanging intimacies, being vulnerable with each other, comforting each other. The conduct of all four male characters undergoes a marked shift when a woman enters their male space. They close ranks against the outsider and treat the woman—even if she is closely connected to another man in the club—as an intruder. The physical space of the boys' club allows and even protects a set of behaviors that might be criticized if performed in public. The boundaries of male-only space are rigidly and harshly enforced.

Dominic Lennard finds that the "retrograde narrative preference for masculine spaces and the confinement of romantic expression within those environs" in *The Wire* functions to interrogate straight male-male friendship (293). These television boys' clubs permit, foster, naturalize, and celebrate misogyny and patriarchy in spaces that are safe for men and threatening to women.

This foreclosure of women is carried to its ultimate conclusion in the same-sex but asexual marriage of Denny and Alan and the flirtations with life partner coupling between Christian and Sean. Not only do these two television bromances celebrate male friendship and homosocial bonding, they also attempt to extend its value into heterosexual romantic bonding while trying to sidestep issues of homosexual romantic love. A previous discursive silence in television around the homosexual possibilities of intense homosocial pair bonding is fractured.

Denny and Alan and Sean and Christian are not hinting at homosexuality or pretending to ignore the tensions between straight-up heterosexual masculinity and the border dance of bromances: in *Nip/Tuck*, Sean and Christian actively fantasize about homosexual romance, and in *Boston Legal*, Denny and Alan legally marry. These bromances and marriages offer Denny and Alan and Sean and Christian a respite from their professional stresses, and could present a celebratory view into deep and true friendship, if not homosexual love. However, these television bromances fully embrace neither devoted friendship or same-sex marriage; they coyly sidestep direct engagement. Lennard argues that, though such televisual moments depict genuine affection between the men, there is also open recognition that these moments are performances (279).

While these parodies may work to naturalize same-sex marriage, they also reveal troubling, retrograde gender politics and are respectful to neither heterosexual nor homosexual marriage. These bromances may work to broaden acceptance of close homosocial relationships and "soften the ground" of popular acceptance of gay marriage, but resistance to being thought of as gay is also clear in these programs.

Christian's therapist asks him, "Ever consider the possibility you're in love with your partner?" and Christian feels his lovemaking has been criticized. A serial killer threatens Sean's life unless Christian cuts off his own hand—and Christian nearly does it, causing the killer to remark, "This is really beautiful, you two really love each other" ("Madison Berg" 3.10). Self-awareness about what they feel for each other comes and goes; it is sometimes recognized and expressed, but it is also sometimes treated as if being mistaken for gay is a shameful matter. Sean becomes angry when Christian gets engaged to be married: "She's taking him away from me right now, when I really need him," he says, and then thinks, "Jesus—you'd think we were gay" ("Diana Lubey" 4.12). Worried that his sleek apartment looks too gay, Christian hires a decorator to "butch it up" ("Cindy Plumb" 4.1).

These contradictory attitudes complicate simple claims that the bromances in these two programs celebrate and advance same-sex marriage. As Mary Vavrus argues about seemingly progressive gender role representations in media that actually shelter regressive gender politics, Helene Shugart argues about *Will & Grace* and other television shows with gay characters, what appear to be subversive and gender-bending relationships on camera can actually be reinforcement of traditional patriarchal attitudes and privilege.

As Christian prepares for his wedding, his bride cannot attend the cake tasting or the invitation ordering, so Sean stands in for her. The two men sample frostings and fillings, examine typefaces, and select floral arrangements, and when they are mistaken for a gay couple ("One of the most loving couples I've ever seen," gushes the cake lady) they unhesitatingly play along with it, holding hands and making eyes at each other. Before the wedding, Sean announces his plans to leave the practice. The camera makes much of the two men's almost-touching hands as Sean ends the conversation with: "I don't know who I am without you and I need to leave to find out" ("Madison Berg" 3.10). After Christian is left standing at the altar by his bride and all the guests have gone home, it is the two men, dressed in wedding tuxedos, who sit together amid ornate flowers on the church steps. Sean comforts Christian and holds him. When Christian weeps that he will always be alone, Sean tells him he was never alone. Then Sean announces he will return to the practice and be a team with Christian once again. Christian, cheering up a bit, asks, "You mean that?" Sean answers: "I do." ("Madison Berg" 3.10). This mimicking of the marital vows is obvious, deliberate, and telling.

The possibility that the two are actually in love is directly explored in season four. Christian appears thoughtful and puzzled. He fantasizes about taking Sean to a gay vacation resort where they wear matching Speedos and lounge in a cabana drinking umbrella drinks ("Faith Wolper, PhD" 4.6). Back in "reality," when Sean discovers his unborn son has a physical deformity, he weeps in Christian's arms and there is a one-beat-too-long moment before they pull apart ("Conor McNamara" 4.8). Later, Christian surprises himself by turning down sex with a stranger at a bar; we are left to think he is dreaming of Sean. The music fades from the scene revealing just the noises of a bar closing in the wee hours, the lonesome sounds of single and closeted life. Sean is preoccupied with jealous thoughts of Christian's romantic interest in a female patient and lies awake at night, mulling, next to his oblivious wife, Julia ("Blu Mondae" 4.2). There is nothing shadowy about season four's exploration of an actual homosexual love affair between Christian and Sean. Both characters wrestle with the "But are we gay?" dilemma, daydreaming of idyllic romantic scenes and agonizing over disappointments with heterosexual relationships and entanglements. These are not scenes of homosocial friendship between characters that are unquestionably heterosexual. These scenes move beyond presenting nonsexual bromance to packaging taboo homosexual intimacy in ways that production companies and networks may imagine are acceptable to desirable television demographics in this particular historical and cultural moment.

To clear things up, Sean visits Christian for a face-to-face confrontation: "I love you, Christian, I always will, but we're brothers, we're best friends. But not like that." Christian pretends a romantic thought about their relationship has never crossed his mind, and frets, "Have I been doing something different lately, walking weird or something? Is it my eyebrows? Because I tell you, if I don't wax, I get this whole uni-brow thing and it looks ugly. But just because I groom, doesn't mean I've gone Brokeback." Ultimately, the pair finds a resolution of sorts:

> *Christian:* I liked thinking about having feelings for you. I never thought I was gay. I just think I have intimacy issues with anyone in my life that I love. (beat) That sounded really gay, didn't it?
>
> *Sean:* Yeah.
>
> *Christian:* Well, screw you. (beat) Seriously, I love you.
>
> *Sean:* I know. I love you, too. ("Diana Lubey" 4.12).

The affection between the two men is genuine and affecting. Television bromances deliver deeply fulfilling, decades-long committed "marriages" between men, contrasting with the reality that many men find it extremely difficult, if not impossible, to make and maintain even mildly intimate friendships. Eve Kosofsky Sedgwick's identification of a continuum between the categories of homosocial and homosexual assists in explicating why suspicions of sexuality arise in heterosexual, homosocial friendship rituals (1).

While men long for friendship, they find it problematic and challenging to maintain. Kimmel argues that "friendship is a counterfeit currency, based on suppression of emotion, false bravado, and toughness . . . developing a genuine friendship—a real one—is difficult, perhaps the biggest risk a guy can take. It means being strong enough to show vulnerability, independent enough to brave social ostracism, courageous enough to trust another. A male friend reminds you that you are a man; he validates your gender identity" (*Guyland* 278).

Part of the power of the bromance is the visible, palpable yearning for connection between the characters. It is clear that the men want a connection, that it carries deep meaning for them, and that it troubles them deeply to negotiate homophobia that is social, cultural, and personal.

Boston Legal not only flirts with the idea of heterosexual male marriage; in the finale of its final season, Denny and Alan travel to Massachusetts, where same-sex marriage was legal at the time the show was written, and marry each other. Denny, descending into advanced Alzheimer's, asks Alan to marry him to give Alan the right to make Denny's medical decisions and to allow Denny to pass on his wealth to Alan. People have married for worse motives, the men reason. "I've always wanted to remarry before I die," says Denny. "And like it or not, you're the man I love." It is a double wedding, with Denny's ex, Shirley, also marrying an old flame and firm partner, Carl Sack (John Larroquette). Denny's passion for Shirley has lasted decades, so perhaps the double wedding offers heterosexual reassurance that if Shirley were available, Denny would choose a woman. Together on the balcony in the final scene of the series, the tuxedo-clad men slow dance together. Denny Crane utters the final line of the program: "It's our wedding night" ("Last Call" 5.13).

There is recognition in the act of heterosexual male-male marriage that gives voice to same-sex marriage arguments, but it also silences women and elides the value of heterosexual female-male marriage. It is possible to read a thinly concealed rage against women hidden beneath the veneer of homosociality. The ambivalence toward strong, feminist, and accomplished women—the attraction/repulsion expressed toward Shirley and Liz, for example—is resolved by avoidance. Particularly in the case of Christian and Sean, the homosocial relationship trumping all heterosexual ones may represent an extension of adolescence and a delayed assumption of certain adult responsibilities.

The marriages between men may be a statement that only men are capable of understanding other men fully and may be a minimizing and trivializing of the marriages and relationships between men and women. These television marriages may draw a line in the sand about just how intimate a man will and can be with a female partner, contrasting those hetero unions with lifetime commitments between soul buddies. Even when these men have relationships with strong women, they seem to have to choose between male friendships and marriage to a woman, and suffer both homosocial and heterosexual anxiety over making that choice. Yet female relationships are neither contained nor examined in this same way. There is hope here for an expanded acceptance of a wide variety of masculinities, but there is also a familiar backlash into eliding women to make men feel more secure.

Bromantic marriage and its contradictory acceptance of same-sex affection while rejecting same-sex sexuality reaffirms the compulsory heterosexual claim on masculinity. Kimmel argues that Freud missed "a piece of the puzzle . . . [a boy] sees his father as his mother sees his father, with a combination of awe, wonder, terror, *and desire*" (275), and the early homoerotic desire becomes suppressed into homophobia. Yet, Kimmel writes, every man knows that his real soul mates are his "brothers" (*Guyland* 13). The resulting rejection of close friendship bonds with other men reveals what Kimmel calls "the great secret of American manhood: *We are afraid of other men*" ("Masculinity as Homophobia" 277–78). These television bromances are brave in the sense that these four men are openly vulnerable about that fear and yet face it in order to be together. Their togetherness is not unproblematic, and it is, in some ways, radical.

The bromance narrative arc is at least conversing with the politics of gay marriage and suggesting possibilities of homosexual coupling. Perhaps the packaging of these male unions as being steadfastly heterosexual—even when the men admit to attraction and/or actually marry each other—offers some measure of social recognition and acceptance of gay marriage. However, that step still falls short of representing and honoring the actual romance and commitment of homosexual matrimony. The media representation of heterosexual male-male marriage emasculates gay marriage and cancels out the romance and desire present there. It diminishes both gay marriage and heterosexual friendship.

These television bromances also intimate that men are capable of only one important relationship in their lives and must choose between a best friend and a wife, rather than enjoy both. This casts both marriage and friendship in an aberrant light: if a man chooses a wife, he has rejected male companionship, and if he chooses a friend, he has rejected the possibility of a wife.

The heterosexual couples of these television dramas extend the exclusion of women already present in the boys' clubs beyond the workplace and into the home. The act of a man joining with a woman becomes enforced as an act of rejecting his peers, his buddies, his friends, his bros. Marriage becomes the dichotomous opposite to friendship. The only way to remain connected with other men is to disavow women, even at the altar. Loving a romantic mate—male or female—is positioned as being antithetical to honoring and maintaining a deep and meaningful relationship to a true friend. Choosing a mate is, in some manner, choosing to accept less autonomy—and less masculinity—than is choosing to hang with a buddy.

These two programs complicate postfeminist masculinity and heterosexual friendship by conflating them with homosexual sexuality. Homosexuality is stripped of its eroticism and is presented as intense friendship between men who do not express their romantic feelings for each other in a physical manner. The television bromances of *Nip/Tuck* and *Boston Legal* create a space in which male friendship is honored, but at the expense of heterosexual or homosexual romantic bonding, and at the expense of relationships with women that are without rancor or objectification. Bromances here do not add homosocial relationships to otherwise fulfilling lives, they elide other relationships and insist that bromance must replace romance (both hetero- and homosexual), that it cannot co-exist alongside it. The men in these bromances become, in the end, faithful only to each other. Until death do they part.

NOTES

1. See Rodino-Colocino 2012; Levine 2001, 2008; Negra 2004; Vavrus 2002; Projansky 2001.
2. See Hamad 2014; Nettleton 2009.

WORKS CITED

Becker, Ron. "Becoming Bromosexual: Straight Men, Gay Men, and Male Bonding on US TV." *Reading the Bromance: Homosocial Relationships in Film and Television.* Ed. Michael DeAngelis. Detroit: Wayne State University Press, 2014. Print.

DeAngelis, Michael. "Introduction." *Reading the Bromance: Homosocial Relationships in Film and Television.* Ed. Michael DeAngelis. Detroit: Wayne State UP, 2014. 1–28. Print.

Forster, Peter. "Rad Bromance (or *I Love You, Man,* but We Won't Be Humping on *Humpday.*" *Reading the Bromance: Homosocial Relationships in Film and Television.* Ed. Michael DeAngelis. Detroit: Wayne State University Press, 2014. 191–212. Print.

Hamad, Hannah. *Postfeminism and Paternity in Contemporary US Film: Framing Fatherhood.* New York: Routledge, 2014. Print.

Kimmel, Michael. *Guyland: The Perilous World Where Boys Become Men.* New York: HarperCollins, 2008. Print.

———. *Manhood in America: A Cultural History.* 2nd ed. New York: Oxford UP, 2006. Print.

———. "Masculinity as Homophobia." *The Masculinities Reader.* Ed. Steven M. Whitehead, Frank Barrett. Malden, MA: Polity Press, 2005. 266–87. Print.

Lennard, Dominic. "'This Ain't About Your Money, Bro. Your Boy Gave You Up': Bromance and Breakup in HBO's *The Wire.*" *Reading the Bromance: Homosocial Relationships in Film and Television.* Ed. Michael DeAngelis. Detroit: Wayne State UP, 2014. Print.

Levine, Elana. "Toward a Paradigm for Media Production Research: Behind the Scenes at *General Hospital.*" *Critical Studies in Media Communication* 18 (2001): 66–82. Print.

Lotz, Amanda. *Cable Guys.* New York: New York UP, 2014. Print.

Negra, Diane. "Quality Postfeminism? Sex and the Single Girl on HBO." *Genders* 39 (2004). Web. 30 Sep. 2014.

Nettleton, Pamela. "Rescuing Men: The New Television Masculinity in *Rescue Me, Nip/Tuck, The Shield, Boston Legal,* and *Dexter.*" U of Minnesota Digital Conservancy. 2009. Web. 30 Sep 2014.

Projansky, Sarah. *Watching Rape: Film and Television in Postfeminist Culture.* New York UP: New York, 2001. Print.

Rodino-Colocino, Michelle. "Man Up, Woman Down: Mama Grizzlies and Anti-Feminist Feminism During the Year of the (Conservative) Woman and Beyond." *Women & Language* 35, no. 1 (2012): 79–95. Print.

Sedgwick, Eve Kosofsky. *Between Men: English Literature and Male Homosocial Desire.* New York: Columbia UP, 1985. Print.

Shugart, Helene. "Reinventing Privilege: The New (Gay) Man in Contemporary Popular Media." *Critical Studies in Media Communication* 20, no. 1 (2003): 67–91. Print.

Vavrus, Mary. *Postfeminist News: Political Women in Media Culture.* Albany: SUNY P, 2002. Print.

9

Some Assembly Required: Joss Whedon's Bridging of Masculinities in Marvel Films' *The Avengers*

Derek S. McGrath

The Avengers (2012) is an unprecedented film. The movie provides not only a massive crossover of some of Marvel Comics' most popular superheroes but also serves as the sequel to five different films: *The Incredible Hulk* (2008), *Thor* (2011), *Captain America: The First Avenger* (2011), and both *Iron Man* films (2008, 2010). While building upon the narratives begun in those films, *The Avengers* also continues the work that these earlier films accomplished, in varying degrees, at providing representations of postfeminist masculinity as multivalent rather than one-dimensional.

The Avengers, as a superhero team, is unique in how they differ from traditional homosocial teams found in other action franchises, such as Batman or Lethal Weapon. Bringing together male protagonists exceptional enough to lead their own franchises or television series, this homosocial group is truly collaborative rather than hierarchical. Director-writer Joss Whedon faced an ambitious challenge, bringing together divergent plot threads. The difficulty of coordinating so many storylines parallels the task facing Nick Fury (Samuel L. Jackson), director of the paramilitary organization SHIELD and the creator of the Avengers Initiative. Like Fury, Whedon needed to bring together protagonists molded by directors with differing aesthetics: Jon Favreau[1] (*Swingers*) first developed Tony Stark (Robert Downey Jr.), Phil Coulson (Clark Gregg), Nick Fury, and Natasha Romanoff (Scarlett Johansson); Kenneth Branagh (*Henry V*) contributed Thor (Chris Hemsworth) and Loki (Tom Hiddleston), with a cameo by Clint Barton (Jeremy Renner); and Joe Johnston (The Rocketeer) shaped the old-fashioned Captain America Steve Rogers (Chris Evans). Whedon added another no-nonsense member to the team, Agent Maria Hill (Cobie Smulders), while rebooting the Hulk, Bruce

Banner (Mark Ruffalo). Instead of hiding these sutures, Whedon highlights their conflicting styles, often through the snarky commentary of Tony Stark: for example, when he interrupts a scene between Thor and Loki, Stark characterizes it as "Shakespeare in the Park." With this lack of hierarchy between characters, varied masculine styles (including that of female characters), Whedon presents a thoroughly heterosocial ensemble.

Having drafted Thor, Iron Man, Captain America, and the Hulk into his army, Fury struggles to guide these bickering (and often battling) superheroes against the supervillain and Norse god Loki. Fury's relinquishing of a linear chain of command—which necessitates his break with his own "superiors"—allows the Avengers not only to save the Earth but, in surprising ways, also directly to appreciate more fluid and varied gender roles. Susanne Kord and Elisabeth Krimmer argue that "[s]uperhero films are centrally concerned with concepts of masculinity" (109), yet recent cinema, especially in postfeminist discourse, reflect forms of masculinity that resist conventional masculine-feminine binaries. I argue that the more fluid approach to masculinity (as performed by male and female characters) in *The Avengers* is integral to how Whedon's cinematic narrative justifies the titular team's victory against Loki, a villain who comes to represent the staid bureaucratic structure that tends to embody traits of traditional masculine hierarchal command structures. Employed by the galactic warlord Thanos, Loki uses a magical artifact, the Tesseract, to open a portal that will admit his extraterrestrial army, the Chitauri, to invade the Earth. Working as a team, the Avengers demonstrate a model of heterosocial collaborative masculinity that contrasts against the hyper-masculine that is traditionally associated with other superhero stories.

Thanks to Whedon's guidance, the film responds productively to a long history of comics that minimizes the importance of anyone who is not a hyper-masculine, emotionally isolated white male on the superhero team. It is significant that two of the Avengers, Stark and Thor, are in intimate relationships with professional women. However, in dismantling that patriarchy, the Avengers risk re-inscribing reductive strategies that still depend on situating some forms of masculinity as privileged above others—the heroes' more muscular physique and greater height celebrated over that of the shrill, androgynous build of the defeated villain Loki. Furthermore, the film establishes which forms of masculinity are better—more heroic, if you will—on the basis of race: villains such as Loki and the Chitauri, and even the green-skinned Avenger Hulk, are coded as different in ways that are symbolic of contemporary racialized (potentially racist) discourse.

Whedon's film exemplifies productive models of gender, as to be expected given his overall body of work in print and on screen, especially *Buffy the*

Vampire Slayer (1997–2003). *The Avengers* identifies how the superhero genre, with its emphasis on untapped potential, unrealistic bodies, and super-human abilities, overall a movement away from the everyday, continues to serve as a productive albeit under-developed space for reassessing gender in narrative and in life.[2] Whedon's dry wit keeps the film from taking itself too seriously when it expects audiences to relate to adults engaging in fisticuffs and Manichean dualism while dressed in tights and capes. David Greven has argued that the 1990s, when Whedon's television work flourished, saw masculinity in popular cinema as "subject . . . to a different kind of light—the light of ironic knowledge. . . . In this era, masculinity became aware of itself as both monolith and joke" (16). Treating the superhero likewise as both a monolith and a joke, *The Avengers* can both edify the noble ideals of mas-culinity—honor, responsibility—and laugh at its failings. In the context of issues of masculinity in the turn-of-the-millennium, *The Avengers* as a film represents struggles of competing forms of masculinity as embodied by men and women toward establishing a more productive heterosocial structure that dismantles patriarchal hierarchical structures. The team dynamic to this film exemplifies models of collaborative masculinities—embracing (while cri-tiquing) multiple masculine ideals—in contrast to hyper-masculine posturing traditionally associated with many superhero stories.

This chapter will highlight the questions raised in *The Avengers* concern-ing these heterosocial interactions, noting that these questions of masculinity and genre are never fully answered in this film: gender remains an act of ne-gotiation or—to borrow from the film's advertising slogan—some assembly required.

CONFLICTING GENRES AND GENDERS WITHIN *THE AVENGERS*

In the process of destabilizing hyper-masculine power structures, the Aveng-ers are on the one hand positioned as a mercenary force hired by SHIELD, on the other hand a set of free agents not under SHIELD's authority. This tension is summarized in one of the film's deleted scenes, when SHIELD agent Maria Hill complains of Fury, "We're at war, and he thinks about superheroes." Much as Hill questions the authority of her male superior yet comes to realize the correctness of his decision, Whedon's film raises provocative questions about gender, albeit settling by story's end to an uneasy position without any firm answers. To quote Whedon, the film feels as much as a "war film" as it does a superhero summer blockbuster ("Commentary"), emphasized by mili-tary commander Fury's insistence on referring to the Avengers as "soldiers." Such bellicose language echoes the film's own difficulties in incorporating its five prequels as well as its wide array of contrasting genres: action, comedy, drama, and fantasy.

Some critics chastised Whedon for the lack of diversity in his proposed Avengers team, catering to a male audience desiring "cartoonish male bonding, a lot of stuff blowing up, and hot-chick eye candy," in a year that included numerous action blockbusters featuring female leads such as *The Hunger Games* and *Brave* (O'Hehir). While the Avengers team in the comics features a large number of female characters, numerous reviewers think Whedon's film failed to actualize that potential gendered (as well as racial) diversity. The film includes only two prominent and named female heroes, only one of them, Natasha Romanoff, alias the Black Widow, on the Avengers team itself; the few remaining female characters serve as love interests for male leads. This dearth of gendered diversity is particularly surprising given not only Whedon's television series *Buffy the Vampire Slayer*, and the comic books he has written, but also the demographics of the film's viewers: evidenced by the number of women present at theatrical screenings, fan conventions, and comic book shops, superhero films are hardly a boys-only crowd.

Despite its limited inclusion of female characters, *The Avengers* demonstrates the complex gender construction that Whedon brings to his works in comics, film, and television. Whedon's male characters, particularly *Buffy*'s Spike, *Firefly*'s Malcolm Reynolds, and singing mad scientist Dr. Horrible, all negotiate between old and new models of masculinity and femininity. Similarly by incorporating into this movie styles seemingly antithetical to tights-and-capes stories—war films, soap operas, and, as he proudly proclaims, Noël Coward plays ("Commentary")—Whedon develops *The Avengers* into a film that opens complicated questions regarding the places men and women occupy in the larger superhero genre.

As these superheroes duke it out, their exploits, regardless of their gender, show that superheroes come in many forms. At the same time, when read within the context of their genders, their actions demonstrate more fluid constructions. Male characters appear as more flawed, subject to bouts of self-doubt and assuming roles as nurturers to their peers regardless of gender; female characters appear as more combative, taking roles as leaders and questioning the authority of their peers. By the time of the final battle, each Avenger plays their individual position, based on their unique talents—as Captain America says "as a team."

Credited in part to Whedon's feminist cachet, *The Avengers* engages in larger discussions about performativity, refusing to present any character as wholly comfortable with their gendering. Granted, *The Avengers* directs the male gaze upon its female characters, with Romanoff's form-fitting spy suit and Pepper Potts's short shorts, but the film also directs attention to its male characters: witness Captain America's taut white undershirt, Hawk-eye's bare and toned arms, even Banner's naked body. Building upon his previous works in fantasy and science fiction, Whedon traces how gender in the superhero genre need not be wholly traditional nor wholly progressive (Jowett). Characters in *The Avengers* must adapt in order to negotiate with this discomfort. Otherwise, these characters will not develop beyond their limitations—gendered and cultural ones as well—to face these global and extraterrestrial threats. These confrontations can be read allegorically for the audience, as the extraterrestrial film, the war film, and the family film bring battling definitions of gender into the superhero narrative.

"KIND OF FAMILIAR": VETERAN CHARACTERS AND RE-FASHIONING WAR FILM TROPES

The Avengers deploys war film tropes within Whedon's self-reflexive take on the superhero genre, destabilizing those static constructions of masculinity associated with both genres, allowing superheroes, war heroes, and secret agents to occupy ambiguous gendered roles. Upon first arriving at the SHIELD base, US soldier Steve Rogers, better known as Captain America, engages *The Avengers* with more traditional war narratives when he notices not men in capes but soldiers running drills. "This is actually kind of familiar," he says to Banner. However as an army captain coping with war trauma and temporal displacement, Captain America embodies traits that are traditionally held in opposition to film portrayals of the successful military veteran. Whereas "[w]ar rhetoric thrives on jumbled chronologies"—films produced are influenced not only by their moments of representation but their moments of reception (Kord 135)—Rogers embodies an early twenty-first-century distrust of power rather than, as he had for many adolescent readers of comics during World War II, nearly unquestioning support of American governmental and military policies.

Rogers's willingness to work against authority owes in part to his unconventional story: unlike war films that show characters emerging into their physical, emotional, and moral self through battle, Rogers's heroism was pre-established, whereas his body was not yet created. Blond and blue-eyed, thirty-year-old Rogers was originally a short, scrawny, and asthmatic kid, transformed through scientific experiments to heal faster, run faster, and fight longer against Nazi troops during World War II. His physique owes as well to his morality: thanks to comic book logic, the Super Soldier Formula administered to him augments those innate qualities of its subject, explained by the formula's inventor Dr. Abraham Erskine (Stanley Tucci), "good becomes great; bad becomes worse." Rogers's portrayal presents paradoxical inconsistencies, particularly in his evident inexperience at romancing women. Instead of a traditional warrior, Rogers personifies an idealized American spirit of uncompromising, naive innocence.

This intensely moralistic quality assists Whedon in exploring traditional notions of masculinity in both the war film and the superhero genre, presenting Rogers as pure to the point of being virginal. Frozen in the northern tundra after miraculously surviving a World War II suicide flight and thawed out in the early twenty-first century, Rogers remains old-fashioned, dressed in 1940s fashion and slow to grasp contemporary popular culture references. Despite his pessimism that "the world hasn't changed" for the better after World War II, Rogers retains a pure innocence actually suited to twenty-first-century understandings of "new masculinity," "combining both 'masculine' and 'feminine' characteristics" toward an understanding of gender equality and a refutation of outdated male chauvinism, which is in keeping with how Whedon has explored models of new masculinity in his other works (Jowett 124).[3]

The allegorical reading of Rogers's sexual frustrations and his artificial enhancement is applicable as well to one of his teammates, Tony Stark, alias Iron Man. Injured by terrorists using weapons from his own company, Stark invents a miniaturized arc reactor. This super-powered pacemaker doubles as a revolution in clean energy, sustaining his shrapnel-pierced heart while powering an Iron Man exo-suit to fight terrorism worldwide. Claiming to have "privatized world peace," Stark competes with the US government's Rogers for that title of "the First Avenger." Despite describing himself to Rogers as an isolated "billionaire playboy philanthropist," his movies present Stark as slowly learning he need not be alone, coming to depend more on corporate assistant and eventual girlfriend Pepper Potts (Gwyneth Paltrow) and his company's military liaison James Rhodes (Terence Howard, then Don Cheadle). *The Avengers* presents Stark's next step as learning to work with a team.

Stark embodies hyper-masculine propensities: he prefers isolation, using sarcasm and both his physical and robotic might to fight his opponents with minimal assistance. Yet Stark resists emotional closeness or dependence at least in part because he feels emasculated. It is through his engagement with the Avengers, in a film drawing narrative cues from the traditional war story, that Stark experiences the loss of an ally, practices more collaborative teamwork with other superheroes to avenge that death, and ultimately discovers a deeper purpose to his role as a hero.

Where Rogers is like Ernest Hemingway's Jack Barnes due to the shock of war, Stark resembles Barnes due to a similarly emasculating wartime injury—his chest wound representing his lack: upon injuring his heart, Stark's "former womanizing days came to an end" (DiPaolo 229). In interviews Paltrow mused that, despite dating for some time, Stark and her character Potts have not "consummated yet" their relationship (qtd in Wilding), making him as celibate as Rogers. As a pampered corporate executive, Stark's rugged vigilante superheroism is offset by his scrupulously managed personal life: he is fastidiously metrosexual in his manicures and coiffed hair. Yet Stark remains self-aware of his uncertain masculine position in homosocial groupings, telling Fury regarding the Avengers, "I don't want to join your super-secret boy band" (*Iron Man 2*).

Stark's meticulous attention to his physical appearance and his contentious personality invites a queer reading into his antagonistic relationship with Rogers. Stark shares more screen time with Rogers than his own girlfriend in *The Avengers*.[4] This sexual tension between Rogers and Stark is emphasized by their shared metrosexual qualities. "And you're all about style, aren't you?" chastises Rogers, whereas Stark identifies Rogers's own hypocrisy: "Of the people in this room, which one is, A, wearing a spangly outfit, and, B, not of use?" Furthermore, Rogers and Stark's verbal sparring is teeming with sexual subtext. Having befriended Banner—another character who alternates between intellectual and physical prowess—Stark defends him against fears that the scientist would become enraged and "Hulk out." As the playboy says, "Why shouldn't the guy let off a little steam?," he places a disingenuously friendly hand on Rogers's shoulder, prompting the soldier to brush off his hand and shout, "Back off!" Responding to Rogers' rebuff, Stark mocks Rogers's frustration by challenging him to a superhero fistfight, with a line reflecting intense homoeroticism: "I'm thinking I want you to make me."

At one point, Stark directly articulates the homoerotic subtext of his partnership with Rogers. After successfully repelling Loki's extraterrestrial army in an air battle, Stark falls from the sky and crashes back onto Earth, potentially dead. Like a re-awakened Snow White, Stark opens his eyes to see handsome Rogers, as well as the Hulk and Thor. Stark is genre-savvy enough to comment on this queer potential of his Prince Charmings: "Please tell me nobody kissed me."[5] In his protestations, Stark outwardly resists his homosocial partnerings, while moving toward greater intimacy and trust than previously with his primarily hierarchical relationship with Rhodes.

Rogers and Stark overcome their spat once they redefine their mission—or have it redefined for them by Nick Fury—as one of avenging a lost colleague, Phil Coulson, Fury's top SHIELD agent. Present in previous Marvel films as a bit player, Coulson gains increased depth in Whedon's script, his previously affectless demeanor undercut by his man-crush on Rogers: a fan since childhood, Coulson recently completed his collection of vintage 1940s

Figure 9.1.   Nick Fury (Samuel L. Jackson) struggles to calm tensions between Avengers, including Steve Rogers (Chris Evans) and Tony Stark (Robert Downey Jr). *(The Avengers)*

Captain America trading cards. Yet through his stoic personality and wry humor, Coulson presents a secure yet understated masculinity, leading other characters to underestimate him.

The development of Coulson's character makes him more sympathetic before his death, fighting off Loki in a scene infused with violent sexual imagery. While confronting the illusionary image of the supervillain with a very large firearm, he does not realize the real Loki is behind him. Loki penetrates Coulson, his phallic scepter piercing the agent's chest. Now sporting a similarly emasculating chest wound like Stark's, Coulson falls limp against the wall. The resulting profusion of blood gives birth to the Avengers: struggling to finish his incomplete thought to Fury, Coulson says the team was "never going to work, if they didn't have some[one] to" *avenge*. As a man capable of working within a team without losing his agency, Coulson understands the narrative value of sacrifice.

In their responses to Coulson's death,[6] Stark and Rogers exemplify how Whedon plays with masculine tropes within the war film and in relation to the superhero genre. Viewers might expect Stark to rebuff Coulson's death with his usual snark: "He was an idiot," Stark initially remarks. When Rogers asks whether "this is the first time you have lost a soldier," Stark finally snaps: "We are not soldiers!" Stark tries to hide a sadness that a soldier must not reveal when it comes to war films: soldiers' mourning is instead best expressed through a victory against the enemy as "dedicat[ed] to the deceased comrade"

(Donald 178). Coulson serves as that figure for Stark, pushing Stark to reveal a more nuanced sense of superhero masculinity than his previous playboy ways. Whereas he earlier joked that Coulson's first name was "Agent," when Stark confronts Loki, he refers to the late soldier by name: "[T]here was one other guy you pissed off. His name was Phil." Stark is now able to acknowledges his role in a team as well as the value of homosocial connections.

Stark's maturation demonstrates how *The Avengers* both adheres to and subverts the tropes of war films. Like many entries in that genre, Whedon's film is "prone to portray war as an arena of male maturation" (Kord and Krimmer 138). The films and television series developed from *The Avengers* as part of Marvel Studios' cinematic continuity do not ignore the challenges of post-war life and do not treat masculine maturation as complete or even necessarily positive. Rogers, Stark, and Coulson—who, thanks to extraterrestrial fluids and covert government programs, is resurrected after the events of *The Avengers*—all cope with varying degrees of PTSD in *Captain America: The Winter Soldier* (2014), *Iron Man 3* (2013), and *Agents of SHIELD* (2013 to present), respectively. Life for these men cannot stay the same after war. Whedon manages to evoke these models of war-film masculinity, while mapping their limitations—as well their need for team members whose more fluid masculine qualities complement theirs.

"YOU HAVE HEART": A MANLY BLACK WIDOW, A WOMANLY HAWK, AND COMPROMISED GENDERING

The Avengers also disrupts the conventional masculine-feminine binary by juxtaposing two SHIELD agents—former Russian assassin Natasha Romanoff, alias Black Widow, and sniper and expert marksman archer Clint Barton, alias Hawkeye—who each assume a mix of masculine and feminine traits and yet are tipped in favor more to the gender that is not the one traditionally associated with their sex. Whereas Barton is referred to as more parental, even motherly, despite his stoic demeanor, Romanoff assumes more masculine qualities and even masculine symbols that defy attempts by villains to refer to her as a weak woman.

When the Avengers seem beaten by Loki—Coulson pronounced dead, and Thor and Hulk tossed mid-battle from the SHIELD aircraft base—Rogers realizes that it is time to put differences aside with Stark, and even former enemies. Rogers retrieves SHIELD agent Natasha Romanoff, for a last assault, and discovers her with their previous opponent (as Loki's brainwashed lackey), her fellow agent Clint Barton, now ready to fight with and not against the Avengers.

Barton is an expert assassin for SHIELD—quiet, bitterly sarcastic, and emotionally distant because, as an archer and a sniper, he must be physically distant. When Loki captures Barton, he holds his magic scepter to Barton's chest to commandeer his will, saying to the archer, "You have heart," sounding more like a question than a statement. Loki's understanding of Barton confirms that behind the archer's unwavering stoicism is a man burdened with the frailties of a human heart, particularly guilt over the murders he has committed. Loki's question elucidates the larger processes by which characters have their hyper-masculine identities, as Romanoff puts it, "compromised."

This complex gendering builds upon Whedon's previous work in fantasy and science fiction, to present characters like Barton and Romanoff whose personalities do not fit within society's more rigid definitions of masculine and feminine. "There's a connection," Whedon admits, between Barton and Romanoff, "but that bond is based on the fact that they are both loners" (qtd in Boucher). Romanoff's relationship with Barton actually reveals an empowered female position, as she stands as his physical and mental superior. Her empowerment owes partially to assuming masculine properties more naturally than Barton and Loki. She is physically more powerful than Barton, and during a key interrogation scene, she manipulates Loki more adeptly than this supposed god of illusion can manipulate her. Although women in *The Avengers* are presented as subordinate to either Fury's leadership of SHIELD or Rogers's command of the Avengers, Romanoff and fellow agent Maria Hill remain kick-ass agents who are stoic and skilled with firearms, engaging in fisticuffs primarily against men. Hill seems to spend as much time arguing with Fury as battling Loki's agents, showing her confidence in her own ability to make command decisions.

In comparison, the archer Barton is feminized, coincidently when *The Avengers* was released in a year when other action films and superhero stories associated the penetrating phallic arrow not with men but with women, for example, Katniss Everdeen in *The Hunger Games* and the aptly named Artemis Crock in DC Comics' animated series *Young Justice* (2010–2013). Barton admits to Loki that he is better with the bow than a handgun, whereas it is Romanoff who handles firearms, and at one point even Loki's scepter: she commands the more destructive and powerful phallic symbols that Barton cannot. The reserved Barton wears a cat-suit similar to the more aggressive Romanoff's, yet lacks her gun, coding him as emasculated in his dress, his weapons, and his actions. Barton's last battle scene in *The Avengers* emphasizes his powerlessness—supine, mouth agape, and groaning quietly, disrupting traditional modes of masculine representation that show the male action hero able to take a punch yet keep fighting.

Barton's feminization is reinforced by his first line of dialogue in *The Avengers*. A sniper physically isolated from fellow SHIELD agents, he explains to Fury that he "see[s] better from a distance." This distance leads one of Barton's peers to mockingly refer to him as "the Hawk" who perches in his "nest," like a mother bird tending to her young. Throughout the film, law enforcer Barton's role as the maternalized protector casts him as a redeemer of fallen persons, such as former criminal and assassin Romanoff. This "civilizer" role in Whedon's works such as *Buffy the Vampire Slayer* is applied to men and women assuming similarly feminized roles, such as self-proclaimed "love's bitch" Spike and "butt monkey" Xander Harris, who console depressed slayer Buffy and dark witch Willow Rosenberg (Jowett 98–99). In *Avenger*'s: sequel *Age of Ultron*, it is revealed that Barton is literally a family man, a father of three children and happily married: his wife recognizes how much these "gods" depend on her more ordinary (less overtly masculine) husband.

As her redeemer, Barton saves Romanoff—and she returns the favor. Hardly following a romantic plot desired by fans who cast her as Barton's girlfriend, Whedon treats Barton and Romanoff as allies only. "Is this love, Agent Romanoff?" Loki mocks her regarding her relationship with Barton—before she removes Loki's mind control over Barton by kicking the brainwashed archer in the head, knocking him out. However, she is at his side when he awakens. Their special intimacy is maintained in subsequent films, with Romanoff wearing an arrow pendant in *The Winter Soldier*. Yet their relationship remains heterosocial, eschewing the trajectory in television female-male partnerships that push them toward the romantic and heterosexual.

It is these agents' closeness with each other that allows Whedon to apply narrative structures commonly associated with female protagonists, such as the rape-revenge story, but with male characters. This gender-bending conceit allows Whedon to explore Barton's masculinity as it contrasts with conventional representations of masculinity. When Barton awakens in a SHIELD infirmary—bound to his bed because he is still under suspicion having gone rogue as Loki's lackey—Whedon uses the aftermath of his subjugation to apply a rape-revenge structure to the character's redemption. Barton implies his servitude to Loki was a mind-rape, asking Romanoff, "Have you ever had someone take your brain and play? Pull you out and stuff something else in? Do you know what it's like to be unmade?" She confirms: "You know that I do."[7] Defining his experience in terms of penetration, Barton, like many rapists in rape-revenge movies, is "positioned in places traditionally reserved for women" (Lehman 106), with Barton as analogous to the victim.

This re-casting allows Barton to demonstrate qualities of the female protagonist in such rape-revenge stories. Much as the acts of torture and murder potentially masculinize such women, Barton is postured in a way to reclaim his manhood after Loki manipulated him. Like the avenging women in rape-revenge narratives, Barton desires to penetrate Loki, fixating on tearing out his eyeball with his own phallic shaft: "Well, if I put an arrow through Loki's eye socket, I would sleep better, I suppose." Barton comes close to fulfilling his rape-revenge narrative when, during the Manhattan battle, Barton—in close up—aims, smirks, and fires at Loki's face. The camera follows the arrow: just as it reaches Loki's eye, the villain catches it before penetration. The music stops, and Loki looks over his shoulder to mock Barton. Then the (previously unconfirmed) explosive arrow bursts, tossing Loki toward Banner—another character mentally manipulated by Loki—now transformed into a very angry Hulk. Barton relinquishes his personal desire for physical revenge, choosing instead strategy and collaboration. Whedon presents these more gender-fluid characters of Barton and Romanoff as foundational to the Avengers team, assisting their teammates as they negotiate of their more restrictive masculinities.

"YOU COME HOME": RACE, ISOLATION, AND UNCONVENTIONAL FAMILIES

In light of journalists' reading of the Hulk's earlier rampage in the film against Romanoff as drawing from sexual violence and "the unchecked male rage that so often victimizes women" (Snyder), Banner's attack against Loki satisfies both his and Barton's revenge against their mind-rapist, reformulating the rape-revenge narrative with men, not women, as those suffering from Loki's mental manipulation. While Barton may promote a more fluid masculinity, characters such as Loki and the Hulk take on hyper-masculine performances that compromise how *The Avengers* negotiates racial identity and the concept of family.

The climax to *The Avengers*, as it occurs in midtown Manhattan in front of numerous symbols of US corporations and New York landmarks draws together the numerous intersections of gender that the film has broached only lightly: nationality, race, and even corporate identity. Drawing on Stark Industries' Tower as a power conduit to transport the Chitauri to Manhattan, Loki's fight takes on allegorical implications: the Avengers fight against the alien Chitauri to protect not only humanity but also implicitly Western-led economic governance, represented by Stark's company and SHIELD's paramilitary operations—with Stark's eponymous skyscraper an attractive target.

As the six white superheroes fight in front of Stark Tower (as well as outside bank branches of Citi and Capital One), *The Avengers* reads as a film that rallies around humanity—or at least the United States—in its defeat of the evil foreign invader Loki, who is too ambiguously gendered and raced to win against such white, primarily American, and seemingly hyper-masculine heroes. In a film that draws upon both traditional and progressive representations of masculinity and femininity, the Avengers as a team otherwise maintain the status quo, a problem that the superhero genre contends with frequently (DiPaolo 41–42), which raises disconcerting questions regarding how this film, and the larger superhero genre, can enact productive gender portrayals while still adhering to problematic portrayals of class, nationhood, and race.

Loki, humanized by a self-loathing motivated by how he sees himself in terms of his race and gender, is a character who reflects twenty-first-century concerns about masculine inadequacy. While Tom Hiddleston's performance makes the character one of the most humanized villains in Marvel's films, Loki is very much not a human but actually a deformed blue frost giant from the alternate dimension Jotunheim. Too short to be a giant, Loki is abandoned by his father Laufey (Colm Feore), then adopted by his family's enemy, Odin (Anthony Hopkins)—father of Thor, and King of the dimension Asgard. In his adulthood, Loki, who used his shape-shifting abilities to blend in with his adopted family, is outed as a frost giant by his blue skin. Loki's discomfort with his own complexion allows the film *Thor* to explore feelings of national and racial isolation. While Loki's character arc is in part related to his conception of his race, as a shapeshifter he does not consider embodying a race other than white, despite Asgard's multiracial court.

Whedon's *The Avengers* emphasizes the almost sexual violence the self-hating Loki takes against numerous human characters: Romanoff, whom he calls the "mewling quim"; Barton and Banner, upon whom he violates mentally; and Coulson, whom he penetrates with his scepter. Even then, this hyper-masculine posturing is mocked by other characters as mere grandstanding. Romanoff, assuming the role of faux helpless female victim, lulls Loki into false complacency until he is bragging about his master plan—which is exactly the secret she wanted him to reveal. Even Coulson, bleeding to death, still fires his oversized firearm to send Loki hurtling through a wall. Coulson taunts, "You lack conviction." Loki's hyper-masculinity prevents him from reading the more subtle threats by Romanoff and Coulson.

Like Loki, Banner's hyper-masculine performances in *The Avengers* can be read productively against themes of race and nationalism. The Hulk's assault upon Loki is foreshadowed when the latter refers to the former's alter ego, Bruce Banner, as "a mindless beast [who] makes play he's still a man." Stark likewise prods Banner—not just with a (friendly?) jab of a miniaturized electric rod but verbally: "You're tip-toeing, big man—you got to strut."

This "strut" refers not only to a tougher masculine performance from the meek scientist, but also throws into relief Stark's greater privilege: Stark has the wealth and resources to "strut," and Banner does not. With little control over his body and emotions, Banner could lose all reason and harm everyone around him. The restraint Banner performs throughout the film allegorizes struggles of presenting a certain masculine performance that is nonthreatening—while still preserving his ability.

That Banner is referred to by Loki and others (and even by himself) as more animal than human demonstrates how he is positioned as Other. Banner provides his services to SHIELD in exchange for amnesty. Banner's enlistment in Fury's army follows a history of Americans who have joined the US military for the sake of being recognized as equals, whether black American soldiers enlisting during the Civil War, or according to more recent immigration reform proposals, for aliens to receive citizenship in exchange for enlistment. Like Loki, Banner's shame is linked, in part, to passing as human, and the conception that his alter ego is not human. Ang Lee admits that in developing Banner's character for his 2003 film adaptation *Hulk*, that he saw the scientist as representing problems facing Asian and Asian American persons. As Lee emphasized, the Hulk's struggle with embracing an interior sense of self against societal pressures reflects the larger "subcurrent of repression" (qtd. in Yang), allegorized in Banner's struggle to, as the character puts it, "behave." In Whedon's film, Banner represses that part of himself, referring to it not by its more popular name "the Hulk," but the aptly named "*other* guy" as he struggles to pass as human.

Whedon emphasizes the differences between his characters in terms of their gender, race, even humanity, to bridge those gaps, appealing to, of all tropes, those of the family film. When interrogated by Fury, Loki addresses his concerns of isolation onto the film's heroes, taunting Fury, an older African American battlefield soldier and spy now serving a largely administrative role within SHIELD, for having "call[ed] on such lost creatures to defend you." Loki knows what it feels like to be that lost creature, as can be heard in how he analyzes each superhero's limitations at integrating into society: an Asgardian who would rather be more human (Thor); a "beast who makes play that he is still a man" (Banner); a World War II soldier re-awakened in the twenty-first century, as "a man out of [his own] time" (Rogers); assassins who cannot begin to "wipe out that much red" blood from their criminal records (Barton and Romanoff); and an immature playboy who does not work well with others, to the detriment of his emotional development (Stark).

Paradoxically, these superheroes are brought together by this common trait—Fury himself referring to the Avengers as "isolated, unbalanced even"—which allows Whedon to imitate the structures of blended families.

They are bonded by their individual understandings of the constraints of their masculine behaviors, marked by their ambiguous relationship to being human. In defining *The Avengers* in the press, Whedon emphasized why such a movie should be impossible to write or direct, unless refashioned into a family movie: "[T]hese people shouldn't be in the same room let alone on the same team—and that is the definition of family" (qtd in Downey). Whedon caps off the family movie dynamic with the film's post-credit sequence in which the heroes dine at a shawarma restaurant. Gathered around the dinner table, their meal is quiet because these soldiers are exhausted following the intense Chitauri war. But in that quietness the characters' body language reveals their intimacy with each other: Barton has his left leg propped against Romanoff's behind as he leans back in his chair, and even the self-admitted "always angry" Banner is chuckling at the absurdity of seeing Rogers seated next to the ever boisterous Thor, his mouth full yet taking another huge bite from his meal. This bizarre family dinner emphasizes how the superhero genre can be invigorated by exploring well-worn tropes of other genres.

Such superhero films grant these characters, as superhuman as they can be, those human moments that provide alternative understanding of conventional social structures. The family dining scene resituates the characters in ways that can speak to readers' own understanding of their problems. This motif is then put into relief in the outer space continuation of the Avengers, *Guardians of the Galaxy* (2014), as Peter Quill, alias Star-Lord, forges an inter-species family of bounty hunters, murderers, and ex-cons in his fight against Loki's employer Thanos. By emphasizing the theme of family, *The Avengers* as well provides a moment for decompression that, while hilarious, also identifies a complicated idea about family that both allows for intimacy and separation. As Thor loses Loki as his family, he gains a new family in the Avengers.

The film's last image before the credits also emphasizes this familial closeness, as Stark and Potts are rebuilding Stark Tower, with blueprints for apartments within the building for each Avenger—as if Stark is moving each member of his new adoptive family into his house. By suspending this family dynamic until the end of the film, Whedon forestalls closure for future installments of the Avengers franchise. With this open ending, Whedon allows *The Avengers* to serve as an exploration of film genres including that of superheroes, wars, and family. These concerns are saved for later consideration in sequels: Loki and Thor seem to mend their strained relationship in the sequel *Thor: The Dark World*, World War II veteran Rogers continues to acclimate to the twenty-first century in *Captain America: The Winter Soldier*, and future battles against new enemies and future alliances with new superheroes await the Avengers in *The*

Age of Ultron (2015). As these stories are ongoing, so too do their individualized masculinities in these superhero films remain an act in progress. Whedon is now leaving the Marvel Comics Universe, allowing future directors to continue these conversations without his direction.

By appreciating the nuanced approach that Whedon takes to gendering men in *The Avengers* after his portrayals of women as action leads in Buffy the *Vampire Slayer*, *Dollhouse* (2009–2010), and *Firefly* (2002–2003), he invites greater attention to the construction of gender in superhero stories overall. Work remains to be done, however. Producers at Marvel Studios tease whether they will develop individual films centered on Avengers characters such as Romanoff and Hill, or other Marvel Comics characters such as Wanda "Scarlet Witch" Maximoff and Jane "Wasp" van Dyne. Marvel has announced the release of a film centered on Carol Danvers, alias Captain Marvel, and released a television series around Captain America's first partner (and first love), in *Agent Carter* (2014 to present). Moreover, the character Jessica Jones appears in two upcoming series from Marvel and Netflix.

Though delayed, Marvel is now addressing the large number of women that are part of these superheroes films' fanbase, fans drawn in part by the more fluid presentations of masculinity and genre in the Avengers universe. These fluid presentations are also what male fans may now expect and appreciate. Through *The Avengers* (and its sequel), Whedon keeps these heterosocial masculinities in conversation. Much as these narratives are ongoing, so too does gender in these superhero films remain an act in progress, some assembly required.

NOTES

1. Jon Favreau maintains an executive producer credit for Whedon's *The Avengers* and *Avengers: Age of Ultron*. With the recasting of Mark Ruffalo as the Hulk/Bruce Banner, Whedon is less tied to Ang Lee and Louis Leterrier's visions.

2. Aaron Taylor's "He's Gotta Be Strong" is an excellent review of how both idealized and mutated masculine bodies come to be not limitations to gender forms but can identify a set of "queered" bodily types that provide a broader range of engendered appearances.

3. Lorna Jowett's *Sex and the Slayer* is especially evocative in how she traces the development of alternative masculine models in Whedon's *Buffy the Vampire Slayer*.

4. And as Whedon reveals, Paltrow's character was included in his script at Downey's insistence ("Commentary").

5. That an earlier draft of Whedon's script had Romanoff say this line in a different context further emphasizes Stark's ambiguous gendering (Whedon "Commentary").

6. Coulson technically dies in *The Avengers*—only to be resurrected by Fury in the film's follow-up television series Agents of SHIELD.

7. Her remark may hint at the flashback in *Age of Ultron*, revealing her brainwashing as a child to become an assassin, culminating with sterilization, which as actions performed against her will parallels the violation Barton feels.

WORKS CITED

Boucher, Geoff. "'Avengers': Joss Whedon Says Jeremy Renner's Hawkeye Is a 'Loner.'" *Hero Complex* 16 Apr. 2012. Web. 23 Aug. 2013.

Butler, Judith. *The Psychic Life of Power*. Stanford: Stanford UP, 1997. Print.

DiPaolo, Marc. *War, Politics and Superheroes: Ethics and Propaganda in Comics and Film*. Jefferson: McFarland, 2011. Print.

Donald, Ralph R. "Masculinity and Machismo in Hollywood's War Films." *The Masculinities Reader*. Ed. Stephen M. Whitehead and Frank J. Barrett. Malden: Blackwell, 2001. 170–83. Print.

Downey, Ryan J. "Comic-Con: Joss Whedon Talks 'Avengers' at EW Visionaries Panel." *MTV Splash Page* 22 July 2010. Web. 23 Aug. 2013.

Greven, David. *Manhood in Hollywood from Bush to Bush*. Austin: U of Texas P, 2009.

Jowett, Lorna. *Sex and the Slayer: A Gender Studies Primer for the Buffy Fan*. Middletown: Wesleyan UP, 2005. Print.

Lehman, Peter. "'Don't Blame This on a Girl': Female Rape-Revenge Films." *Screening the Male: Exploring Masculinities in the Hollywood Cinema*. Ed. Steven Cohan and Ina Rae Hark. New York: Routledge, 1993. 103–17. Print.

Kord, Susanne, and Elisabeth Krimmer. *Contemporary Hollywood Masculinities: Gender, Genre, and Politics*. New York: Palgrave, 2011.

O'Hehir, Andrew. "'The Avengers' and Hollywood's Gender Wars." *Salon* 2 May 2012. Web. 23 Aug. 2013.

Snyder, Daniel D. "Scarlett Johansson Has the Most Human Moment in 'The Avengers.'" *The Atlantic* 7 May 2012. Web. 23 Aug. 2013.

Taylor, Aaron. "'He's Gotta Be Strong, and He's Gotta Be Fast, and He's Gotta Be Larger Than Life': Investigating the Engendered Superhero Body." *The Journal of Popular Culture* 40, no. 2 (2007): 344–360.

Whedon, Joss. "Commentary to *The Avengers*." *The Avengers*. Disney, 2012. DVD.

Wilding, Josh. "Robert Downey Jr. and Gwyneth Paltrow on the Return of Pepper Potts in *The Avengers*." *Comic Book Movie* 31 Mar. 2012. Web. 23 Aug. 2013.

Yang, Jeff. "Look . . . Up in the Sky! It's Asian Man!" *San Francisco Chronicle* 1 June 2006. Web. 23 Aug. 2013.

LOVING ANTI-HEROES

10

The Falling Man: Nostalgia and Masculinity as Genres of Composure in *Mad Men*

Maureen McKnight

I've always been fascinated by the visually arresting opening credits for AMC's critically acclaimed television series. It depicts a suited man, Don Draper, in silhouette as office walls crash down around him. Fretful violin music underscores the ominous implication as Don begins plummeting downward, past mid-century advertisements of happy consumers. When I first saw this opening sequence for the show's 2007 debut, I was reminded of Richard Drew's "the Falling Man," the agonizing photograph of a man falling from the North Tower of the World Trade Center during the 9/11 attacks. In the decade following the terrorist attacks of September 11, 2001, *Mad Men*'s haunting opening credit's imagery conjures Drew's photograph, seeming to direct theories about Don Draper's likely death, for it—and its worried-sounding score—portends disaster.

Two key details disrupt this supposition about Don's eventual demise. One is fairly obvious: The opening credits actually conclude not with the death of the falling silhouetted man but with Don Draper's commanding figure, pictured from behind as he's seated on a couch, casually holding a cigarette with one outstretched arm. Don's posture suggests a confidence that contrasts the out-of-control descent of the previous sequence; indeed, in each year of the show, viewers have witnessed many examples of Don's corporate and romantic prowess.

The other disruption is more complicated, for it resides in *Mad Men*'s treatment of time itself, and my work here will consider that treatment. As *Mad Men* fans know, the series' first three seasons are heavily invested in nostalgia in its many forms—pitching it, displaying it, producing it—much to the delight of twenty-first-century viewers. Our own nostalgia in watching the show provides us with not only pleasure but also with a way to articulate what's happening to Don during the tumultuous 1960s.

In later seasons, however, the show focuses less on nostalgia and more, as I see it, on what Lauren Berlant calls the "ongoing now" (196), a revised understanding of the present moment, one that's increasingly dominant for contemporary viewers caught in the precarity of twenty-first-century capitalism. What interests me about *Mad Men*'s consideration of time is its capacity, especially in its later seasons, to refashion the present moment into what Berlant calls "an impasse." Rather than experiencing the present moment as a stable, concrete event, she explains, an impasse occurs when one feels "adrift" and "discovers a loss of traction" in life (200). Berlant introduces the idea of an impasse as both "a formal term encountering the duration of the present, and a specific term for tracking the circulation of precariousness through diverse locales and bodies" (199).

This notion of an impasse compels me because it becomes "a space of time lived without a narrative genre" (199), creating a link between Berlant's figuration of the precarious impasse of early twenty-first-century life and Don's mid-century plummet from the Manhattan skyscraper. His fall never reaches conclusion: rather, it symbolizes his attempt to adapt to the era's anomie, instructive to contemporary viewers regarding how we might also manage our feelings of dislocation. Don Draper, the central protagonist, acts as a bellwether, having to live, as we all do, in the ongoing now of the present moment, a precarious state that is "at once overpresent and enigmatic" and that continually "requires finding one's footing in new manners of being in it" (196). I argue here that Don's free-fall visually signals his work to manage this emergent understanding of time, this impasse, for he exists in "the unbound temporality of the stretch of time" (199). As Lauren M.E. Goodlad, Lilya Kaganovsky, and Robert A. Rusing contend, the show "defamiliarize[s] a millennial condition" (11), a defamiliarization that creates "not a tragedy, with its powerful sense of an ending, but dramatic irony, with its intimation of lessons learned and resolutions still to come" (27). Don's free-fall portends not his tragic death, but how he—and how we—might feel as we negotiate new social norms regarding, among other modes of identity, masculinity. After a consideration of *Mad Men*'s treatment of time first with nostalgia and then with the "ongoing now," my work here will conclude with a discussion of how Don's masculinity and his efforts to find his footing as a man in the 1960s function as a harbinger for present-day viewers.

THE NARRATIVE OF NOSTALGIA

Mad Men's early seasons' emphasis on nostalgia brings into relief not only this emotion's capacity for providing coherence but also its ability to manage dislocation. As Jeremy Varon reasons, "the show is more plausibly the staging of a fantasy than the rendering of history" (258). With its midday boozing, freelance womanizing, and post-WWII capitalist expectations, *Mad Men*'s depictions of Madison Avenue advertisers of the early 1960s invite viewers into a look back that at once seeks solace in the presumed "good ol' days" while at the same time interrupts that romanticized version of the past with jarring realities. Early on, Betty Draper struggles in a pre-Betty Friedan era, the Draper children grow up largely unattended mainly in front of the family television, and Don Draper, though a corporate hero, agonizes to connect with his lovers, his family of origin, and his immediate family. Viewers of *Mad Men* know that "Don Draper," having been born as Dick Whitman, steals a dying man's identity to escape the Korean War. Despite any familial or corporate successes, despite his desire to belong and be loved, Don remains in exile from any kind of home, whether literal or metaphorical.

One might postulate that *Mad Men* is a nostalgic show but, though it is "told in hindsight" (Siska 204), it is not a show filled with characters seeking to restore lost homes, and Don's recollections of his childhood are not pleasurable. Varon notes that the show remains "captive to the condition it diagnoses, equipping neither its characters nor—as yet—its viewers with the internal resources or genuine historical inspiration to find a way out" (258). Don knew he was a "whore child," and he does not reminisce gaily about such events as his mother's death in childbirth, his rigid stepmother, his "dishonest" father, or his whorehouse upbringing. Even the "regressively 'boyish' behavior of the men at Sterling Cooper," as William Siska notes, "has never been a desire to recapture authentic feelings of childhood. None of the men, so far as we know, had an idyllic upbringing" (204).

Rather than trying to restore a lost past, Don's nostalgia is more thoughtful, more focused on the pain of his upbringing itself. In *The Future of Nostalgia*, Svetlana Boym distinguishes between two modes of nostalgia: restorative and reflective. Restorative nostalgia, Boym argues, "does not think of itself as nostalgia, but rather as truth and tradition" while reflective nostalgia "dwells on the ambivalences of human longing and belonging and does not shy away from the contradictions of modernity" (xviii). Reflective nostalgia "thrives in *algia*, the longing itself, and delays the homecoming—wistfully, ironically, desperately" (xviii). Thus, Don is brooding and introspective while remembering his past as he contemplates its traumas, delaying any lasting homecoming. In sifting through his memories, his nostalgia emphasizes the algia, or longing, rather than restoring any lost home. Don thus uses nostalgia to manage his feelings of exile.

In this way, *Mad Men* differs from other recently produced period shows that involve a "look back," including short-lived series such as *Pan Am* (2011) and *The Playboy Club* (2011), as well as *Boardwalk Empire* (2010–2014), *Mr. Selfridge* (2013–), *Masters of Sex* (2013–), and most notably *Downton Abbey* (2010–).[1] The agency of nostalgia in *Mad Men* lies in its repeated encounters with mid-twentieth-century alienation in time, inviting viewers to experience two supposedly stable types of temporality: the past of the 1950s and 1960s and the twenty-first-century present. *Mad Men* provokes a twinned temporality in both Don and its audience to generate narrative power, for nostalgia structures Don's life and assures viewers about the stability of a linear timeline. As Lynne Joyrich argues, the show "can both engage and disavow" both history and presence, "subjecting the past to its aestheticized view," "rais[ing] issues for interrogation yet also allow[ing] for their evasion" (217). In this way, *Mad Men*'s enchantment with yesteryear differs from pre-agricultural television fantasies such as *Game of Thrones* (2011–), *The Walking Dead* (2010–), and *Revolution* (2012–2014), for his awareness of his own ontological and temporal estrangement—and its value—both structures his and our views and makes it possible for him to become a brilliant ad man. Don uses his painful longing at the same time the show makes it available to its audience, and its evocation placates viewers into understanding time as fixed and intractable. Our restorative nostalgia's evocations of Don's reflective mode of nostalgia establish a "that was then, this is now" sensibility, or, as Mark Greif calls it, Now We Know Better.[2]

Nowhere in *Mad Men* is Don's brilliant engagement with nostalgia more evident than in the episode "The Wheel" (1.13), the finale of season one. In his pitch to Kodak regarding its new "wheel" technology for projectors, Don demonstrates his understanding of sentiment's power in advertising and nostalgia's ability to re-narrate the past. Kodak representatives want the new technology of their machine emphasized in its marketing, and Don acknowledges that technology "is a glittering lure," but he seeks a deeper engagement, one that goes "a level beyond flash," which occurs when consumers "have a sentimental bond with the product." Don's former coworker, an "old pro of a copywriter, a Greek, named Teddy," informs Don's understanding of this deeper possible bond. Teddy advised that one means to creating a bond is to make the product "new. . . . It creates an itch." Another way is through nostalgia, for, as Don says slowly, it is "delicate, but potent."

Don's admittedly heavy-handed reference to his former coworker's definition emphasizes, both for Don and for viewers, nostalgia's ability to produce and manage sentiment. For Don, nostalgia is useful both as a way to experience desire and as an advertising strategy. As Fredric Jameson notes desire underwrites capitalism, for its force, rather than "undermin[ing] the rigidities of late capitalism" is "very precisely what keeps the consumer system going in the first place" (202). Generating desire for goods and services is advertising's bailiwick, and its effects—and Don's aptitude—are powerful. Don's nostalgia reinforces both his pleasure and power, strengthening his advertising skills and making him an award-winning ad executive. His reflective nostalgia is thus twinned with a restorative one, and these multiple registers of nostalgia make available—to him and to viewers—a linearity of his life, a concrete temporality that offers a pleasurable sadness.

Mad Men's audience delights in witnessing Don's skill and recognizing Don's pathos, especially in this episode, which aired within a year of the Great Recession's beginning. After explaining the importance of nostalgia, Don shows slides of himself and Betty as they eat hot dogs in the sunshine, frolic with the children, and kiss in a frozen embrace. In a voiceover, Don says,

Teddy told me that in Greek, nostalgia literally means the pain from an old wound. It's a twinge in your heart, far more powerful than memory alone. This device isn't a space ship, it's a time machine. It goes backward, forward. It takes us to a place where we ache to go again. It's not called a wheel, it's called a carousel. It lets us travel the way a child travels. Round and around, and back home again. To a place where we know we are loved.

Don's use of his own family's photographs are one part of the appeal in his pitch to Kodak; a second appeal involves the low camera angle that confirms Don's authority, with first an establishing shot, followed by a medium close up that culminates, finally, in a close up of Jon Hamm's handsome and intense face; a third appeal involves the quiet intimacy of Hamm's voice and his unblinking but engaged stare; and a fourth involves the music—long, tense whole notes—that emerges in the scene just as the technology of the wheel is engaged. These lures underwrite the scene itself with a painful longing. When Don announces "this device isn't a space ship; it's a time machine," he could be referencing *both* Kodak's carousel *and* the nature of nostalgia itself.

MODES OF COMPOSURE

Nostalgia thus functions as a "mode of composure" (Berlant 197), one that makes sense of disparate, inchoate experiences by ordering them according to a linear storyline. When Don describes Kodak's projection carousel as a "time machine," he's wishing he too could find a place of belonging, as a son, as a lover, as a husband, as a man—and, in so doing, he creates a past to which he can point. In longing for home, he manufactures a narrative of an identifiable past and a concrete present. This structure of feeling "lets us travel the way a child travels. Round and around and back home again to a place where we know we are loved."[3] With his identity as Dick Whitman hidden, Don's nostalgia for his past involves not only a cyclical desire for desire itself but also the creation of a discernable past and present.

That's because nostalgia must occur in a timeline. As Heidegger notes, the past nostalgia "seeks has never existed except as narrative" (qtd. in Frow 81). Nostalgia as an emotional response thus broadly signals attempts to negotiate new territories either of place, feelings, or thought. Those territories must be negotiated through narrative, for it is through narrative that nostalgia fashions the past as temporally distinct and stable. All narratives of nostalgia, Nicholas Dames explains in *Amnesiac Selves*, might be broadly characterized "as the set of sites and temporal processes that reflect, and manage, *dislocation*—experiences of dissonance, disconnection, separation from past spaces and certainties" (12). Dislocation, Dames argues, "is the dilemma nostalgia is invented to solve" (12), and it characterizes both the 1960s' post-WWII affect in the United States as well as the early-twenty-first century's "fading of security and upward mobility" (Berlant 200) during a nearly decade-long, jobless recovery from a massive recession.

With an ever-changing Manhattan workplace, without a family of origin that he can claim, without an authentic childhood-to-adulthood identity, Don feels dislocated. If dislocation "is the dilemma nostalgia is invented to solve," Don's nostalgia functions as a narrative device to manufacture, exacerbate, heighten, yet manage his desires. At the same time, it makes possible a stable identity for Don, especially regarding his place in the world as a man. Nostalgia neatly organizes his life into discrete and recognizable eras: past and present. Don's recognition of his own temporality as malleable makes it possible for him to generate structures of affect that appeal to his clients, his lovers, and anyone he meets.

SEASONS OF DRIFT

That is until season four, during which the institutions that have defined him—marriage and the advertising agency renamed Sterling Cooper Draper Pryce—change radically, leaving his footing even less secure than before. In the first scene of that season's premiere, "Public Relations" (4.1), a reporter from *Advertising Age* asks Don, "Who is Don Draper?" This question frames the 2010 season and indicates the ontological and narrative dilemma Don faces—how to move forward, even after his secret identity has been revealed to Betty and even as the late 1960s' structures regarding masculinity and identity are challenged. As Brett Martin notes in *Difficult Men*, whether and how any of the characters "would survive the onrushing ruptures of the sixties" functions as "one of *Mad Men*'s most suspenseful ongoing mysteries."

The modus operandi of the show pivots away from a nostalgia that constructs a stable self, then, to consider "life simply *happening*, much the way it actually does, tough truths included" (Martin). Don must face what Tony Soprano faces when, as he comes to understand that "every day is a gift," Tony wonders, "does it have to be a pair of socks?"

In these subsequent seasons of drift, Don struggles immensely, and he loses the footings that nostalgia once offered him. We get some glimpse into whether Don might face life's hard facts when he begins to journal at the beginning of season four. In "The Summer Man" (4.8), a mid-season episode that immediately follows Don's personal nadir, Don works to exert an unusual control over his own story not only through a decrease in his drinking and an increase in exercise but also through writing. Newly sober, viewers hear him say that his "mind is a jumble" and that he "can't organize [his] thoughts." We get access to Don's inner monologue through an initially jarring voiceover narration. Don writes that he wants to gain a "modicum of control over the way [he] feel[s]." With his marriage in ruins, with the loss of major client Lucky Strike, Don seeks by the end of season four to create a new narrative for himself.

Without nostalgia as a guide, he seeks out other modes of composure. Drinking continues to provide a haven to Don, but it fails as a way for him to gain control over his life. His journaling is his first attempt to regain authorial control, but for Don it's too private to have sustainable effects. It's telling that when Don writes a public letter renouncing Big Tobacco it is in no less than the *New York Times*, for his recreation of self cannot occur in isolation. In fact, to write this very public letter, he tears out his private journal entries to make room in his notebook. This move contrasts his inability to write either a letter of reference for or an apology to his secretary Allison after their failed dalliance at the beginning of the season. Direct and revealing, Don's letter addresses not only why he's quitting Big Tobacco, but also his failed marriage and his former lover Midge's sickening dependency on heroin. As always, Don's pitch functions both as advertising and as a window into his feelings. Don writes of his devotion in his "long relationship" with Lucky Strike, claiming that he now realizes that tobacco "never improves, causes illness and makes people unhappy." Though tobacco, his former wife Betty, and Midge's art have offered tremendous rewards (money for the company, domestic stability, cultural capital), Don acknowledges his previous limited narrative control when he says about Lucky Strike that "[w]e knew it wasn't good for us, but we couldn't stop." It is at this point Don hints he wishes to stop desiring desire itself, to get off the carousel of his yearning and reach for something, someone, some place solid—a home, one that's real and stable, not manufactured through nostalgia.

Figure 10.1.   Throughout *Mad Men*, Don Draper (Jon Hamm) longs for—and fears—a
stable self.

But having to face the precarity of the ongoing now almost thwarts Don's professional abilities, and in the end he once again leans on nostalgia to frame his worldview and his pitch. In speaking with the American Cancer Society Board, he stumbles to articulate why he "suddenly" wrote his public letter renouncing tobacco. Sensing his own weakness in front of the client, he adds an insightful coda: "I think in my heart it was an impulse because I knew what I needed to do to move forward." He then invokes nostalgia because he knows it will make teenagers feel mournful for their lost childhoods, despite their hatred of their parents. When faced with the board members' doubt about teenagers' nostalgia, Don explains, "they're mourning for their childhood more than they're anticipating their future, because they don't know it yet, but they don't want to die." He's so certain of nostalgia's power that he assures the board that Big Tobacco companies will hate the approach. Again, Don speaks as much to the company's needs as his own, ultimately relying on nostalgia as that lure beyond technology, newness, or sex to stop teenagers from smoking.[4] Don can't quit nostalgia; it's his wheelhouse, a more powerful organizing principle than any other force in his life. He knows how to use it to produce a coherent narrative that not only fuels his own and others' desires but also helps him to avoid the present moment as an impasse, as "the unbound temporality of the stretch of time" (Berlant 199). In an impasse, "one keeps moving, but one moves paradoxically, in the *same place*" (199). In season four, we see Don's struggle in place to manage his anomie.

EVERY DAY IS BRAND NEW

As such, when Don seeks to "change the conversation" by the end of season four, he first rebrands Sterling Cooper Draper Pryce and then, tangentially, rebrands himself. This reboot becomes his "chance to be someone who could sleep at night." It's no surprise that this line occurs so publicly in the *New York Times*—for both the agency's sake as well as Don's. Don seeks to create a new form of masculinity for himself that can manage the anomie he's feeling. It's also an allusion to the drifter, the "gentleman of the rails" from "The Hobo's Code" (1.8), who "freed" himself from family because he "couldn't sleep at night tied to" what he had once: "a wife, job, a mortgage." Don takes an interest in this hobo who "gave up the conventional life to be free." Don takes his cues from the drifter, seeking to free himself so he could, as the drifter did, see "brand-new place[s], people, what have you." That way, as the drifter explained, "every day is brand new," and the newly freed man can "sleep like a stone." The drifter lives contentedly in the impasse, and that satisfaction appeals to Don.

But Don's mistake is that, to start anew, he proposes to Megan, his twenty-five-year-old secretary who's modern, beautiful, and maternal. This shocking turn—which does not actually surprise Joan—demonstrates how quickly Don thinks he can "get out of here and move forward," as he explained to Peggy after she gave birth. He's attracted to Megan because she offers what Betty so desperately wants (and her new husband Henry tells her no one can have), "a fresh start." An impasse causes confusion because the normative guidelines fall away. Though he does not know himself, Don believes Megan when she claims, "I know who you are now." He reaches for her in a desperate moment, when he feels very much alone.[5] In his proposal to Megan, with a dreamy, faraway look in his eyes, Don declares his love for her by saying, "I feel like myself when I'm with you, but the way I always wanted to feel." Having felt alone and adrift, he reaches for any genre of composure—in this case, marriage—that will help him (seem to) move forward. As with Kodak's carousel, he loves a projection of himself, and, with his marriage proposal to Megan, Don proposes becoming a new man. Without the complications of the past, without having to, as Faye Miller recommends, "take [his] head out of the sand about the past," Don can reinvent himself. That way, he won't be, as Faye fatally states, "stuck trying to be a person like the rest of us." Don's version of masculinity disentangles him from not only facing his true self but also the sometimes-dull ontological obligations of living in the present moment—in other words, the tedium of a pair of socks.

PRECARIOUS MASCULINITY

When Don suspends his reliance on nostalgia as a way to manufacture a narrative of his life (by entering his second marriage), he must negotiate new territories of masculinity. In committing to Megan, Don doubles down on a stable masculine identity. His subsequent struggle to adapt to changing times and his efforts to "change the conversation" about who he is as a man signal his difficulty in comprehending the social constructedness of identity emergent in the 1960s. Don's strengths and weaknesses as a 1960s' man have simultaneously fascinated and repulsed twenty-first-century viewers. In *Difficult Men*, Martin makes clear that "*Mad Men* is about a transitional generation—caught between the upheavals of World War II and the youthquake of the 1960s—written by another such generation, one growing up under the shadow of the baby boomers' self-mythologizing, but too near to claim something new as their own." It's misleading, however, to assume a stability of the two "generations" mentioned, as both are porous. I agree with Martin that *Mad Men* is about transition, but not about the transitions from one decade or generation to another; rather, I see *Mad Men* as a meditation on the precarity evident in the ongoing now, especially given the recent recession's heavy toll on men. As Joyrich states, *Mad Men* "reveals how selves might be revised . . . how subjectivities are both envisioned and re-viewed" (231). We can see this tenuousness also prompts viewers' fascination with Don Draper's version of masculinity, which was dominant in the late 1950s but which becomes, masculinity studies has explained, only one of many versions by the late 1960s.

Born out of the work feminists such as Judith Butler and Eve Kosofsky Sedgwick have done with femininity, masculinity theory articulates a non-biological, performative definition of masculinity. It seeks "to treat masculinity not as the normative referent against which standards are assessed but as a problematic gender construct" (Kimmel "Intro" 10). As such, masculinity functions not as an invariable gender category but as part of an identity that is socially constructed through discourse. Looking back to the 1960s, contemporary viewers can see Dick Whitman's mode of masculinity as a stellar performance, a mode R. W. Connell notes was generally "defined through an opposition with femininity and institutionalized in economy and state" (248). Just as Dick Whitman assumes (or dons) the identity of veteran and hero Don Draper, he also performs the role of former high school football star, of corporate titan, and of disengaged father in such a way that befits the 1960s. Through *Mad Men*'s multiyear run, viewers can witness Don's efforts to adapt to change. Don's early 1960s' version of masculinity functions well, prompting a restorative nostalgia in contemporary viewers for a time when masculinity operated cohesively with dominant structures. It may even emphasize, as Sarah Banat-Weiser argues in "'We Are All Workers': Economic Crisis, Masculinity, and the American Working Class," the gendered nature of the 2008 Great Recession for contemporary viewers.[6] Kimmel explains that the "old standard" of manhood that was "rooted in the life of the community and the qualities of a man's character gave way to a new standard based on individual achievement" ("The Birth" 138). The early 1960s' Don excels at individual achievement, given his striking romantic and professional aptitudes, and that excellence appeals to contemporary viewers.

Yet, as much as Don's successful manliness attracts *Mad Men* fans, his struggles also hail us, demonstrating the penalties of resistance to change. By the late 1960s, neither Don's nostalgia nor his other attempts to navigate the ongoing now of ordinary life serve him well. Even Don's impulse to flee rather than face his fears is yet another genre of composure that fails him. Like Huck Finn, Don seeks to "light out for the territory"—first with Midge, then with Rachel Menken, then with his kids' teacher, then even with Megan. Each woman but Megan rejects him, so he's forced to travel within himself, remaining in the present moment. In the early 1960s, Don can use his sense of dislocation to enhance his pleasure and his work, becoming a paragon of mid-twentieth-century career success by deploying the power of sentiment to enhance his male power and appeal. But Don's late 1960s' struggles do not suggest that he participates in the "undercurrent of macho masculinity" with Marlon Brando, James Dean, and Jack Nicholson, among others, in the ways these post–1950s' American men "'deconstruct[ed]' macho rather than play[ed] it straight" (Bordo 112). Instead Don flails about, seeking a foothold but finding none. By the end of *Mad Man*'s season four, when he proposes to Megan, Don reaches for familiar "gestures of composure" to frame his life (199). The subsequent seasons depict a Don Draper who seems lost without an adaptive masculinity that reflects changing cultural norms. It's this lost Don who picks up the needle from the Beatles' record just as John Lennon sings, "love is all and love is everyone, it is knowing" in "Tomorrow Never Knows."

PRECARIOUS BODY

This sense of insecurity, of anomie, regarding the 1960's social and economic ruptures permeates *Mad Men*. Thus when Don seeks other genres of composure besides nostalgia, he makes himself available to "an intensified and stressed out learning curve about how to maintain footing, bearings, a way of being, and new modes of composure amid unraveling institutions and social relations of reciprocity" (Berlant 197). In seeking a stable masculinity, Don reveals his disinclination to consider its performative nature, its being in time. Don's flailing after he disengages from nostalgia's narrative suggests he's not yet ready for the late twentieth-century discussions of identity that "proceed through analyses of its temporal complexity" by "conceptual shuttle movements that endlessly weave between the future and the past" (Sedgwick 68). If as Sara Ahmed explains, "the word 'emotion' comes from the Latin, *emovere*, referring to 'to move, to move out'" (11), then we might better see Don's free-fall and his search for a genre of composure as symbolic of his ontological drift.

It's no surprise, then, that the last scene of season four shows a newly engaged Don and Megan in bed, with Megan sleeping peacefully and Don staring longingly out a window, one of the show's motifs for Don's alienation. In this significant moment of his life, Don chooses stasis. He marries Megan and works diligently to manufacture a stable identity as husband, worker, and father—an identity he has imagined would bring him happiness. This kind of masculinity offers a narrative that might order Don's life in the same way nostalgia once did. Megan knows his past, but it doesn't affect her love for him, so duplicity will not distract Don from the ongoing now of his life. During his marriage to Megan, Don desires a stable home life that will fulfill its promise of happiness. When that falls short, neither heavy drinking nor adultery assuages his anxieties, as they only numb him from his reality. Even his former haven of professional achievement offers no solace: He has lost his footing. After Megan leaves the agency to pursue acting, after Peggy seeks to capitalize on her talents away from SCDP, and after Sally loses respect for her father upon finding him with Sylvia Rosen in flagrante delicto, Don begins to realize that no such stable masculinity is possible. His rebranding, his search for a stable stronghold, does not get him off the carousel and it does not help him to manage his anomie.

Thus Don Draper is a "precarious body," emblematic of the twentieth century's creation of a supposedly stable masculinity, one that prefigures a neoliberal "aesthetic shaped by the fraying of norms . . . [and] genres of reliable being" (Berlant 196). His flawed search for a stable manhood implies Don's difficulties in adjusting to changing times, times during which normative social structures guiding behavior break down, and contemporary viewers can see Don's precarity. Precarity, Berlant argues, emerges within what she calls the "neoliberal feedback loop" of the last half-century, involving a sense of insecurity that "provides the dominant *structure* and *experience* of the present moment, cutting across class and localities" (192). Therefore Don's disturbing free-fall in the opening credits portends not his eventual destruction but the late twentieth and early twenty-first century understanding that masculinity, the economy—really any category—is precarious, malleable, changeable. At each episode's beginning, as Robert A. Rushing notes, viewers are reminded that "Don falls, his world disintegrates, [and] identity is a construction that, when peered at too closely, opens up into a terrifying and vertiginous abyss of nothingness" (208). It signifies not a headlong pitch to death but, to borrow Berlant's words, the "adaptive imperative" at work in the "new precarious public sphere" of late capitalism (195).

Don might not fully understand his need to adapt, but *Mad Men*'s fans can see it. Our own backward glance at Don's version of masculinity is of course pleasurable; at the same time, though, it teaches contemporary viewers about the precarity of Don's reliance, and our own, on a stable masculinity—or any stability, even what we think of as the present moment. *Mad Men*'s striking opening image of a man freefalling past mid-century, dream-like advertisements produces a sensation thus shared between Don and *Mad Men* viewers, all of whom work to manufacture a stable past and present through nostalgia, each one "waiting quietly for the catastrophe of [one's] personality to seem beautiful again, and interesting, and modern."[7] After searching through various genres of composure for some stable self, for the real man named

Don Draper or Dick Whitman or otherwise, *Mad Men*'s protagonist, and the viewers as well, must face a reality much more precarious—the ongoing now, which is made and remade continuously, as in an impasse, right along with other socially constructed modes of being.

NOTES

1. Though endearing, *Downton Abbey*'s emphasis on melodrama undercuts any critique of the cultural work of a reflective nostalgia, allowing viewers to reminisce with escapist pleasure about Edwardian England, its pageantry and fashions, and its easily placated class conflicts. Matthew Crawley initially expressed reservations at accepting an elevation in class status, but the romance plot quickly overwhelmed his objections.

2. As Goodlad, Kaganovsky, and Rushing note, Sady Doyle, Benjamin Schwarz, Daniel Mendelsohn, and Mark Greif engage in an analysis of *Mad Men*'s "illusion of moral superiority" regarding the past (8). Greif argues, "We watch and know better about male chauvinism, homophobia, anti-semitism, workplace harassment, housewives' depression, nutrition and smoking. We wait for the show's advertising men or their secretaries and wives to make another gaffe for us to snigger over." As Michael Bérubé observes, Greif's comment is the "single most annoying criticism of *Mad Men*" (345).

3. A July 8, 2013 *New York Times* article "What Is Nostalgia Good For? Quite a Bit, Research Shows' details the popularity of this affective move.

4. Don has made the case for sentimental appeal before. When Peggy, in trying to find an angle to advertise Mohawk Airlines in "For Those You Think Young" (1.2), suggests "sex sells," Don makes clear his disdain for that approach: "Says who? Just so you know, the people who talk that way think that monkeys can do this. . . . YOU are the product. You *feeling* something. That's what sells. Not them. Not sex. They can't do what we do, and they hate us for it." As with Mohawk Airlines, with Kodak Don wants to manufacture a felt response that's deeper than the flash of technology or the "glittering lure" of sex. Don's job, then, is to make people feel something, a task at which he excels.

5. In "The Suitcase" (7.4), Don grieves over Anna Draper's death because, as he tells Peggy, she was the "only person in the world who really knew me."

6. By looking at branding strategies, Banat-Weiser analyzes a "crisis trope, one that encapsulates culture beyond crisis but is still enmeshed in the ongoing impact of recession by using a recuperative, capital friendly narrative to mobilize and authorize American working-class men to deal with the crisis individually, rather than call a flawed capitalist structure into question" (83).

7. Don Draper recites the poem "Mayakovsky" by Frank O'Hara at the end of "For Those Who Think Young" (2.1).

WORKS CITED

Ahmed, Sara. *The Cultural Politics of Emotion.* New York: Routledge, 2004. Print.

Banat-Weiser, Sarah. "'We Are All Workers': Economic Crisis, Masculinity, and the American Working Class." *Gendering the Recession: Media and Culture in an Age of Austerity.* Ed. Diane Negra and Yvonne Tasker. Durham: Duke UP, 2014. 81–106. Print.

Berlant, Lauren. *Cruel Optimism.* Durham: Duke UP, 2011. Print.

Bérubé, Michael. "Change Is Gonna Come, Same As It Ever Was." *Mad Men, Mad World: Sex, Politics, Style, and the 1960s.* Ed. Lauren M. E. Goodlad, Lilya Kaganovsky, and Robert A. Rushing. Durham: Duke, 2013. 345-59. Print.

Bordo, Susan. *The Male Body: A New Look at Men in Public and in Private.* New York: Farrar, 2000. Print.

Boym, Svetlana. *The Future of Nostalgia.* New York: Basic, 2001. Print.

Connell. R.W. "the History of Masculinity." *The Masculinity Studies Reader.* Ed. Rachel Adams and David Savran. Malden, MA: Blackwell, 2002. 245–61. Print.

Dames, Nicholas. *Amnesiac Selves: Nostalgia, Forgetting, and British Fiction, 1810–1870.* Oxford: Oxford UP, 2001. Print.

Frow, John. *Time and Commodity Culture: Essays in Cultural Theory and Postmodernity.* Oxford: Clarendon, 1997. Print.

Goodlad, Lauren M. E., Lilya Kaganovsky, and Robert A. Rushing. "Introduction." *Mad Men, Mad World: Sex, Politics, Style, and the 1960s.* Durham: Duke UP, 2013. 1-31. Print.

Greif, Mark. "You'll Love the Way It Makes You Feel." *London Review of Books* 23 Oct. 2008. Web. 17 July 2014.

Jameson, Fredric. *Postmodernism, or, The Cultural Logic of Late Capitalism.* Durham: Duke UP, 1991. Print.

Joyrich, Lynne. "Media Madness: Multiple Identity (Dis)Orders in *Mad Men.*" *Mad Men, Mad World: Sex, Politics, Style, and the 1960s.* Ed. Lauren M. E. Goodlad, Lilya Kaganovsky, and Robert A. Rushing. Durham: Duke UP, 2013. 213–37. Print.

Kimmel, Michael S. "The Birth of the Self-Made Man." *The Masculinity Studies Reader.* Ed. Rachel Adams and David Savran. Malden, MA: Blackwell, 2002. 135-52. Print.

———. Introduction. *Changing Men: New Directions in Research on Masculinity.* London: Sage, 1987. Print.

Martin, Brett. *Difficult Men: Behind the Scenes of a Creative Revolution: From* The Sopranos *and* The Wire *to* Mad Men *and* Breaking Bad. New York: Penguin, 2013. Digital.

Rushing, Robert A. "'It Will Shock You How Much This Never Happened': Antonioni and *Mad Men.*" *Mad Men, Mad World: Sex, Politics, Style, and the 1960s.* Ed. Lauren M. E. Goodlad, Lilya Kaganovsky, and Robert A. Rushing. Durham: Duke UP, 2013. 192–210. Print.

Sedgwick, Eve Kosofsky. *Touching Feeling: Affect, Pedagogy, Performativity.* Durham: Duke UP, 2003. Print.

Siska, William. "Men Behaving as Boys: The Culture of *Mad Men*." *Mad Men: Dream Come True TV*. Ed. Gary R. Edgerton. London: Tauris, 2011. 195–208. Print.

Tierney, John. "What Is Nostalgia Good For? Quite a Bit, Research Shows." *New York Times*. 8 July 2013. Web. 15 July 2014.

Varon, Jeremy. "History Gets in Your Eyes: *Mad Men*, Misrecognition, and the Masculine Mystique." *Mad Men, Mad World: Sex, Politics, Style, and the 1960s*. Ed. Lauren M. E. Goodlad, Lilya Kaganovsky, and Robert A. Rushing. Durham: Duke UP, 2013. 257–78. Print.

11

"Out Like a Man": Straddling the Postfeminist Fence in *Dexter* and *Breaking Bad*

Brenda Boudreau

In an interview with *Vulture*, *Breaking Bad* creator Vince Gilligan defended his female character Skyler White against the vitriolic responses generated among some fans: "We've been at events and had all our actors up onstage, and people ask Anna Gunn, 'Why is your character such a bitch?' And with the risk of painting with too broad a brush, I think the people who have these issues with the wives being too bitchy on *Breaking Bad* are misogynists, plain and simple" (Brown). It is this same Gilligan, however, who described the series' finale as having a fitting end for Walter White (Bryan Cranston): "As bad a guy as he has been, and as dark a series of misdeeds as he has committed, it felt right and satisfying and proper to us that he went out on his own terms; he out like a man" (Hudson). There is a contradiction underlying both these statements that mirrors the conflicting cultural attitudes toward masculinity and femininity that underlie both *Dexter* and *Breaking Bad*, both of which continue to generate colliding critical responses. Walking that line between anti-feminism, feminism, and postfeminism in paradoxical, even schizophrenic ways at times, is precisely what makes these series postfeminist texts worthy of interrogation as we consider what these series show us about our cultural attitudes to masculinity in the twenty-first century.[1]

In *Postfeminism: Cultural Texts and Theories*, Benjamin Brabon and Stéphanie Genz describe the postfeminist man as being "slightly bitter about the 'wounded' status of his masculinity," which has been affected by second wave feminism:

> He is a melting pot of masculinities, blending a variety of contested subject positions, as well as a chameleon figure still negotiating the ongoing impact of feminism on his identity. In short, the 'postfeminist man' is defined by his

problematic relationship with the ghost of hegemonic masculinity as he tries to reconcile the threat he poses to himself and the social systems he tries to uphold (143).

In *Dexter* and *Breaking Bad*, this "ghost" is even harder to pin down because Dexter (Michael C. Hall) and Walter White embody conflicting subject positions. I would suggest that this is even more complicated by both characters' roles as fathers and husbands, roles that really do become "ghosts of hegemonic masculinity."

Hegemonic masculinity is never quite fixed within either series, and stereotypical masculine roles are both contested and reinscribed, which is why the ghost metaphor seems so apropos. These are men, as Amanda Lotz notes in *Cable Guys: Television and Masculinities in the 21st Century*, who are pulled between patriarchal masculinity and feminist masculinity (35). The contradictions inherent in the series' trajectories, then, and the contradictory responses they elicit from audiences toward both the male and female characters, point to series that are straddling the postfeminist fence, and examined over the course of several years, what emerges is ultimately a troubling depiction of hegemonic masculinity as it relates to women.

Brabon and Genz write that postfeminism is "context-specific and has to be assessed dynamically in the relationships between its various manifestations and contexts" (5). Lotz takes this even further to suggest that hegemonic masculinity is series-specific and that the definition is constantly changing (40). I would suggest that we see this changeability even within the series' trajectories, particularly if they are long-running, as were *Breaking Bad* (six years) and *Dexter* (eight years). This instability of hegemonic masculinity is a key point from which to consider these two series, which are filled with contradictory masculinities—the distant 1950s patriarch to the sensitive 1980s "new man" who wants to be a genuine partner to his wife, to the 1990s selfish, narcissistic frat-boy who is happiest when he is removed from the company of women, to the twenty-first-century anti-hero who interacts with the world through violence and aggression.

Dexter and Walter are weirdly positioned within this postfeminist landscape as being influenced by postfeminist hegemonic ideals of marriage and fatherhood, while also demonstrating parodic nods to pre-second wave, 1950s families to 1990s fantasies of complete erasure of women who are too demanding. Dexter and Walter, then, are something a bit different from the heroic Hollywood father since they are "both victim and criminal": "This amalgam of features invites a complex reaction on the part of the audience— part envy, part identification, part empathy, part loathing, and part guilt for liking the guy" (Smith 395).[2] Both of these series complicate these reactions in highly troubling ways through the depiction of Walter's wife Skyler and

Dexter's wife Rita (Julie Benz), both of whom become scapegoats for the ambivalence audiences felt toward the antiheroic "heroes" of the series.

Amanda Lotz suggests that *Dexter* and *Breaking Bad* fit a particular paradigm of the post second-wave male-centered series that explore men who want to be good husbands and fathers, even though they ultimately fail. Lotz also suggests that women are not blamed for the confusion these male characters feel: "The men's relationships with the women in their lives are often troubled, but this is most commonly acknowledged as a result of the men's failure to live up to what the narrative presents as reasonable expectations of them" (88). I would argue, however, that neither series lets the women off the hook quite so easily, and whether intentional or not, the series' narratives led audiences to have a love/hate relationship with both Skyler and Rita. This in turn led to wildly divergent responses toward both wives, ranging from vitriolic blame for the wives' roles in their husbands' failures as men to sympathy for the male characters' inability to straddle the competing (and unrealistic) expectations placed on them within the family. Amanda Marcotte writes that the "anti-Skyler brigade seems to be part of larger trend of fans loathing wives on television—especially if they're married to anti-heroes—and this antipathy stems from underlying sexism that comes rushing out in the socially acceptable terms of hating a fictional character" (Marcotte). This is most decidedly true in both *Dexter* and *Breaking Bad* and forces us to interrogate what both series were trying to say in the postfeminist landscape of the twenty-first century.

DEXTER: PERFORMANCE OR PARODY?

Dexter is the character whose masculinity seems the most unstable given his own sense of self-identity divorced from the heteronormative world. Each season of the show presented a new model of hegemonic masculinity which did not always align very well with each other, and, when taken together, point to our cultural anxieties about masculinity. This may have been part of the point that the writers were trying to make, but it was unsettling for many viewers at the time, trying to reconcile how they were supposed to respond to their beloved anti-heroes. We are positioned to feel sympathy for Dexter as a "damaged" man whose murderous impulses were thrust upon him when he watched his own mother cut into pieces with a chainsaw when he was only three years old.

His stepfather, Harry (James Remar), helped Dexter to channel his need to kill in a "socially responsible" way—by only killing proven criminals who somehow managed to dodge the justice system, and throughout the series we see him as "just" serial killer whose violence is necessary, even desirable. It is no accident that so many of Dexter's victims are rapists, or the sexual and physical abusers of women and children. As Isabel Santaularia writes, "The society that serves as his hunting ground is presented as deficient, if not rotten to the core, so his role as Dark Defender is even more justifiable in the series' diegesis" (61). Dexter then, develops a superhero persona, which, like Clark Kent, is hidden from everyone around him. Before a kill, he dons green cargo pants, a tight green shirt, leather boots, and leather gloves, cuing the viewer that he has switched identities. In these clothes, Dexter is extremely strong, aggressive, and lethal, and despite his gruesome murders, we applaud his vigilante justice: "Within a representational world where dominant masculinity is synonymous with violence (and particularly violence toward women), this opens a space for Dexter's unusual heroism" (Arellano 13).

Dexter's proclivities make it almost impossible for him to connect in meaningful ways with other human beings, other than his now deceased wife and his sister Deb (Jennifer Carpenter). Dexter's social isolation begins to erode in the second season, however, when he meets Rita Bennett, and literally becomes her savior when he plants evidence to send her abusive, drug-addicted ex-husband to prison. He also becomes the protector of Rita's children, another role that allows him to feel more like a father. So, for example, one day at the grocery store he sees Astor (Christina Robinson) talking to a man, and thinks, "My highly honed senses detect another predator sniffing around one of my cubs" ("The Lion Sleeps Tonight" 3.3). This man, will of course, end up on Dexter's kill table when Dexter verifies that he is a pedophile. When Rita becomes pregnant, Dexter has to decide if he wants a conventional life enough to risk detection. Dexter is less in love with Rita and her family than he is with the idea of fitting into some kind of traditional family role, one that he had assumed was not open to him. Dexter makes it clear through his voiceovers that he is an actor performing a role, one that might become "real" if he is convincing enough to others and himself.

To really understand hegemonic masculinity within the series, however, we have to analyze Rita as a character. Like Walter in *Breaking Bad*, Dexter ends up with a woman who is his intellectual inferior, at least as she is presented within the show. Rita is in many ways a stereotypical dumb blond, initially buying Dexter's flimsy and frequent excuses for his absences and disappearances. Dexter knows that Rita is a victim of an emotionally and physically abusive husband because his sister Deb had saved Rita's life after a domestic violence call. Dexter likes Rita because she is somewhat passive and undemanding and is not particularly interested in physical intimacy given her previous relationship. During the four seasons she was in the show, Dexter emerged as a more positive man, one who really did seem to want to be a good husband and father. Rita and her children, however, did not integrate well into Dexter's nightly stalking and killing, and audiences started to see

Figure 11.1. Dexter (Michael C. Hall) saw marital therapy as one more unreasonable demand from Rita (Julie Benz). *(Dexter)*

Rita as an obstacle to what Dexter was "supposed" to do, according to his father Harry's code.

Later in the series, Dexter's hegemonic masculinity shifts as Rita becomes more demanding and begins questioning Dexter's absences and excuses, particularly after they marry. So, for example, she is understandably angry when she finds out that Dexter has kept his apartment after they move in together, finding out only when his landlord calls to report a problem ("Dirty Harry" 4.5). Most of Rita's interaction with Dexter is trying to get him to be more communicative and honest with her, but she becomes increasingly more demanding and more suspicious of Dexter's nighttime disappearances, frequently nagging him and checking up on him at work. Dexter finds it increasingly difficult to try and execute his kills when he is up feeding an infant at 2 a.m. or rushing to make appointments with a marital therapist that Rita insists are necessary to save their marriage. Dexter starts to fail as a serial killer, becoming sloppy and careless. As with Skyler White in *Breaking Bad*, websites and fan blogs began appearing that called Rita "annoying" and "whining and controlling," and when Rita was finally killed by the Trinity Killer at the end of season four, many of the posts celebrated her death, feeling that she was dragging down the show.

While *Dexter* often relied on dark comedy, the tone of the initial episodes in season five is troubling. Dexter decides not to call Astor and Cody and "ruin" their Disney vacation with their grandparents with news of their mother's death. When they return, after Dexter tells them he is "sorry for their loss," they sit on the couch in Mickey Mouse ears in shocked silence until Astor blurts out, "Where were *you* when someone was killing her? You should have been there to protect her" ("My Bad" 5.1). This, however, is precisely where the ghost of hegemonic masculinity is pushed to the margins in this particular series since the narrative is filtered through Dexter's perspective. Dexter's voiceovers certainly suggest that he feels a sense of guilt for not having killed the Trinity Killer earlier, but it doesn't take long for him to be relieved that Astor and Cody decide to live with their grandparents and for him to move on. Once he packs up all the boxes in the house he shared with Rita, he muses, "Life seems different, manageable. Everything is in its right place" ("Everything is Illumenated" 5.6). When he has to go out at night for the kill, he has a nanny ready to fill in, one who, unlike Rita, asks no questions and makes no demands.

The first two episodes of season six show yet another new side of Dexter, one in which Dexter becomes a walking contradiction of masculine performativity by being a wounded, widowed husband who lost his wife in a horrific way, but one ready to redefine single fatherhood without looking back toward the past. Dexter is very sweet and gentle with Harrison throughout this season, but he rarely spends much time with him other than to occasionally make him breakfast or to get him ready for bed. In truth, Dexter does very little of the actual day to day parenting of his son, hiring full-time nannies who are willing to work around the clock. Anyone who has spent time with an active two-year-old would laugh out loud when the nanny Jamie says that she is lucky to have the job so she can work on her dissertation. Harrison is not a normal child, however. He sits, practically unmoving most of the time and almost seems like he has been drugged.[3]

Dexter also develops a sexual prowess and confidence that was missing in the other seasons. Thus, when he goes to his high school reunion, purportedly to avenge the death of a woman who was murdered by her husband, Dexter discovers that all of a sudden he is "popular," valorized for his job as a blood spatter expert, sympathized with over the death of his poor wife Rita ("Those Kinds of Things" 6.1). All of a sudden Dexter is "cool" and "sexy." We see the masculine performativity highlighted even further at this reunion when Dexter decides to participate in a flag football game in order to get a blood sample to verify the guilt of his next victim—Dexter the "lab geek" is suddenly the "tough guy" on the field, exciting his father Harry's ghost as he coaches from the sidelines ("Those Kinds of Things" 6.1). As Lotz notes, "Dexter enters into conversation with notions of masculinity, primarily in the way the series makes the performative nature of masculinity more evident than most" (112). Once Rita has been removed from the picture, there is definitely a sense that Dexter can perform a completely different kind of masculinity, and he can avoid the women who may judge him for it.

By the end of season six, Dexter takes on the role of cultural hero to such a degree that he becomes almost a parodic caricature of a superhero, which, like other serial killers' masculinity, "is also related to the preservation of moral values, justice, and/or law and order" (Santaularia 59). Dexter first saves the entire Miami Police department (and his sister Deb) from a poisonous gas attack ("Talk to the Hand" 6.11). Dexter gets dumped into the ocean, narrowly escaping being killed by the Doomsday Killer. When he is picked up by a passing boat filled with refugees, he has to rescue everyone on board when a man tries to rob the passengers ("This Is the Way the World Ends" 6.12). And finally, and most importantly, Dexter has to singlehandedly rescue his son. As Susanne Kord and Elisabeth Krimmer note, "By saddling the Father with the sole responsibility for the son's survival, father films imply that the nuclear family is irrelevant" (51). The final season of Dexter belies this observation, however. Once Harrison becomes a walking, talking human being, he becomes a threat to Dexter, and he is a responsibility that Dexter knows he cannot handle alone. In the final season, Dexter decides that he does not have to continue killing and can create a conventional life as a husband and father, but this decision leads to the murder of his sister Deb. Dexter realizes that he will only ever be a liability to his family. He decides to send Harrison off with his new girlfriend Hannah (Yvonne Strahovski), a former serial killer who purports to love Dexter and Harrison, and whom Harrison clearly loves. Yet even though Hannah is still a manipulative liar and murderer, the audience accepted her more than the non-killer Rita. And Dexter exits the show as a "good" father, even though his choice sends Harrison into permanent hiding in Argentina with Hannah, as she flees US prosecution. (6.12). Dexter's performance of (anti-)hero and family man over this series demonstrates the excuses society is willing to extend to masculinity, and the expectations placed on women to support manly behavior.

BREAKING BAD: TAMING OF THE "BITCH"

As in *Dexter*, *Breaking Bad* also reveals the ghost of hegemonic masculinity given the contradictory masculinities exhibited during the series' six-year run. In what has become one of the most quoted lines from *Breaking Bad*, meth-producing king Gus Fring (Giancarlo Esposito) tries to convince Walter White to cook meth for him, even though Walter is worried that his family is falling apart: "What does a *man* do? A man *provides* for his family—and he does it even when he's not appreciated, not respected, or even loved. He simply bears up. He does it *because* he's a man" ("Mas" 3.5). What defines a man becomes central to *Breaking Bad*, and it obviously was one question that carried through to the end of the series. These lines resonate throughout the series when we consider Walter's wife Skyler (Anna Gunn), who prompted extensive Twitter, Facebook, and blog posts. Skyler becomes the linchpin around which Walt's hegemonic masculinity is constructed, and there is a strong suggestion that Walter had no idea how to respond to the postfeminist masculinity models expected of him. I would agree with Sady Doyle who wrote on the website *In These Times* that responses to Skyler were not simply the fodder of misogynistic interpretation: "Early ideas of Skyler as uptight or nagging weren't just the inevitable result of misogynists seeing a not-completely-submissive wife expressing anger: They were, more or less, built into the script" (Beyerstein and Doyle). Whether they were aware of it or not, then, the writers of the show demonstrated a more entrenched ghost of hegemonic masculinity that positioned Skyler to take the wrath of a lot of fans.

Initially, we sympathize with Walter White, who, despite the fact that he is a high yield meth producer, and later, a murderer, insists that he does so to support his family. Motivated by being given only months to live as a result of lung cancer, Walter White decides to start cooking meth, believing that he can make a lot of money quickly to leave for his wife, disabled teenaged son, and the new baby on the way. He decides that if he is going to die anyway, he at least wants to leave his family enough money to pay for expenses when he is gone, and he settles on the sum of $737,000. At this point his ambitions are fairly modest—he wants to leave his wife with money to pay off the house, and leave money for his son and daughter's college expenses.

At first, we see Walter as a victim of a multiply pronged assault of an economy that has pushed white males to the margins: "Perhaps the most customary marker of authority—wealth, or the ability to earn it—has also changed dramatically for American men over the past generation, with the impact of economic recessions, increasing unemployment, and rising expectations of material possession further impacting the ability of men to achieve the same perceived potency as their forebears" (Shary 2). Walter is a high school chemistry teacher by day, trying to make chemistry interesting to a room filled with bored, disengaged, and often disrespectful students. He makes $43,000 a year in a job he knows he is totally overqualified for, and he has "seen every person [he has] ever known surpass [him] in every way" ("Bit by a Dead Bee" 2.3). He also has a son with cerebral palsy and he and his wife Skyler have an unplanned baby on the way. After school, he is forced to take on another job (presumably because his job as a teacher does not give him enough money to support his family), working at a low level job in a carwash and being pushed around by his Romanian boss, subjected to the humiliation of students' laughter when they spot him shining tires.

In the first three seasons, Skyler is often presented as a nagging, controlling wife who believes Walt needs her to empower him to stand up to his boss, who chastises him for using the wrong credit card, and one who does not seem to have much respect for her husband's self-determination. So, for example, when she hears that Walt has cancer, her first response is to find the best doctor, who is, unfortunately, not part of their HMO. Walt wants to refuse any treatment at all, when he hears the $90,000 price tag, but Skyler will not even talk about options ("Cancer Man" 1.4). Skyler has been described as "emasculating": "She is presented as a hefty percentage of Walter's problem; he needs to take back his manhood from her. Since Walter is our central protagonist, our Everyman to whom we relate, we can't really help seeing Skyler negatively" ("Round Table Discussion: Skyler Hating Online"). There is an obvious suggestion in these first three seasons that there has been a systemic derailment of white male privilege that has caught Walter in its crosshairs, and he has become a victim of the erosion of masculinity, particularly as it is wrapped up in the role of Father and husband. In this series, at least part of the blame is directed to Skyler, which is why lines from Walt to Skyler such as "Will you do that for me honey? Will you please, just once, get off my ass" are spread throughout the Internet on YouTube and other "Best quotes from *Breaking Bad*" sites ("Cat's in the Bag" 1.2). On the surface, it's easy to blame Skyler if we don't analyze why Walter's life is in its current "poor me" state.

Given what we learn about Walter as the series progresses, however, it becomes more difficult to see him solely as a victim of external forces. Walter is a victim of what Stephanie Coontz calls the "masculine mystique," which "encourages men to neglect their own self-improvement on the assumption that sooner or later their 'manliness' will be rewarded" (Coontz). Walter does not take an active role in improving his lot in life, and if anything, his complacency is juxtaposed to his earlier premarital successes. He cofounded a hugely successful biotech company called Gray Matter with his friend Elliott Schwartz (Adam Godley). So the question becomes why Walter would have chosen to go teach in a high school. Whatever motivated him to move away from Gray Matter, the way other scientists talk about his amazing research at Elliott's birthday party ("Gray Matter" 1.5) suggests that Walter could have found another job easily in another lab.

Part of Walter's hegemonic masculinity ghost, then, is as a beleaguered and oppressed man, but it doesn't really make sense when we hear more about his past. It's never entirely clear why he sold off his shares in the company for $5,000, other than a vague disagreement with his then girlfriend Gretchen (Jessica Hecht), who eventually married Elliott. Later, Walter tries to insist to Gretchen that she and Elliott cut him out of the company and stole his ideas, but she suggests that Walter walked out the door one day with barely any explanation, walking away from the company and from his relationship with her. So though Walter may believe he deserves better from life, he has blocked possibilities for financial or professional reward.

Walter seems to have internalized the ghost of hegemonic masculinity even more so than Dexter because he has very traditional ideals about what his role as father and husband entails—namely, being a provider for his family. He is intensely proud and does not want to accept money from anyone, not even a loan from his brother-in-law. He is furious when Skyler tells Gretchen and Elliott that he has cancer (1.5). Again the reality of the situation does not seem to align with Walter's characterization of the pair, who seem genuinely happy to see him and sincere in their offer to give him a job so he can tap into their excellent health insurance. Walter refuses to accept any kind of money from them, even if it might mean hastening his death, so when he continues to cook meth, we know he chooses this option to protect his own ego. This is not the first time we see the large chip on his shoulder that Walter is carrying, and it won't be the last.

Skyler feels trapped by this empty machismo, given her desperation to keep Walt alive. Walt's lies get progressively more complex and far-fetched, adding insult to injury for Skyler, who predictably felt insulted and furious by Walter's lack of respect for her intelligence. This is highlighted in Walter's lies about a second cell phone. Skyler is ultimately smarter than Rita because she at least pushes for the truth about Walt's erratic behavior, but she is also left feeling deeply disappointed when he is physically and emotionally unavailable to her during her pregnancy. Virtually all of the attention is on Walt given his cancer diagnosis and treatment, but as Rebecca Price-Wood notes, Skyler would have been extremely worried about the birth of a second child given she and Walt's ages and the fact that her first son had a birth defect (133).[4] Walt goes to very little effort to care for Skyler during her pregnancy, and indeed, Walter decides to ignore Skyler's texts and calls announcing that the baby is coming, instead making a meth deal. It is her boss Ted Beneke (Christopher Cousins) who takes Skyler to the hospital and is still there when Walter finally arrives, long after his daughter has been born. Walt expresses very little apology for not being there for Holly's birth, other than a lame excuse that he got caught in a traffic jam, which Skyler accepts without argument.

Responses to Skyler White were even more vitriolic than to Rita Bennett, and blogs and wikis and Facebook pages described Skyler as a passive aggressive bitch who had no faith in or respect for her husband. Anna Gunn, the actress who played Skyler, even wrote an open letter to the *New York Times* expressing frustration with the hatred fans openly expressed in a variety of forums and a fear about the way these feelings were being transferred to her as the actress rather than just the character she played: "I finally realized that most people's hatred of Skyler had little to do with me and a lot to do with their own perception of women and wives. Because Skyler didn't conform to a comfortable ideal of the archetypical female, she had become a kind of Rorschach test for society, a measure of our attitudes toward gender" (Gunn). Marcotte writes that the "anti-Skyler brigade seems to be part of larger trend of fans loathing wives on television—especially if they're married to anti-heroes—and this antipathy stems from underlying sexism that comes rushing out in the socially acceptable terms of hating a fictional character." This sexism, however, seems to very deliberately refuse the reality of Skyler's very real physical and psychological situation.

Very few Skyler haters have pointed to Walter's control of his wife, including his insistence that he control Skyler's body throughout her pregnancy. For example, Walt is furious when he finds out that Skyler has smoked a few cigarettes while being pregnant and tried to flush the remaining pack down the toilet: "I'd like an explanation. You're pregnant for God's sake!" ("Gray Matter Technology" 2.5). He also berates her for eating frozen paninis without his permission: "I thought we nixed those? Aren't those the ones with the off-the-chart sodium?" (2.5). The suggestion in these two scenes is that this kind of bodily control has been ongoing, and Skyler is afraid of Walt's response, strongly alluding to psychological abuse. In one very disturbing scene in season two, Walter even attempts to rape Skyler who is wearing an avocado skin mask, pushing her face violently against the refrigerator and forcing down her underwear, until she manages to pull away in anger and horror, telling him that he cannot take out his anger and frustration on her ("Seven Thirty-Seven" 2.1). Even here, some fans posted disgust at Skyler's refusal to excuse her obviously sick and terrified husband.

Hatred was also directed toward Skyler when she does not divorce Walter but instead decides to help him launder the money he has made by buying a car wash; many viewers saw her as a hypocrite and a gold-digger. Her affair with Ted Beneke, however, was the catalyst that really sent Skyler haters over the deep end as an "action more reprehensible that marital rape" (Rosenberg). By this point in the series, however, Skyler had seen a dark and controlling side of her husband, and no doubt she believed that jealousy might be a way to drive Walter out of the house after he refuses to grant her a divorce.

Walt's understanding of hegemonic masculinity in terms of fatherhood also tried to marginalize his wife, despite the fact that he was ultimately a bad parent. While his role as father is key to Walter's identity, he rarely communicates with his son in any deep and meaningful way and seems largely disconnected from him. This is highlighted in season two when Walter Jr. (R. J. Mitte) changes his name to Flynn; Walt finds this out when a friend of Walter Jr.'s comes to the door asking for him. When Walt tells Skyler that he doesn't understand what's wrong with Walter Jr., Skyler says, "Don't take it personally. He wants his own identity" ("Down" 2.4). While Walter Jr. considers his father a "great dad," he valorizes his "bad-ass" Uncle Hank (Dean Norris), the DEA agent, over his own father in a way that fuels Walt's anger and jealousy. Clearly reacting after hearing the news that his cancer has gone into remission, Walter pours both Hank and Walter Jr. a shot of tequila ("Over" 2.10). Significantly, Hank is again regaling Walt Jr. with stories of his DEA successes. When Walt pours a second shot for his son, Hank starts to express concern: "The kid's sixteen! What are you doing, going for Father of the Year?" When Hank tries to walk off with the bottle, Walt stands up to him for the first time: "Bring that bottle back! My son, my bottle, my house," smiling slightly when he hears his son vomiting behind him into the pool.

In many ways, this is a turning point for Walter because it is not his son's welfare that is uppermost in his own mind, but proving his own masculinity to his brother-in-law. Indeed, the series was filled with children being put in danger. As Emily Nussbaum notes, audiences of *Breaking Bad* seemed willing to look the other way with the amount of times that *Breaking Bad* put children in danger, trusting Walter to do his best to protect them: "The audience has been trained by cable television to react this way: to hate the nagging wives, the dumb civilians, who might sour the fun of masculine adventure. 'Breaking Bad' increases that cognitive dissonance, turning some viewers into not merely fans but enablers" ("Child's Play"). This is one of many examples that suggests that contradictory hegemonic masculinity pushes outside the boundaries of the show, reflecting a deeply troubling response to gender roles.

By season five, Walter has also become, like Dexter, a caricature of power. He has adopted the persona of Heisenberg, his meth producing pseudonym, more completely, with his shaved head, goatee, black clothing and hat, even at home. Skyler by this point is fully involved in his "business venture" and when she expresses nervousness about the danger, he responds, "Do you know how much I make in a year? I am *not* in danger. I *am* the danger. *I* am the one who knocks" ("Cornered" 4.6). Now he is making more money than he knows what to do with, spending it recklessly. He buys his son a flashy sports car; when Skyler insists that he return it, he and Walter Jr. blow it up, completely disregarding the nearly $50,000 it cost him.

He no longer makes any pretense about cooking meth exclusively for his family. He kills Gus Fring, his key competitor, and he kills his new partner Mike, paving the way for himself to be king of the meth production in the southwest and beyond. It is no longer for the money (which is stacked, un-used, in a storage bin) ("Gliding All Over" 5.8). As Jason Landrum notes in "Say My Name," "Walt's ceaseless drive to succeed as a criminal is a fantasy of masculinity liberated from symbolic dissatisfaction that mobilizes the hidden enjoyment lurking behind our post-millennial culture" (104). He has become "bad," and he's okay with that—as long as he continues to be the breadwinner of his household and the father to his children. This hegemonic masculinity really is a specter by this point in the series, however.

When Walter insists that he is going to keep cooking meth even after he and his remaining partner Jesse (Aaron Paul) have the potential to pocket five million dollars, Walter explains that that he is now in the "empire business" ("Buy Out" 5.6). Clearly the power that Walt inherits after Gus's death has gone to his head, and he no longer makes any real pretense of wanting to keep the family together, telling Jesse, "She [Skyler] made me kick my own kids out of the house. She told me she was counting days until my cancer came back. This business is all I have left now. And you want to take it away from me?" ("Buyout" 5.6). It is surprising that Walt wants to keep Skyler close to him because she makes it very clear that she can't stand him and is a "hostage" in her own home, feeling obligated to let Walter into her bed to keep her children absent and safe.

As with *Dexter*, *Breaking Bad* began its final season with the family teetering on the edge of destruction. Things unravel very quickly for Walter— Skyler hates him; his partner Jesse can't stand him and, in fact, is willing to make a deal with Hank and the DEA to take Walter down. Walter Jr. is barely talking to him for allowing Skyler to send the kids to live with Hank and Marie. By the end of the season and of the series, Walter's cancer returns, but before he dies, he inadvertently takes his family down with him, despite finding a way to leave millions for his son. When Hank figures out that Walter is Heisenberg, he and Marie also figure out that Skyler has known for a long time, making Marie hate her sister. Jesse is kidnapped and tortured by Walter's main competition and forced to produce the blue meth. He is "rescued" by Walter, but he is left with nothing to show for the pain Walter had put him through. Hank and his partner are killed by Walt's rival drug dealers. Walt finally admits to Skyler that he did everything not for the family but because he liked it and it made him feel "alive" ("Felina" 5.16), showing his lack of regard for her. When Walter Jr. finds out that his mother knew exactly what was going on, he says, perhaps, rightly, that she is "just as bad" as Walter ("Ozymandias" 5.14). Even though Walter gives Skyler information with which to make a deal with the police, there is no doubt that Skyler is going to go to prison at least for some time, leaving her son and daughter behind.[5] No one touched by Hank has any reason to feel grateful to him.

Neither man presumably was able to see that their criminal activities would ultimately put their families directly in harm's way, and when push came to shove, they really were incapable of caring enough to stop their behaviors. Even at the end of the series when we see Walter dying alone after being shot, and Dexter alone in a logging camp in Oregon, we feel conflicted: are we meant to applaud their final apologies and admittance of guilt? Are we supposed to respect their willingness to sacrifice themselves for their families' well-being or are we supposed to hate them for their narcissistic selfishness that put their family members in harm's way in the first place? These were series built on the contradictory personas of their main characters, and this lack of answers may be why many viewers were so disappointed in the series' finales.

As Matt Zoller Seitz said in *Vulture*, at the end of *Breaking Bad*, Walter remains "a horrendously manipulative, dishonest, coldblooded, violent, destructive person, and now he's reaping the consequences of all the ill-advised or outright evil choices he has made" and yet audiences were still rooting for him. The same could be said of Dexter. Harrison has been left fatherless after Dexter stages his own death and disappears into a logging camp, and Harrison will be in permanent hiding in Argentina with Hannah, a woman who may or may not remain loyal to her promise to Dexter to care for his son. To return to Vince Gilligan's quote at the beginning of this chapter that Walter White "went out like a man," he also said in an interview that he felt that there was some redemption at the end of the series: "Walt has failed on so many levels, but he has managed to do the one thing he set out to do, which is a victory. He has managed to make his family financially sound in his absence, and that was really the only thing he set out to do in that first episode. So, mission accomplished" (Snierson). Given the number of dead bodies and shattered lives, this seems like a small accomplishment. Ultimately, if we focus on the audience's response to the wives of these so-called anti-heroes, neither series leaves us feeling very settled about postfeminist masculinity at the turn of the century, suggesting that the "ghost of hegemonic masculinity" has yet to be exorcised.

NOTES

1. I will use the term postfeminist here, following Benjamin Brabon and Stéphanie Genz's assertion that "In its various manifestations, postfeminism exhibits a number of relations to feminism ranging from complacency to hostility, admiration to repudiation" (12); even though I would agree with Amanda Lotz in *Cable Guys* that the term is "fraught with contradictory meanings" (23). This analysis will focus on precisely these contradictory meanings within each series.

2. In the last two decades, several studies have been done examining masculine anxiety manifested in fatherhood and the way Hollywood chooses to explore it. See, for example, Michael Kimmel, *Misframing Men: The Politics of Contemporary Masculinities*. Stella Bruzzi, *Bringing Up Daddy: Fatherhood and Masculinity in Post-*

War Hollywood, London: BFI, 2005, Nicola Rehling, *Extra-Ordinary Men: White Heterosexual Masculinity in Popular Culture*. Plymouth, UK: Lexington Books, 2009; Donna Peberdy, *Masculinity and Film Performance: Male Angst in Contemporary American Cinema*, New York: Palgrave Macmillan, 2011; Timothy Shary, *Millennial Masculinity: Men in Contemporary American Cinema*. Detroit: Wayne State, UP, 2013, Joel Gwynne and Nadine Muller, eds. *Hollywood Fatherhood: Paternal Postfeminism and Contemporary Hollywood Cinema*. New York: Palgrave Macmillan, 2013.

3. Note: very few critics have suggested that Harrison might also be suffering from PTSD, having witnessed his mother's murder and being left sitting in her blood, crying, a scene obviously reminiscent of Dexter and his brother witnessing their own mother's death and left there for three days.

4. Price-Wood also suggests in "Breaking Bad Stereotypes about Postpartum: A Case for Skyler White" that Skyler was no doubt suffering from a period of postpartum depression mood disorder that virtually no critics have explored that would have explained some of her irritation and anger (135), as well as her decision not to leave Walter after she finds out the truth about his meth cooking in order to protect her son (138).

5. Emily Nussbaum, among others, have noted that Walter gave a "gift" to his wife with a final, horrifying phone call, which, while it gave Skyler an alibi, also let Walt say what he felt: "that Skyler is a whiner, a nag, a drag, responsible for anything that happened to her . . . he relishes calling her a bitch" ("That Mindbending").

WORKS CITED

Arellano, Lisa. "The Heroic Monster: Dexter, Masculinity, and Violence. "*Television & New Media* (2012): 1527476412450192. Web. 7 May 2015.

Beyerstein, Lindsay, and Sady Doyle. "Breaking Bad's Skyler White: Villain or Victim?" *In These Times*. 28 Aug. 2013. Web. 5 May 2015.

Brown, Lane. "In Conversation: Vince Gilligan on the End of Breaking Bad." *Vulture*. 12 May 2013. Web. 14 May 2015.

Coontz, Stéphanie. "The Myth of Male Decline." *New York Times*. 29 Sept. 2012: n.pag. Web. 14 May 2015.

Genz, Stéphanie and Benjamin A. Brabon. *Postfeminism: Cultural Texts and Theories*. Edinburgh: Edinburgh UP, 2012. Print.

Gunn, Anna. "I Have a Character Issue." *New York Times*. 23 Aug. 2013. Web. 5 May 2015.

Hudson, Laura. "Die Like a Man: The Toxic Masculinity of Breaking Bad." *Wired*. 5 Oct. 2013. Web.

Kord, Susanne, and Elisabeth Krimmer. *Contemporary Hollywood Masculinities: Gender, Genre and Politics*. New York: Palgrave Macmillan, 2011. Print.

Landrum, Jason. "Say My Name: The Fantasy of Liberated Masculinity." *The Methods of Breaking Bad: Essays on Narrative, Character and Ethics*. Ed. Jacob Blevins and Dafydd Wood. Jefferson, NC: McFarland, 2015. 94–107. Print.

Lotz, Amanda D. *Cable Guys: Television and Masculinities in the 21st Century*. New York: New York UP, 2014. Print.

Marcotte, Amanda. "Breaking Bad TV Expectations." *The American Prospect*. 17 Aug. 2102. Web. 13 May 2105.

Nussbaum, Emily. "Child's Play: 'Breaking Bad's' Bad Dad." *The New Yorker*. 27 Aug. 2012. Web. 11 May 2015.

———. "That Mind-Bending Phone Call on Last Night's 'Breaking Bad.'" *The New Yorker*. 16 Sept. 2013. Web. 7 May 2015.

Price-Wood, Rebecca. "Breaking Bad Stereotypes about Postpartum: A Case for Skyler White." *The Methods of Breaking Bad: Essays on Narrative, Character and Ethics*. Ed. Jacob Blevins and Dafydd Wood. Jefferson, NC: McFarland, 2015. 94–107. Print.

Rosenberg, Alyssa. "How Anna Gun's Performance as Skyler White Changed Television." *The Washington Post* 26 Aug. 2014: n.pag. Web. 9 May 2015.

"Round Table Discussion: Skyler-Hating Online." *Masculinity in Breaking Bad*. Ed. Bridget Rousell Cowlishaw. Jefferson, NC: McFarland, 2015: 132–38. Print.

Santaularia, Isabel. "Dexter: Villain, Hero or Simply a Man? The Perpetuation of Traditional Masculinity in *Dexter*." *Atlantis: Journal of the Spanish Association of Anglo-American Studies* 32, no. 2 (2010): 57–71. Print.

Seitz, Matt Zoller. "Seitz on Breaking Bad and Why Viewers Need to Whitewash Walter White". *Vulture*. 18 Sept. 2013. Web. 5 May 2015.

Shary, Timothy. *Millennial Masculinity: Men in Contemporary American Cinema*. Detroit: Wayne State UP, 2013. Print.

Smith, Victoria. "Our Serial Killers, Our Superheroes, and Ourselves: Showtime's *Dexter*." *Quarterly Review of Film and Video* 28, no. 5 (2011): 395–400. Print.

Snierson, Dan. "Breaking Bad: Creator Vince Gilligan Explains the Finale." *Entertainment Weekly* 30 Sept. 2013: n. pag. Web. 7 May 2015.

12

Last Men Standing: Will Smith as the Obsolete Patriarchal Male

Elizabeth Abele

In the twenty-first century, Will Smith built on his exceptional position in Hollywood as "King of the Fourth of July" to move to films where he represents the last adult male of his kind: *I, Robot* (2004), *I Am Legend* (2007), *Hancock* (2008), and *After Earth* (2013). These science fiction fantasies offer conversations about the potential and limitations of traditional masculinity, conversations in which Smith's race exists only as a subtext. His protagonist in *I Am Legend* is of particular interest since it is set in a seat of Western patriarchal power—Manhattan—and because it intersects with US and British millennial zombie films. *I Am Legend* joins these zombie films in asking which men can (or should) survive in the face of a zombie apocalypse.[1] In a related fashion, in his millennial roles, Smith serves as the ultimate representative of American male power and prowess—whose own exceptionalism may make him obsolete, unlike the male survivors of zombie films.

At the time that Sidney Poitier (1960s) and Eddie Murphy (1980s) became major Hollywood stars, they were unique as African American leading men.[2] However, when Will Smith emerged as a box-office star, he joined the company of Denzel Washington, Laurence Fishburne, Morgan Freeman, and Wesley Snipes, who were likewise headlining action films in the mid-1990s. *Bad Boys* (1995) directly acknowledges this context, as the characters played by Martin Lawrence and Will Smith compare themselves to Morgan Freeman ("you could be driving Miss Daisy") and Wesley Snipes in *Passenger 57* (directed by African American Kevin Hooks). These quips demonstrate that by the time Smith hit the big screen, a range of African American males images were available. The blockbusters of Smith's early career presented him as a cool (black) male protagonist with the potential to energize traditionally male genres and American masculinity—*Bad Boys*, *Independence Day* (1996),

Men in Black (1997), *Wild Wild West* (1999). In these films his race is referenced, but more often as an asset than a defining characteristic.

Smith's protagonists are secure in who they are, insisting on bringing their own values into their jobs, rather than allowing the job to transform them. In *Men in Black*, as Agent K (Tommy Lee Jones) trains Agent J (Will Smith), J challenges K to bring humor and compassion to the job. And ultimately, Agent J is not being trained as a partner (sidekick), but is in fact being groomed to replace K: even K realizes that his stoic version of masculinity is outdated. In *Independence Day*, Hiller refuses to sacrifice his commitment to his stripper-girlfriend and her son for military advancement; again, it is his maverick qualities and sense of style that transform the military (and save the world), not the other way around. David Magill characterizes Will Smith as operating in these films as a "racial trickster" (131), who recodes "black hipness as accessible to white mainstream audiences" (129)—and particularly useful in defeating Europeans and aliens.

Smith first merged this hipness and confidence with fatherhood in his early films *Independence Day* (1996) and *Enemy of the State* (1998). Hannah Hamad notes how Smith's protagonists moved from "fatherlessness" to "father figure," culminating in his father role in *Pursuit of Happyness* as "a model of postfeminist fatherhood, . . . which negotiates discourses of postracialism and neoliberalism, coalescing around the figure of the upwardly mobile African American postfeminist father" (132). However, in Smith's most recent roles, he has moved away from this progressive position to join the ranks of traditional masculinity—often to his characters' detriment. His protagonists' fatherhood has become stale and confining, particularly as the commander in *After Earth*.

From presenting a more fluid solution to the challenges of traditional (white) masculinity at the end of the twentieth century, Smith's twenty-first-century characters more often embody patriarchal authority. The move of these characters reflects Herman Gray's observation that in this century "a small but highly visible cohort of black cultural workers enjoys access to institutional resources, especially the forms of legitimization, prestige, and recognition that such institutions bestow" (13). In these postracial worlds of these films, Smith's protagonists demonstrate the traps of traditional masculinity—traps to men in power that are presented as equally open to black men. In *The Will to Change: Men, Masculinity, and Love*, bell hooks writes of the damage of patriarchal control on the men who wield it: "Being the boss does not require any man to be emotionally healthy, able to give and receive love." (57). Supporting this seeming paradox, in these later Will Smith films, less "exceptional" males may achieve more than Smith's heroic protagonists.

I, Robot (2004), *I Am Legend* (2007), and *After Earth* (2013) join other films of the past decade that present the potential destruction of humanity, often linked to the excesses and failures of a traditionally patriarchal (capitalistic) society. A vibrant sub-genre within these apocalyptic films has been the zombie film, including *28 Days Later . . .* (2002), *Shaun of the Dead* (2004), *Grindhouse: Planet Terror* (2007), *Zombieland* (2009) and *World War Z* (2013), as well as the *Walking Dead* graphic-novel and television series. Some critics expand the definition of the genre to include films that feature other infections that result in a loss of agency, like *Invasion* (2007) and *The Happening* (2008). The challenges faced by Robert Neville, a virologist and military officer, in *I Am Legend* are shared by the protagonists of other zombie apocalypse films, a mini-genre of the millennium. However, the less exceptional male protagonists of these films survive their narratives, while Neville must die for society to be saved. Neville's uncompromising version of masculinity is shared by his protagonists in *I,Robot* (2004), *Hancock* (2008), and *After Earth* (2013).

This chapter will examine Will Smith's sole male survivor of a zombie apocalypse in *I Am Legend*, within the context of the protagonists of zombie films *The Happening* and *Zombieland*. As in his film *I, Robot* (2004), these protagonists struggle to maintain their humanity in a world where the rules of survival demand a new way of living. The position of Smith's protagonists as the obsolete male becomes clear when placed in the context of the (living) male protagonists of other zombie films. This chapter will explore the significance of Will Smith's emergence as both the representative of the exceptional man as well as the demonstration of the limits of American exceptionalism.

THE MILLENNIAL ZOMBIE APOCALYPSE

Unlike a typical action hero who must save the lives of countless others, survival itself is a heroic feat, as the undead in films such as *28 Days Later . . .*, *Grindhouse: Planet Terror* and *Zombieland* (2009) are a nearly unstoppable force. These films in many ways resemble 1970s disaster films like *Poseidon Adventure* (1972), *Towering Inferno* (1974), and *Jaws* (1975), which critics have noted emerged from an underlying cynicism about American society and about the possibility of heroism.[3] In both genres, as the microcosm of survivors strive to live to the end, the narrative demonstrates who deserves to live, as well as who must be sacrificed to bring the world back into balance.

However, zombie films differ from disaster films in several key ways. First, the threat resembles human beings. Therefore, zombie films become a critique of the community itself, as the "community" gradually becomes dangerous. Second, the survivors face the constant potential of themselves becoming monstrous. Not only are their former friends now monsters, but individuals must face their own capacity for violence and must take steps to actively preserve their agency and humanity. As Anna Froula describes, cinematic zombies "are both victim and monster, dramatizing the horrors of brainwashing and enslavement," as survivors face "violent encounters with soulless monsters that look human" (196). These dynamics add to the gauntlet that survivors must overcome—not only must they live, but they must remain human, avoiding contamination. And if the survivors remain technically human but lose their humanity, have they truly survived?

While in the films *Planet Terror* and *I Am Legend* the zombie infections have an identifiable source (tied to the hubris of respectively the military and science), in other films the source of the infection is unknown. Even then, the suspicion remains that the infection is tied to the excesses of post-capitalist society, to humankind's need to consume obsessively—almost a mirror-image of the zombie-like plague that some critics see as eroding twenty-first-century humanity. For example, Michael Kimmel, in his 2008 book *Guyland: The Perilous World Where Boys Become Men*, describes today's common trance-like addiction to video devices: "All these distractions together comprise a kind of fantasy realm to which guys retreat constantly" (147). This repetitive, virtual existence cuts them off from interaction with people as well as from direct experience, removing the opportunity for spontaneous joy. Zombie films take this voluntary loss of agency to a more frightening level.

While the zombie genre overall may function as a critique of US society, these films specifically join with critiques of contemporary US masculinity. Kimmel notes that many young American men take advantage of their reduced responsibilities to women, to society, and to the economy—choosing to remain "guys" rather than making the transition to "manhood." In 1960, almost 70 percent of men had reached the markers of manhood—leaving home, getting an education, finding a partner, starting work and becoming a father—by thirty. Today, less than a third of males that age can say the same (41). But after a zombie epidemic, the boy-man may mature while the less flexible men die. As Gretchen Bakke observes in recent action films: "whiteness, deadness, and maleness are all under strident attack" (402). In zombie films, those responsible for the infection are clearly tied to whiteness and adulthood, while the "deadness" that accompanies the relative easy routine of twenty-first-century life is part of what has made the general population susceptible to slipping into the zombie state.

A key trait shared by male protagonists in millennial Hollywood zombie films is their ability to be objective. In *I Am Legend*, Smith's Robert Neville is a military scientist; *The Happening*'s Elliot (Mark Wahlberg) is a biology teacher, a character who thinks in terms of hypotheses; and *Zombieland*'s Columbus (Jesse Eisenberg) is a phobic graduate student who survives by living by his own rules. Though these men are not emotionally hardened, they still possess the masculine quality to control emotions and to act rationally.

The second trait they *initially* share is their ability to separate themselves from others. Zombie movies often present other human beings as a threat to individual survival: in *Night of the Living Dead* (1968), Ben (Duane Jones) successfully survives zombies and hysterical survivors, only to be shot by a posse that mistakes him for a zombie. These millennial survivors are more self-protective: in *I Am Legend*, Robert Neville sends his family away to protect them and to focus on his duty. As Manhattan is being evacuated, Neville ignores the pleas of strangers, using his military privilege for his wife and daughter only. Likewise, *The Happening*'s Elliot deliberately limits his concern to his wife and his best friend's family. In *Zombieland*, all the survivors avoid real names to keep from becoming attached.[4] False connections, particularly connections to acquaintances they can't save, become lethal in landscapes with zombie infections: emotionally shallow connections in these films become literally dead weight.

A common feature of the ultimate survivors in a zombie film is a reconstituted "family," often not connected by sex or blood. David Carruthers connects this closure to Northrop Frye's definition of the mythos of comedy, "wherein the fated lovers' *saturnalia* is impeded by the imposition of the conservative *senex*. What better way to typify the rule-obsessed aged, of course, than by means of the undead!" (8). The closure of these films also resonates with Frye's formulation of "a new society to crystallize around the hero" (qtd. in Carruthers 8). The surviving figures at the end of the film have renounced the society prior to the infection, with their commitment to each other providing the basis for a new order.

In M. Night Shyamalan's *The Happening* protagonist Elliot must learn to commit to relationships that matter, while letting go of the petty concerns that have separated him from his wife. In *The Happening*, the infection that sweeps the Northeastern United States does not lead the population to feed on each other. After disorienting their mental faculties, the neurotoxin released by plants causes them to kill themselves. In many ways, *The Happening* is an inversion of traditional zombie films: an early television report graphically shows an infected man inviting zoo lions to rip his arms off, rather than the common scene of zombies ripping off the arms of others.

The male protagonist is thirty-something biology teacher Elliot, who tries to get his wife Alma and his best friend Julian (John Leguiziamo)'s family to safety. While Neville represents a man stuck between traditional and postfeminist versions of masculine duty, Elliot is more like one of Kimmel's "guys," a thirty-something man who has not hit all the markers of being adult. Though he has a responsible job, he has only recently married, and they have not yet had children—Alma does not think he's "grown up" enough to start a family.

While overall the film preaches self-containment as essential to survival—the infection occurs whenever there is a mass of people—the ultimate test, after the main characters have divested themselves of all "virtual" connections, is to truly commit. Though Alma and Elliot's marriage at the start of the film was plagued by ambivalences and doubts, by the end they are fully committed to each other and to the orphaned Jess. Seemingly the antidote for somnambulist destruction of life is a commitment to love and to life.[5]

Zombieland offers two male protagonists, with very different masculine codes and experiences prior to the zombie apocalypse: their movement from survival to living may be even more deliberate than Elliot's. With its voice-over narration and playful titles throughout, *Zombieland* is the most direct in spelling out exactly the discipline that it takes to survive a zombie apocalypse. Opening two months after the virus first hits, the film follows Columbus, a graduate student, as he chronicles first his survival and then his move toward connection: first his uneasy partnership with Tallahassee (Woody Harrelson), and then his more complicated encounter with grifter-sisters Wichita (Emma Stone) and Little Rock (Abigail Breslin).

Like Neville and Elliot, Columbus is objective and orderly, as he formulates a numbered list of rules based on his zombie experiences. Though in his mid-twenties, Columbus has hit even fewer of Kimmel's adult markers than Elliot. Though living in an apartment distant from his parents, he has never had a girlfriend or a full-time job, existing largely on pizza and Mountain Dew. When he is taken prisoner by twelve-year-old Little Rock, he defends himself by saying "girls mature faster than boys"—though he is chronologically no longer a boy. However, in a world where zombies are an active threat, being an overgrown adolescent has proven valuable, making it easy for him to survive by his rules. As he admits, he "avoided people like zombies *before* they were zombies." Only now that there are no people left does he find that he misses them, that he is ready for connections, ready to grow up.

The audience knows even less about Tallahassee. He lives by a more hyper-masculine, instinctual code, but one that likewise keeps him isolated and alert. He takes a joy in killing zombies, creatively using whatever tool is at hand. Initially, Tallahassee's masculinity feels like a throwback: at one point, he plays the theme song from *Deliverance* on a banjo. However, it is ultimately revealed that Tallahassee's bravado and isolationism are not due to frozen immaturity like Columbus, but a reaction to ultimate loss: the death of his son. He rejects false connections in Zombieland because he has known true connection.

When Wichita and Little Rock put themselves in danger, chasing a childhood fantasy, Columbus and Tallahassee are forced to acknowledge their own bond, before they can put themselves at risk for the sisters. Columbus also learns that even the most important rules are meant to broken: in an instant, "*Don't* be a hero," becomes "*Be* a hero." Or as Tallahassee would say, it became "time to nut up or shut up." These "guys" ultimately choose to be men, risking their own survival to save what has become the first family they have known in a long time. Working together, Columbus and Tallahassee save the sisters, and the four drive off together. Columbus is rewarded by learning Wichita's name—it is time for real attachments. As Columbus states as they drive off together, "Without other people, you might as well be a zombie."

While Smith's protagonists in *I, Robot* and *I Am Legend* fight to remain human in the face of robot and zombie hordes, their rigid versions of masculinity may make the difference between man and non-man slight. In surveying recent zombie films, Simon Cooper suggests that what makes this genre so frightening is how easy it is for people to shed their humanity:

> In the age of biotechnologies, where the very essence of our humanity is capable of being broken down, transplanted or transcended, the idea that our life is something able to be rendered soulless . . . resonates profoundly (26).

In millennial zombie films—and related films like *I, Robot*—surviving, not just literally, but as a *human* requires conscious effort and discipline, declining the "virtual" human connections that lead contemporary people to forget who they are. Despite the major differences in tone and the definition of the infections, these zombie films surprisingly are very similar in their conversations about the masculine qualities achieved by their everyday protagonists, which might provide the best hope for humanity.

REMAINING HUMAN—WILL SMITH AS THE LAST MAN

Will Smith in *I Am Legend* joins the protagonists of *The Happening* and *Zombieland* in dramatizing the specific challenges that contemporary men face in balancing humanity and masculinity, connecting to his other millennial roles in questioning the future of American patriarchal masculinity. Though the Dark Seekers of *I Am Legend* may differ somewhat from the Hollywood zombie, the novel and its previous adaptations were a major influence on George Romero, the creator of *Night of the Living Dead* and its sequels. This 2007 adaptation blends elements of the original novel with the current zombie genre.

While Smith's dramatic turns in *Ali* (2001) and *Pursuit of Happyness* (1996) directly focus on the historical challenges and achievements of African American men, his science fiction characters (*I, Robot*, *I Am Legend*, *Hancock*, and *After Earth*), have moved into worlds where the marked difference is not skin color. In *I, Robot*, his character is prejudiced against robots;

in *I Am Legend*, his character carries out Nazi-like experiments on zombie-like creatures; and in *Hancock*, the title character faces the isolation of being the only one of his kind—a superhero.[6] In *I Am Legend*, *Hancock*, and *After Earth*, Smith moves from Poitier's exceptional black man to being the exceptional *man*, unique in the full sense of the word: respectively the only human in Manhattan, the only male super-being, and the only adult male on the abandoned planet Earth.

Related to his position among zombies in *I Am Legend*, Will Smith's protagonist in *I, Robot* (2004) fights for humanity in a society increasingly dependent on technology. Instead of surviving the near-extinction of humankind, Del Spooner is the one man who remains aware of the risk to humanity from its dependence on servile robots. Though at the beginning of the film, there is only 1 robot to every five human beings, with their super strength they have the potential to dominate and exterminate as quickly as a zombie swarm.

As with Smith's other exceptional protagonists, Spooner (even though it is 2035), embodies stereotypical qualities of traditional twentieth-century masculinity: he is a detective, whose focus on his work has left him divorced, childless and surly. He prefers to work alone, with the closest thing he has to a friend his police lieutenant (Chi McBride). While everyone around him, including his mother, embraces the way that robots have improved the ease of life, Spooner is suspicious of decision-making based solely on circuitry. As part of his desire to hold onto the purity of his humanity, he prefers retrograde music (Motown) and shoes (Chuck Taylors), as well as a stereo without voice control (manual buttons). While his fellow citizens are not zombies, their comfort with robots and other computer-assists connect them to Kimmel's description of the partial numbness of virtual existence over human activity. Instead of his robotic, prosthetic arm making him more appreciative of robots, it has only intensified his insistence on the human and his prejudice against robots.

It is his deep suspicion of the robotic which led Dr. Lanning (James Cromwell) to select him as the only man who could recognize and resist the rebellion organized by the virtual intelligence VIKI. However, to succeed Spooner must also develop a more flexible masculinity, partnering not only with scientist Susan Calvin (Bridget Moynihan) but more importantly with Lanning's prototype-robot Sonny (Alan Tudyk). Ironically, the white CEO criticizes Spooner for his hatred of robots (who have snow-white faces and blue eyes): "Prejudice never shows much reason. You probably just don't like their kind." Spooner must move beyond his prejudice to recognize Sonny's humanity—and to accept his friendship. While Spooner's traditional masculinity is a barrier to his personal happiness, his commitment to being human—and ironically recognizing the humanity in Sonny—is what gives him the ability to halt this apocalypse. Only by expanding his own humanity to collaborate with others different from himself—letting go of his privilege as a man—does he become a man who can do more than survive.

I Am Legend's Dr. Robert Neville is consistently marked as exceptional, with ties to public and private power structures. A prominent scientist and military colonel, heralded on the cover of *Time* magazine (which he still keeps posted to his refrigerator), Neville is the sole human resident of Manhattan after a virus has created a race of mindless, aggressive zombie-like creatures, living in a communal nest like rodents, avoiding sunlight due to their loss of pigment. Hannah Hamad notes the "evasively neoliberal image" of Smith's Neville as "the exemplary embodiment of the postracial ideal" (129). As a virologist stationed in New York City, Neville was involved in the initial quarantine and battle against the Krippin virus.[7] Neville is the remaining representative of the military and medical establishments, while continuing as the provider and protector in his home (even if it currently only includes his dog Sam). So while his race may mark him as part of a "neoliberal" universe, his masculinity is tied to patriarchal roles and institutions. While zombie films generally feature ordinary men rising to the task, here we have a heroic man without an audience or dependents.

His only avenue to fulfill his need to "save" others is to send out a broadcast message, offering protection any survivors out there, and to continue with his search for a cure. Neville does not hunt the Dark Seekers indiscriminately (as in the novel), but instead captures "samples" for anti-viral trials—which have over the past three years, inevitably ended in the test subjects' torturous deaths. In the dozens of photos he has of his failed "test subjects," they are all gaunt and in pain—leaving the question open as to whether he is truly dedicated to saving humanity or whether he has become a Dr. Mengele. Gerry Canavan notes how zombies films serve as an allegory for populations that are no longer deemed worthy of survival or protection, with their "imaginary racial demarcation into *life* and *anti-life*" (173); this distinction justifies any violence that Neville commits against the Dark Seekers, an albino race.

Overall, Neville actively struggles with the consequences of being a traditional, successful man, who puts his duty before all, believing in his own omnipotence. In flashbacks, we learn that Neville sent his wife and daughter away—ignoring his wife's pleas for them to stay together. He believed his duty came first: "this is my post. I can still fix this. I'm not gonna let this happen," he tells her. Instead of "saving" his family, however, he watches helplessly as their helicopter explodes in mid-air. The responsibility he feels for their deaths is evident through his constant flashbacks to their last hours throughout the film. And three years later, he still has not "fixed this." Perhaps if—instead of playing the lone, stoic hero—he had allowed his family to stay with him, he could have protected them better; or their love and support might have helped him find a cure for the plague sooner. Instead, Neville put imagined connections to "humanity" before his very real connection to his family.

Bakke presents Neville as part of the trend of black (super) heroes who kill white men.[8] And the threat in this film is obviously coded as ultra-white: Dr. Krippen is British; and the Krippen virus has made the Dark Seekers lose all pigment. In addition, the Dark Seekers are all played by non-ethnic actors, with the Alpha male (Dash Mihok) appearing particularly Aryan. However, it is hard to see Neville as distinct from the patriarchal order, or representing the alternate masculinity of Bakke's black heroes. Neville is an unquestioning part of both the scientific community and the military, rejecting neither of their methods. His belief in his own abilities—"I can still fix this"; "I can provide you with security"; "I can save you"—reflects the same arrogance as Dr. Krippen. When Dr. Krippen was asked in an early interview if they had cured cancer, she answered unflinchingly: "Yes. Yes, we have." (And despite the unforeseen effects, she was right: dead people don't develop cancer.) Though Neville reveals a warmth, ethics and love of aesthetics that could lead to a revised, postfeminist masculinity, he actively represses these qualities in his service to hierarchy and duty.

While Neville continues his experiments, remaining committed to his post, he does significantly choices to keep himself human. While earlier zombie films show human characters who enjoy looting for consumer goods (most obviously in *Dawn of the Dead*), Neville has filled his home with art: looking at the walls of his brownstone, he has chosen masterpieces by Vincent Van Gogh, Keith Haring, Edgar Degas, Henri Rousseau, Claude Monet, and Amedeo Modigliani to grace his home. Part of his daily routine is to visit a video store, checking out and *returning* DVDs. Though as the sole survivor everything on Manhattan belongs to him, he only takes what he needs to survive—and what he needs to feed his sense of humanity.

A key marker of Neville's humanity is his connection to the music of Bob Marley, for whom he named his daughter. When he finally meets another survivor Anna (Alice Braga), he explains Marley's philosophy, presenting it as similar to his own work as a virologist. Marley worked to cure racism and hate by injecting music and love into people's lives, for example with his lyric: "Light up the darkness." However, Neville may have lost his way and become guilty of "racism" in his insistence of a definition of humanity that excludes Dark Seekers—allowing him to experiment on them without qualms, ignoring their capacity for humanity.

After three years alone, Neville is beginning to lose his ability to recognize human agency. After Neville successfully escapes the lair, a Dark Seeker exposes himself to harmful sunlight to rage against the murder his fellow by Neville. Instead of recognizing the *human* emotion in the Alpha's[9] self-destructive action, Neville sees it as a sign of his social devolution: "typical human behavior is now totally absent."[10] Underestimating his foe, and his foe's desire for revenge, Neville walks into a man-trap, copied from Neville's Dark Seeker trap. Neville fails to recognize the intelligence and agency that this trap demonstrates.

At the same time that Neville fails to see the humanity of the Alpha Male, he makes the further error of confusing virtual connections with real intimacy. While Neville baited his trap with human (his) blood; the Alpha Dark Seeker imaginatively baits his trap with "Fred," one of Neville's mannequin "friends." Though this invented friendship had been a good coping mechanism, Neville has made the serious error of confusing fake with real ones. Shouting "Fred, you better tell me now if you are real," he repeatedly shoots at Fred, seeing the mannequin as the threat, rather than looking for who placed the mannequin—and walking right into the trap. Though Neville eventually escapes, his dog Sam is infected in the struggle, forcing Neville to euthanize her. In over-valuing Fred, Neville loses his true friend Sam.

Having lost his one breathing companion (and "killed" an unbreathing companion), Neville breaks with his cautionary rules that have kept him alive. Abandoning hope, he skips his midday appointment at South Street Seaport and recklessly sets out to attack Dark Seekers at night—knowing full well that for the dozen he may kill, dozens more will appear to tear him apart. In shooting up the Grand Central Station and later embarking on a killing spree at South Street Seaport, Neville abandoned his rules and his objectivity, placing himself and others needlessly in jeopardy.

Instead of rescuing, Neville is rescued. Anna, like female survivors in other zombie films, proves herself equal to the fight, extracting him from his self-destructive rampage against the Dark Seekers. Responding to his broadcast, she has arrived in Manhattan with the boy Ethan (Charlie Tahan). Overall, she challenges Neville's lack of hope and the lapses in his humanity. While Anna has faith that there is a survivors' colony in Vermont, he insists that *everyone* is dead. She counters him by saying that he must believe or he would not have broadcast the message. Most importantly, when he shows her the test subject, he refers to the Dark Seeker as "it" while Anna says "she." Unlike Neville, Anna can tell the difference between an inanimate object ("it") and a human being ("she"). And miraculously, at the moment that they are over-run with Dark Seekers, the test subject visibly becomes a *she*, visibly becoming more human—Neville has found his cure.

While Hamad sees this final trio of Neville, Anna and Ethan as "a reconstituted nuclear family, and as a multiethnic spectacle of postracial

Figure 12.1.   Despite being alone for three years, Robert Neville (Will Smith) chooses to hold onto his duty and his guilt rather than bond with a woman and child over breakfast. *(I Am Legend)*

transcendence showcasing the multicultural ideal" (130), Neville does not embrace Anna and Ethan as a replacement for his lost family. This resistance separates Neville from the protagonists of zombie films like *28 Days Later. . . ,* *Zombieland,* and *The Happening.* Instead of enjoying a "family meal" when Anna cooks him breakfast, he angrily complains that he was saving the bacon for a "special occasion"—not recognizing that the first people who answered his broadcast message are that occasion. His interactions with Ethan are likewise strained, as he recites lines of *Shrek* (2001) in a monotone while the boy is trying to watch the video. Instead of bonding with them as a family unit, he positions himself as their protector. As he sent his wife and child away, he secures Anna and Ethan with the anti-virus, before his kamikaze confrontation with the Dark Seekers. In Frye's terms, Neville is the out-moded father figure that must be furiously "baited and exploded from the stage" for the world order to succeed. As Carruthers observes, "even the most benevolent of paternal figures in the zombie comedy are systematically annihilated by the genre" (10). Smith's paternalism—that he maintains in his last interaction with the Dark Seekers proclaiming that he can "fix" them—may be as damaging as the virus it produced.

In the epilogue, Anna and Ethan deliver the antiviral to the survivors' colony. In voiceover, she eulogizes him as a legend: "We are his legacy." Neville in this narrative is a Moses-figure. Though he takes on the responsibility for delivering "his people," he, like Moses, is personally denied the Promised Land. Perhaps his sin was sending his family away. Perhaps he betrayed Bob Marley through his "racist" experimentation on Dark Seekers. Though Neville did have the masculine discipline to survive, he did not have the qualities required to be a part of the renewed human race (unlike Neville, Columbus or Tallahassee). Anna, because of her faith in God's plan, and the boy Ethan, because of his innocence, pass through the colony's gates in his stead. Neville demonstrates the limits of traditional (exceptional) masculinity.

Will Smith's earned prominence in Hollywood positioned him to move into these millennial roles as exceptional men—roles in which he neither abandons his race nor highlights it. With the exception of *Hancock*, he remains in relationship with black women. In *I, Robot* and *After Earth*, he likewise appears in the context of other powerful black men. In *After Earth*, the prologue sets up humankind's immigration from Earth, to a hostile planet: the Prime Commander who made settlement possible is black though unnamed.

Other African American actors have been cast in (traditionally white) patriarchal roles, without comment: Morgan Freeman played a corrupt CEO in *Hard Rain* (1996) and a US President in *Deep Impact* (1998); Danny Glover played a President in *2012* (2009); and Samuel L. Jackson was an arrogant CEO in *Deep Blue Sea* (1999) and an arrogant news pundit in *Robocop* (2014). While African American director Antoine Fuqua cast white actors as his hero and President in *Olympus Has Fallen* (2013), he respectively cast Morgan Freeman and Angela Basset as Speaker of the House and Secret Service Director. So Hollywood has been projecting images of color-blind masculine power for decades.

However, what sets Will Smith's roles apart from these other powerful figures played by African American actors is that Smith plays the lead protagonist, and unlike the presidents of Freeman and Glover, his characters are secure enough in their position that these films are actually able to explore their characters' vulnerabilities, their discomfort in their roles. So while these films project a neoliberal image of race, they simultaneously critique the "exceptional" man who puts his duty over collaboration and connections to other, trafficking in new forms of prejudice. His persona's complex relationship to race, masculinity, and power makes Will Smith a unique Hollywood figure, beyond his box office records.

In *I, Robot*, *I Am Legend*, *Hancock*, and *After Earth* race may not exist as an issue, but definitions of masculinity are life-threatening, as these films dramatize the traps of traditional heroic masculinity. Though *I Am Legend*'s Robert Neville demonstrates many wonderful, humane qualities—through the love of his family, Bob Marley and art—he still holds onto the privileges of his position, firmly believing in his power and authority, as he repeatedly asserts "this is my post." Even at his death, Neville still sees his personal value lying in his work, the cure for the virus; Annalee Newitz connects men like Neville to capitalistic men: "because they spend so much time working, they feel dead themselves" (2).

Ultimately these Smith films, like *The Happening* and *Zombieland*, promote a more fluid masculinity that may be easier for less exceptional men to practice: his character is the negative example. In Hancock, it is the advertising executive Ray (Jason Bateman) who not only gets the happy family life, but who likewise succeeds in making society more compassionate. Hancock tells him, "Ray, you're going to change the world." After surviving their challenge on Earth, Kitai (Jaden Smith) tells his father Cypher (Will Smith), "I want to work with Mom"—choosing to no longer follow in his father's footsteps as a Ranger; Cypher replies: "Me too." Unlike Neville, Spooner, Hancock, and Cypher survive because they recognize that the less "exceptional" may be more human and valuable. Choosing the less traditionally masculine path at the end of these films is literally and metaphorically life affirming. These Smith films, as well as many zombie apocalypse films, begin to answer bell hooks call: "Until we create a popular culture that affirms and celebrates masculinity without upholding patriarchy, we will never see a change in the way that masses of males think about the nature of their identity" (103). At this point in his career, Will Smith has moved from a "racial trickster" to a "heroic trickster" who indirectly points to a better path for contemporary audiences.

NOTES

1. I first examined masculinity in millennial zombie films in a section of chapter 8, "Living to Get It Right: Home Front Masculinity as the 21st Century Masculine Ideal" in *Home Front Heroes: The Rise of a New Hollywood Archetype, 1988–1999* (McFarland, 2013). This chapter expands and develops this previous material, connecting it to the persona of Will Smith.

2. Ironically, in his first featured performance, Will Smith presented a parody of the exceptional black man in *Six Degrees of Separation* (1993). Paul is a former hustler who now introduces himself to wealthy Manhattan parents as a former prep-school classmate of their kids and the son of Sidney Poitier (Poitier only had daughters): however, the only thing he is after is their acceptance. These white liberals welcome him into their home, charmed by this handsome and well-spoken man,

congratulating themselves on the privilege to offer hospitality to this "exceptional" young man.

3. For example, Peter Lev described these films as presenting the common view of a troubled America, displacing "contemporary problems into simple, physical confrontations" (49).

4. To avoid the attachment of real names, all characters in *Zombieland* are only referred to by their place of origin (with the exception of "Bill Murray"). "Columbus" is from Ohio.

5. However, this optimistic ending is undercut by a second coda with a new Event beginning in Paris. The apocalypse has been paused, not averted.

6. Marking the challenges of his unique status, the screenplay notes that Hancock lost his memory when he was mugged coming out of a screening of *Frankenstein* in 1931. Like the creature, Hancock faces constant rejection as the only one of his kind, which makes it difficult for him to control his bitterness and anger though he would prefer to serve mankind.

7. In classic *Frankenstein* fashion, Dr. Krippin (Emma Thompson) believed that science could control life and death: asserting that she had defeated cancer, the lab-created virus was set free on the general population with fatal results.

8. Bakke specifically connects *I Am Legend* to *Blade* (1998), *The Green Mile* (1999), and *XXX: State of the Union* (2005), but the argument could be extended to other films like *Virtuosity* (1995) and *The Matrix* (1999) where the ultimate villain is hyper-white.

9. Though this zombie figure is not identified by name, the character/actor does appear in the credits of the film as the Alpha Male (Dash Mihok), playing a significant role in several key scenes. The only other films where a zombie appears in more than one scene are when the character is first introduced as a human figure—that is, Barbara's brother John in *Night of the Living Dead* or the father (Robert Carlyle) in *28 Months Later*. Alpha is unusual in that he is not known, but he has a personality and agency.

10. Terence McSweeney notes a similar dynamic in *Land of the Dead* (George Romero, 2005). The first sign that a zombie has evolved is when Big Daddy cries in anguish at the slaughter of his companions. As in *I Am Legend*, the continued aggressions of the human survivors prompt the zombies "to retaliate against their oppressors" (110).

WORKS CITED

Bakke, Gretchen. "Dead White Men: An Essay on the Changing Dynamics of Race in US Action Cinema." *Anthropological Quarterly* 83, no. 2 (2010): 400–28. Print.
Canavan, Gerry. "Fighting a War You've Already Lost": Zombies and Zombis in *Firefly/Serenity* and *Dollhouse*." *Science Fiction Film and Television* 4.2 (2011):173–203. *Project Muse*. Web. 31 Mar. 2012.

Carruthers, David M. "Mechanical-Human-Animal Intersections: Reshaping Identity in the Anxious Age of the Zombie Film." *Northeast Modern Language Association 43rd Convention.* Harrisburg, PA. 9 April 2014.

Cooper, Simon. "the Horror of Assimilation: Zombies and Bio-Capitalism." *Arena Magazine,* June-July 2007: 26–27. Print.

Corliss, Richard. "Zombieland: The Year's Coolest Creature Feature." *Time* 1 Oct. 2009. *General Onefile.* Web. 28 Nov. 2010.

Froula, Anna. "Prolepsis and the "War on Terror": Zombie Pathology and the Culture of Fear in *28 Days Later* . . . ." Reframing 9/11: Film, Popular Culture, and the "War on Terror." Eds. Jeff Birkenstein, Anna Froula, and Karen Randell. New York: Continuum, 2010. 195–208. Print.

Gray, Herman S. *Cultural Moves: African Americans and the Politics of Representation.* Berkeley: U of California P, 2005.

Hamad, Hannah. *Postfeminism and Paternity in Contemporary US Film: Framing Fatherhood.* New York: Routledge, 2014. Print.

hooks, bell. *The Will to Change: Men, Masculinity, and Love.* New York: Atria, 2004.

Kimmel, Michael. *Guyland: The Perilous World Where Boys Become Men.* New York: HarperCollins, 2008. Print.

Lev, Peter. *American Films of the '70s: Conflicting Visions.* Austin: U of Texas P, 2000. Print.

Magill, David. "Celebrity Culture and Racial Masculinities: The Case of Will Smith." *Pimps, Wimps, Studs, Thugs and Gentlemen: Essays on Media Images of Masculinity.* Ed. Elwood Watson. Jefferson, NC: McFarland, 2009. 126–40. Print.

McSweeney, Terence. "The Land of the Dead and the Home of the Brave: Romero's Vision of a Post-9/11 America." *Reframing 9/11: Film, Popular Culture, and the "War on Terror."* Eds. Jeff Birkenstein, Anna Froula, and Karen Randell. New York: Continuum, 2010. 107-16. Print.

Newitz, Annalee. *Pretend We're Dead: Capitalist Monsters in American Popular Culture.* Durham: Duke UP, 2006. Print.

Index

About the Contributors

Elizabeth Abele is an associate professor of English at SUNY Nassau Community College, serving as Executive Director of the Northeast Modern Language Association (2005–2013). Her essays on American culture and masculinity have appeared in *American Studies*, *Scope*, and *Journal of Transnational American Studies*, and in edited anthologies including *Critical Approaches to the Films of M. Night Shyamalan* (Palgrave) and *Deconstructing Brad Pitt* (Bloomsbury). She is the author of *Home Front Hero: The Rise of a New Hollywood Archetype, 1988–1999* (McFarland Press, 2014). For 2014–2015, she was a Fulbright Scholar in American studies at the Universiti Malaya, Kuala Lumpur.

Katie Barnett currently teaches in the Department of Media and Cultural Studies at the University of Worcester, lecturing on film, television, and gender. She completed her PhD at the University of Birmingham in 2013, where she also served as editor of the interdisciplinary *North American Studies* journal, *49th Parallel*. Her research interests focus on representations of parenthood, particularly fatherhood, in popular culture, and how these representations intersect with notions of masculinity, queerness, and nationhood.

Laura L. Beadling earned her PhD in American studies from Purdue University in 2007. She is currently teaching literature, film, and screenwriting at Youngstown State University. Along with Dr. Russ Brickey and Evelyn Martens, she has a book of exercises for the composition classroom, *Practical Composition*, coming out later in 2014 and she is working on a book on Native American filmmakers including Shelley Niro, Georgina Lightning, and Chris Eyre. She lives in Ohio with her husband and two to three small dogs.

Brenda Boudreau is a professor of English at McKendree University in southern Illinois. Her research has focused on gender in film, literature, and television, with her most recent published article "'Sexually Suspect': Masculinity in the Films of Neil LaBute." Her current project explores postfeminism's influence on female characters on cable television.

Dustin Gann is a native Kansan. He earned a PhD. in twentieth-century US history from the University of Kansas in 2012. Gann's research balances an interest in regional and Midwestern history alongside a desire to understand the processes that have shaped national culture during the twentieth century. He currently teaches within the School of Historical, Philosophical, and Religious Studies at Arizona State University in Tempe, Arizona.

Keith Friedlander is a professor of English composition at Humber College in Toronto, Ontario. He recently completed his doctoral dissertation on the early nineteenth-century British print industry through the University of Ottawa. His work compares how creators operating in different modes of expression (including poets, essayists, illustrators, editors, and critics) conceptualize authorial agency. His areas of specialization include British Romanticism, print culture, and comic studies.

John A. Gronbeck-Tedesco is assistant professor and convener of American Studies at Ramapo College of New Jersey. His writing has appeared in *American Quarterly*, *Journal of Latin American Studies*, *Journal of American Studies*, *Studies in Latin American Popular Culture*, and CounterPunch.org. His book, *Cuba, the United States, and Cultures of the Transnational Left, 1930–1975*, is forthcoming from Cambridge University Press.

Mary T. Hartson is assistant professor of Spanish at Oakland University in Rochester, Michigan. Her research centers on images of masculinity in popular cinema of both Spain and the United States, especially regarding its relationship to consumerism. She has published on film and literature from the period of the Francoist dictatorship as well as Transition cinema, and is currently working on the book project *Casting Spanish Masculinity in a Consumer Age*.

Michael Litwack is a doctoral candidate in modern culture and media at Brown University. His research areas include critical race and ethnic studies, comparative media theory, American studies, and television and digital media.

Derek S. McGrath is the recipient of a doctoral degree in English literature from Stony Brook University. In addition to his specialization in nineteenth-century American literature, he researches, presents, and publishes on comics and the superhero genre, with a focus on representations of gender in these works. McGrath was also invited to present a talk at New York University's Poe Room on the use of contemporary popular culture in teaching representations of gender in nineteenth-century American literature, which he has revised for the volume *Teaching Tainted Lit*.

Maureen McKnight is an assistant professor at Cardinal Stritch University in Milwaukee, Wisconsin. Her research focuses on the cultural work of memory and the emotions in American literature. She has published articles on Zora Neale Hurston in *The Southern Quarterly* and Charles Chesnutt in the *Iowa Journal of Cultural Studies*. At Stritch, she teaches American literature, film, literary theory, and African American literature. In 2013, she received the university's Teaching Excellence and Campus Leadership award.

Pamela Hill Nettleton is an assistant professor of journalism and media studies at the Diederich College of Communication at Marquette University in Milwaukee, Wisconsin. Her work is in gender, masculinity, and domestic violence in the media. Her dissertation on post-9/11 television masculinity won the Broadcast Education Association's 2010 Kenneth Harwood Outstanding Dissertation Award. Before earning her doctorate, she was a magazine writer and editor for twenty-five years.

CPSIA information can be obtained at www.ICGtesting.com
Printed in the USA
BVOW08*1518221115

427348BV00003B/3/P